MATHEMATICAL ECONOMICS TEXTS

9

TOWARD A THEORY OF ECONOMIC DEVELOPMENT

MATHEMATICAL ECONOMICS TEXTS

Editors

K. Arrow, Professor of Economics, Harvard University, U.S.A.
F. Hahn, Professor of Economics, London School of Economics, U.K.
J. Johnston, Professor of Econometrics, University of Manchester, U.K.
R. M. Solow, Professor of Economics, Massachusetts Institute of Technology, U.S.A.

Students of mathematical economics and econometrics have two unnecessary difficulties. One is that much of what they have to read is spread over the journals, often written in different notations. The second is that the theoretical and the empirical writings often make little reference to each other, and the student is left to relate them.

The main object of this series is to overcome these difficulties. Most of the books are concerned with specific topics in economic theory, but they relate the theory to relevant empirical work. Others deal with the necessary mathematical apparatus of economic theory and econometrics. They are designed for third-year undergraduates and postgraduate students.

The editors are drawn from both sides of the Atlantic and are people who are known both for their contribution to economics and for the emphasis they place on clear exposition.

Titles in the series

Other titles are in preparation

TOWARD A THEORY
OF
ECONOMIC
DEVELOPMENT

PAUL ZAREMBKA

University of California, Berkeley

Published Under the Auspices
of the Institute of International Studies
University of California, Berkeley

HOLDEN-DAY, INC.
SAN FRANCISCO

ISBN 0-8162-9995-1
Library of Congress Catalog Card No. 75-188130

First published 1972
Copyright © 1972 by Holden-Day, Inc.,
500 Sansome Street, San Francisco, California.

HOLDEN-DAY, INC.
500 Sansome Street
San Francisco, California

Printed in the United States of America

1234567890   MP   798765432

To Renata

PREFACE

Development economics can be usefully divided into two parts, development theory and development planning. Development theory entails an analytic description of the development setting, together with a formulation of the key aspects of the development process. Development planning concerns the design and application of a set of policies to encourage the development process and is ultimately policy oriented. Development theory is an important antecedent to development planning.

This book grew out of the belief that a generally accepted theory of development has been lacking. Although one theory applicable to all developing countries may be unattainable, at least a theoretical framework should be possible. In attempting to provide such a framework, the book can be viewed as the analogue for developing countries of growth theory for developed countries. As such, the focus is upon general and partial equilibrium problems arising in the development context.

Three beliefs underlie the contents of the book. First, development theory must confront nonproportional growth of sectors; that is, the underlying focus must be upon the transformation from agriculture to industry in the process of economic development. Second, the basic analytic premise should be that many of the factors determining the speed of the development process (such as the levels of labor unemployment, of savings, and of technological improvement adoption) are outgrowths of rational responses by individuals to their environment. Third, assumptions made in the theoretical framework should be chosen to capture "first-order" factors, that is, chosen to balance the merits of conceptual simplicity with the nature of a problem at hand and with the requirements of any existing empirical evidence.

Even though the book was written primarily as a contribution to the theory of economic development, it can well be used as a textbook for development courses. The agriculture-industry transformation theme, together with the study of the supplies and demands for outputs and factor inputs, should be at the heart of development courses. The required level of mathematics is limited to basic calculus, symbolic notation relies (where possible) upon well-established or mnemonic characters, and many derivations are relegated to appendices at the end of the book (only Appendix C is more difficult mathematically). Although a careful study of the empirical Chapters 9 and 10 requires a familiarity with basic econometrics, the estimation procedures can be skipped without loss of comprehension of the theoretical implications discussed in these chapters.

In the preparation of this book, I have benefited greatly from suggestions of many people, and my thanks are extended to each of them. Discussions with, and comments by, Avinash Dixit on many chapters, particularly in the early stages, were most helpful in sharpening the focus. Albert Fishlow's penetrating remarks, based on two readings of the manuscript, were very valuable. My wife, Renata Kiefer, greatly assisted by helping me stay in touch with the development context and suggesting numerous improvements throughout the writing of the book. Lon Hanke's reactions to the various drafts aided considerably in understanding the rural situation. Very helpful comments on a draft of the manuscript were given by Bent Hansen (particularly on Chapters 5, 7, and 8), by Bruno Knall (particularly in leading to the incorporation of Chapter 4), by John Letiche (particularly on Chapters 4, 5, 6, and 8), and by Amartya Sen (particularly on Chapter 1). Lance Taylor commented on an early draft of six chapters. Finally, June Flanders, Dale Jorgenson, Ernest Nadel, Georg Tolkemitt, Ted Truman, and Michael Wiseman commented on one or more chapters, and their comments often led to considerable revisions.

The major financial support for the research came from a National Science Foundation grant (GS–2822), beginning in 1969, and from a grant for academic leave in 1970–1971 from the Institute of International Studies at the University of California, Berkeley. Early support was provided by Berkeley's Institute of Business and Economic Research and by the National Science Foundation (through the Project for the Explanation and Optimization of Economic Growth at Berkeley). All of this financial support is gratefully acknowledged.

My thanks also go to C. Christian von Weizsäcker for arranging for me to spend my year's leave at the Alfred Weber Institute at Heidelberg University and to that Institute for the use of their facilities. Hooman Ghavimi provided very useful research assistance during most of the project, with Caglar Keyder giving some additional help. Ellen Mc-Gibbon and Iku Workman carefully and accurately typed the many drafts of the manuscript. Finally, the *Journal of Economic Theory* granted permission to use an article of mine upon which Chapter 2 is based.

Berkeley   Paul Zarembka
February 1972

CONTENTS

TOWARD A THEORY OF ECONOMIC DEVELOPMENT

INTRODUCTION

In all countries there are three principal types of factor inputs used to produce output: natural resources embodied in land, labor of various skills, and capital in many forms and vintages. In developing countries, however, the existing factor inputs lead to output levels implying low per-capita income. The low income may be due to limited quantities of certain factors (e.g., capital) or to relatively inefficient production techniques.

This study of development theory begins with the factor input most often considered to be in abundant supply in developing countries: unskilled labor. In fact, the question of the existence of a labor *surplus* is an important prelude to any theory of development and has become rather controversial in development economics. In Chapter 1 it is shown that the classical surplus-labor approach, associated most often with the names of Lewis and Fei and Ranis, and the neoclassical approach, associated most often with the name of Jorgenson, are limiting cases of a more general description of laborer behavior. Thus, it is possible to test empirically if either approach is an accurate description of reality or if, perhaps, a middle position between the two approaches is more reasonable. In any case, any choice of theoretical approach is probably better decided according to the problem at hand, than as a universal rule.

With the results of Chapter 1 as a basis, the general structure of developing economies is studied in both Chapters 2 (for closed economies) and 5 (for open economies). Several important characteristics of the models in these chapters are worth mentioning here. First, the sectoral breakdown of the economy is always in terms of the dominant factors of production: labor and land in both domestic and export agriculture, labor and capital in the secondary sector, and (in Section 3.3 as an extension of Chapter 2) only labor in the labor-intensive service sector. This breakdown implicitly incorporates another characteristic of developing countries—the rural-urban dichotomy. However, the distinction in much of growth theory between capital goods production and consumer goods production is not included; this distinction in developing countries is less important than that between agriculture and industry.

Second, in these chapters it is presumed that the market mechanism is a very important behavioral characteristic of developing countries. The presumption reflects a personal sense of reality and is also reflected by comments such as those of Bent Hansen (1967, pp. 19–20):

> I am convinced, from my own studies of the wages of agricultural labourers in Egypt, as well as from a growing stream of empirical evidence from other underdeveloped countries, that the problem of deviations of market prices and shadow prices for factors in underdeveloped countries has been exaggerated by academic Western economists. Markets in underdeveloped countries are probably not more imperfect than in developed countries unless they have been made so by government intervention (say, import licensing); also in developed countries cases are known (as for instance in U.S. agriculture) where factor prices have been greatly out of line with marginal product value for long periods. And the fact that divergencies between market prices and shadow prices in developed countries are often related to dynamic developments, while many underdeveloped countries may have stagnated in their traditional forms for centuries during which equality of market prices and marginal product value could slowly be obtained, might even be taken as argument for such divergencies to be more important in developed countries.

Third, the functional forms for the theoretical relationships in production and consumption are the simple log-linear forms. Functional form is not of first-order importance in *understanding* the operation of developing countries, as long as limiting cases are not assumed (such as a constant capital/output ratio). Furthermore, the log-linear form is, in an important sense, a middle ground between fixed proportions and infinite substitutability between independent variables (the implied elasticity in the log-linear form is unity). In any case, the functional form for manufacturing production can be supported by empirical evidence from research by others, while the functional form for food consumption is examined empirically in Chapter 10.

The structure of closed economies is studied in Chapter 2. Because the resulting model is as simple as reality will permit, in this chapter the reader is given an overview of a developing economy and a sharper focus on important problems. A property of the mathematical solution obtained for the model is that the secondary sector is on its steady-state growth path (i.e., the secondary sector capital/output ratio is behaviorally, although not technologically, constant). Any limitation of this property is more apparent than real; Appendix B shows how this solution can be simply reinterpreted for any initial value for the capital/ output ratio other than only the asymptotic one. Furthermore, the model of the *economy*, as opposed to the sector, is not approaching its asymptote; that asymptote would imply that the ratio of rural to urban population approaches zero (which is exactly how growth theory treats the developed economy).

In Chapter 2 the key market that explicitly ties the sectors together is the labor market (although the demand functions for outputs, also, implicitly tie the sectors), but the mechanism of that market is not carefully spelled out. In Chapter 3 we first elaborate on the operation of the rural-urban labor market and study the causes of urban unemployment. We then conclude the chapter by introducing a labor-intensive service sector into the dual economy model.

Although increases in the labor force and improvements in labor skills are important sources of economic growth, another source is certainly savings, particularly if technical progress is embodied in investment. Thus, in an often quoted statement, Arthur Lewis (1954, p. 155) asserts:

> The central problem in the theory of economic development is to understand the process by which a community which was previously saving and investing 4 or 5 percent of its national income or less, converts itself into an economy where voluntary saving is running at about 12 to 15 percent of national income or more. This is the central problem because the central fact of economic development is rapid capital accumulation (including knowledge and skills with capital).

Jorgensen (1967, p. 310) argues that because the secondary sector has the highest savings rates the source of the rise in savings is simply a redistribution of output toward that sector as economic growth takes place. Even so, studying the determinants of the level of aggregate savings leads to some of the most complex problems in general economics and in development economics in particular. As a start toward a fuller theory of savings, in Chapter 4 we present a model that integrates the consumer's survival and profit motives. The model helps explain theoretically why savings among farmers and urban workers are so low.

Chapters 2 through 4 comprise Part Two, "The Closed Economy." Much of the discussion there is equally relevant to open economies. However, because international trade leads to significant changes in the economic structure of many countries, trade has had a prominent role in development economics. Nevertheless, a difficulty in analyzing the impact of trade on development is that modern trade theory is not particularly relevant for developing countries because the theory is basically static and, more important, because the principal exports of developing countries are almost always natural-resource intensive. Thus, in Part Three we open the economy to trade by taking the country's comparative advantage in exporting as given. As such, our approach is more in the Ricardian than the Heckscher–Ohlin tradition of explaining the impact of trade.

Because agricultural products are the predominant exports of developing countries, in Chapters 5 and 6 we study such open economies by building, in part, upon the closed economy model of Chapter 2. Imports are consumer luxury goods in Chapter 5 but are capital goods in Chapter 6. In both cases, particular attention is given to the effects of changing terms of trade on real-income distribution and income growth. Also, in Chapter 6, some attention is given to tariff and export-tax policy for the purpose of maximizing imports of capital goods.

International trade often implies substantial uncertainty in foreign exchange earnings. In Chapter 7 we discuss the sources of this uncertainty, both for countries exporting predominantly a single product and for those exporting two principal products. We also discuss the export-stockpiling policy for the purpose of maximizing export receipts in an uncertain world market.

A crucial result that flows from the developing economy models of Chapters 2, 5, and 6 is that the agricultural sector of low-income countries is a very important, perhaps the most important, sector. This result is certainly consistent with observations of specialists on particular developing areas. For example, Andrew Kamarck (1971, p. 126), in reviewing the African situation, asserts:

The key sector for economic development in most of Africa is still therefore, agriculture. So far, only a few African countries have found and developed mineral resources, the only alternative way, at this stage, of earning foreign exchange. For most African countries, then, it is agriculture that must be depended on: to raise the standard of living of the people initially, to provide the minimum market necessary for manufactures to get a foothold, to earn the necessary foreign exchange to pay for imports, and to provide the revenues to finance needed government services. The improvement of agriculture must be the central part of any development program.

The same observation would also apply to most countries of Asia; it would be a less accurate description of many countries in Latin America.

The book concludes with three chapters (one, mainly theoretical; two, empirical) in which we examine the agricultural sector in much greater detail. First, in Chapter 8 we develop a theoretical framework for studying the supply of agricultural output in developing countries, given the nature of the production possibilities open to the farmer. In particular, growing agricultural output is related to growing aggregate cropped area, to changing variable factor input prices, and to changing labor conditions, marketing facilities, and land-tenure arrangements. Also, an important source of technological change in agriculture, the adoption of new seeds, is analyzed.

Chapters 9 and 10 are the directly empirical chapters of the book. Empirical reasearch is vitally important for understanding economic development because theories of development, in the end, are useful only if they help to explain observed behavior. These two chapters here, both based on microeconomic data, are written primarily to suggest further theoretical work. Thus, in Chapter 9 we report some evidence on the factors of production used to produce output in Indian agriculture. In Chapter 10 we both reexamine the theoretical characterization of the food consumption function and report some econometric evidence on the form of this function.

In Figure I.1 we present a schema for a developing economy, which summarizes the principal topics discussed in this book. The arrows indicate significant commodity or resource flows; less significant flows, such as rural consumption of services, are not indicated.

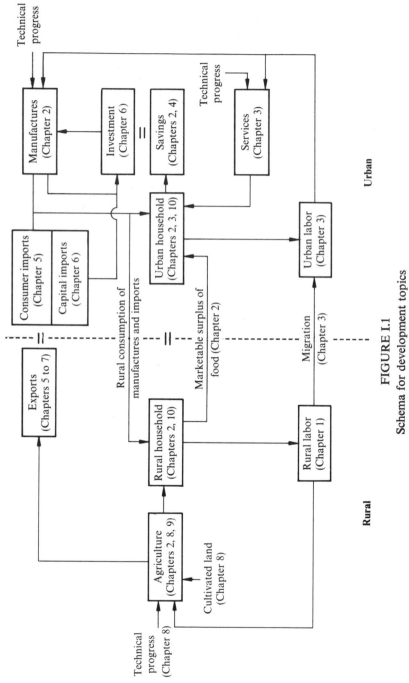

FIGURE I.1
Schema for development topics

6

PART ONE
SURPLUS LABOR

Chapter One

THE THEORY OF SURPLUS LABOR

The popularity of the classical, or labor-surplus, school of development economics arose out of a belief by a large number of economists that wholesale application of neoclassical economic theory to developing countries would lead to a misunderstanding of these countries and to inappropriate policy recommendations. Most economists were willing to accept the fact that much industrial activity in the modern sector is dominated by profit-maximizing behavior, with laborers being paid approximately their marginal productivity and capitalists reinvesting much of their earnings. However, they believed that agricultural activity is traditional in nature, that very often the output of a farm is too low to provide much more than a subsistence level of living, and that, therefore, a survival motivation dominates in agriculture. In fact, traditional agriculture was considered to be so poor that the large labor input required to produce even subsistence income leads to a marginal product of labor close to, or at, zero.

As argued most succinctly by Lewis (1954) and elaborated by Fei and Ranis (1964), the marginal product of agricultural labor near zero implies that industry can obtain unlimited labor from agriculture by paying a constant real wage which need be only somewhat greater than the subsistence wage prevailing in agriculture. Development thus proceeds as industry obtains labor at this constant real cost, capitalists reinvest their earnings, and the demand for industrial labor continually rises. As long as the rate of population growth is not too rapid, eventually the withdrawal of labor from agriculture will raise the marginal product of agricultural labor above subsistence wages. Neoclassical economic theory would then be more relevant.

This description of the agricultural sector bothered other development economists, particularly those most influenced by Marshallian microeconomic theory. Viner (1957), for example, found it most difficult to believe that the marginal product of labor is zero:

> As far as agriculture is concerned, I find it impossible to conceive of a farm of any kind on which, other factors of production being held constant in quantity, and even in form as well, it would not be possible, by known methods, to obtain some addition to the crop by using additional labor in more careful selection and planting of the seed, more intensive weeding, cultivation, thinning, and mulching, more painstaking harvesting, gleaning, and cleaning of the crop.[1]

These economists, furthermore, were troubled that a zero marginal product implied that agricultural workers were spending time working but accomplishing nothing.

In 1961 the debate sharpened when Jorgenson (1961) published a competing theoretical model of the development of a dual economy which he labeled as neoclassical. It differed most importantly from the Lewis model by arguing that the marginal product of agricultural labor is, in fact, substantially above zero so that a withdrawal of labor from the sector would lower output and raise the marginal productivity of the remaining workers. Thus, the supply curve of labor to industry is upward sloping.

At the theoretical level, the Jorgenson model and observations such as those of Viner placed the labor-surplus school on the defensive for a time. However, a cogent defense of surplus labor came in 1966 when A. K. Sen (1966) made a clear distinction between the marginal productivity of a laborer in agriculture and the marginal productivity of a man-hour. Sen, in fact, showed that the marginal productivity of a laborer could be zero even though the marginal productivity of a man-hour is substantially above zero. To establish this, Sen argued that if the "real" cost of a man-hour of work is constant—in particular, if the

---

[1] From the extract in Meier (1970, p. 152).

marginal utility to income is constant and the marginal disutility of work is also constant—then the loss of a worker from a privately operated farm leads others on the farm to work proportionately more hours to make up for the loss.   In other words, explained with micro-economic theory, if the real labor cost is constant with respect to the number of hours worked per worker, then competitive equilibrium for the farm implies constant utilization of factor inputs, including *total* man-hours.   Thus, Sen used neoclassical techniques to argue for the existence of surplus labor by assuming a particular shape for the indifference curve between leisure and income (that it is the straight line of perfect substitutability).

The Sen argument is important because it permits a consistency between the existence of surplus labor and comments, such as Viner's, that the marginal productivity of a man-hour is greater than zero. Furthermore, the argument points out that the Jorgenson neoclassical model implicitly assumes work hours per agricultural worker to be constant because that model makes no theoretical distinction between the number of laborers in agriculture and the number of work hours.

The leisure-income choice in low-income agriculture is examined in detail in this first chapter.   On the one hand, it is shown that the classical, or labor-surplus, description of low-income agriculture obtains not only when the Sen assumption—that the elasticity of indifferent substitution between leisure and income approaches infinity—is satisfied, but also when the elasticity of factor substitution in production between labor and land is zero.   On the other hand, it is shown that the neoclassical description, including a failure to distinguish between laborers and man-hours, obtains when the elasticity of indifferent substitution happens to equal the elasticity of factor substitution.   If the elasticity of indifferent substitution is greater than the elasticity of factor substitution, but both are greater than zero and less than infinity, then a middle position between the classical and neoclassical descriptions is appropriate.

1.1   The Leisure-income Choice in Agriculture

Consider the simplest possible case: private ownership of a family farm where all output is consumed on the farm.   Suppose there are four family members, all working, and one additional worker, a relative,

arrives to live on the farm (the numbers obviously do not matter for the
sake of argument).[1]   If the four members worked 5 hours daily before,
everyone can now work 4 hours and together produce the same total
output as before, with an output per worker that is 80 percent of its
former level.   If all five persons still work 5 hours daily, the labor
input increases by 25 percent, the output increases by less, and the
output per worker is greater than 80 percent but less than 100 percent
of the former level.   Finally, with a sufficient increase in work hours
per worker above 5 hours and a high enough marginal productivity to
labor, output per worker remains constant.

These three cases are represented in Figure 1.1, where P is the maximum amount of leisure possible (zero work hours). MP is the marginal productivity curve for each worker before the addition of a new
family member, assuming that each worker always works the same
number of hours as the others and that output is shared equally.   The
only other input, land, is fixed. $M'P$ is the marginal productivity

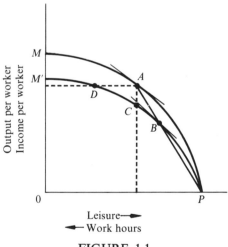

FIGURE 1.1
Output per worker on the farm

---

[1] We study the addition, rather than the withdrawal, of a farm worker because
rising labor/land ratios in low-income agriculture are almost universal today,
but the argument can be reversed.

curve after the addition of a new member; note that it is uniformly below the other curve because the labor/land ratio has increased.[1]

Now, in Figure 1.1 the slopes of the curves at any point A and B intersecting a straight line from P are equal because these correspond to the same total labor hours on the farm. Thus, point B corresponds to a proportionate reduction in man-hours input by each worker upon the addition of a new member. Point C corresponds to the same man-hours input by each worker. Point D may not be attainable (if the vertical distance to M' is less than that to A) but, if attainable, corresponds to a sufficient increase in work hours by each worker to lead to constant output per worker. The decision of hours worked per worker along $M'P$, of course, depends upon the indifference curve between income and leisure.

To study the work-hour decision, first characterize the farm production function in labor hours and land by the CES function

$$(1.1) \qquad y = [\beta(nH)^\rho + \gamma A^\rho]^{1/\rho} \qquad \rho < 1$$

where y is total farm output, n is the number of family members, H is labor hours input per family member, A is land acreage cropped, ρ defines the elasticity of factor substitution between labor and land as $\sigma = 1/(1 - \rho)$, and β and γ are parameters. Constant returns to scale are assumed. The average per-worker product is then

$$(1.2) \qquad \frac{y}{n} = \left[\beta + \gamma\left(\frac{A}{H}\right)^\rho n^{-\rho}\right]^{1/\rho} H$$

The marginal per-worker product is therefore

$$\frac{\partial y/n}{\partial H} = \left[\beta + \gamma\left(\frac{A}{H}\right)^\rho n^{-\rho}\right]^{1/\rho} - \frac{1}{\rho}\left[\beta + \gamma\left(\frac{A}{H}\right)^\rho n^{-\rho}\right]^{1/\rho - 1} \rho\gamma\left(\frac{A}{H}\right)^\rho n^{-\rho}$$

$$= \beta\left[\beta + \gamma\left(\frac{A}{H}\right)^\rho n^{-\rho}\right]^{(1-\rho)/\rho}$$

or, using (1.2),

$$(1.3) \qquad \frac{\partial y/n}{\partial H} = \beta\left(\frac{y}{nH}\right)^{1-\rho}$$

---

[1] A technical point: The curves are drawn assuming that zero output is associated with zero labor input; but if the production function in labor hours and land is, for example, a CES function with an elasticity of substitution greater than 1, then land is productive without labor input.

This relation describes mathematically curve MP in Figure 1.1. When new family members are included so that n becomes n' ($n' > n$), then

(1.4)
$$\frac{\partial y'/n'}{\partial H'} = \beta \left(\frac{y'}{n'H'}\right)^{1-\rho}$$

which describes curve $M'P$ in Figure 1.1.

Now, assume that the indifference curves between income and leisure are homothetic (constant marginal rates of substitution along any ray from the origin) and can be described by a CES function

(1.5)
$$I = \left[b(H_0 - H)^{\rho_0} + c\left(\frac{y}{n}\right)^{\rho_0}\right]^{1/\rho_0} \qquad \rho_0 < 1$$

where I is utility (we are only interested in ordinal utility, and so this could be any monotonically increasing function of utility, not utility itself), H_0 is maximum possible leisure time (distance $0P$ in Figure 1.1), ρ_0 defines the elasticity of indifferent substitution between leisure $H_0 - H$ and income per worker y/n as $\sigma_0 = 1/(1 - \rho_0)$, and b and c are parameters. Then, the marginal rate of substitution of leisure for income MRS is

$$MRS = \frac{\partial y/n}{\partial H}\bigg|_{I_{\text{constant}}}$$

$$= \frac{\partial [I^{\rho_0} - b(H_0 - H)^{\rho_0}]^{1/\rho_0} c^{-1/\rho_0}}{\partial H}$$

$$= \frac{1}{\rho_0}[I^{\rho_0} - b(H_0 - H)^{\rho_0}]^{1/\rho_0 - 1} c^{-1/\rho_0} b\rho_0 (H_0 - H)^{\rho_0 - 1}$$

or

(1.6)
$$MRS = \frac{b}{c}\left(\frac{y/n}{H_0 - H}\right)^{1-\rho_0}$$

After a new family member has arrived,

(1.7)
$$MRS' = \frac{b}{c}\left(\frac{y'/n'}{H_0 - H'}\right)^{1-\rho_0}$$

At the initial equilibrium point A, Equation (1.3) equals (1.6), or

$$\beta\left(\frac{y}{nH}\right)^{1-\rho} = \frac{b}{c}\left(\frac{y/n}{H_0 - H}\right)^{1-\rho_0}$$

Thus,

$$\beta^\sigma\left(\frac{y}{nH}\right) = \left(\frac{b}{c}\right)^\sigma\left(\frac{y}{nH}\frac{H}{H_0 - H}\right)^{\sigma/\sigma_0}$$

so that

(1.8)
$$\left(\frac{H}{H_0 - H}\right)^{\sigma/\sigma_0} = k\left(\frac{y}{nH}\right)^{1-\sigma/\sigma_0}$$

where $k = (\beta c/b)^\sigma$ and $y/(nH)$ is average output per worker per hour. Likewise, because (1.4) equals (1.7) in equilibrium,

(1.9)
$$\left(\frac{H'}{H_0 - H'}\right)^{\sigma/\sigma_0} = k\left(\frac{y'}{n'H'}\right)^{1-\sigma/\sigma_0}$$

Comparing (1.8) and (1.9), if $\sigma = \sigma_0$, then equilibrium hours of work per worker do not change when new family members arrive (point C obtains). If $\sigma < \sigma_0$, then equilibrium hours of work decrease (a point to the right of C); and if $\sigma > \sigma_0$, then equilibrium hours increase[1] (a point to the left of C). Thus, the following proposition has been established.

Proposition: Given a privately operated farm, as described above, with a constant elasticity of factor substitution between labor and land σ and a constant elasticity of indifferent substitution between leisure and income σ_0, the addition of new working family members affects equilibrium working hours per family member H' with respect to the previous level H as follows:

(1.10)
$$H'\begin{Bmatrix}<\\=\\>\end{Bmatrix}H \quad \text{accordingly as} \quad \sigma\begin{Bmatrix}<\\=\\>\end{Bmatrix}\sigma_0$$

In other words, if the elasticity of indifferent substitution happens to equal the elasticity of factor substitution in production, then work hours are constant with respect to changes in the number of family members on the farm; that is, no distinction need be made between laborers and man-hours in developing agriculture. If indifferent substitution is greater, then work hours per worker decrease as new members enter the farm [a special case of this result is that of Sen (1966),

---

[1] Derived by taking the σ/σ_0th root of both sides of the equations and noting that $H'/(H_0 - H')$ increases faster than $y'/(n'H')$ with respect to H'.

as we shall see in a moment].   Finally, if indifferent substitution is lower, then work hours increase.

In his article, A. K. Sen (1966) [see also Berry and Soligo (1968)] established what amounts to a corollary to this proposition.

Corollary 1:   If there is perfect substitutability between leisure and income (real labor cost is constant) so that $\sigma_0 \rightarrow \infty$, then work hours per worker decline proportionately to the increase in new family members (point *B* in Figure 1.1).[1]

Algebraically, this result can be derived from Equations (1.8) and (1.9) by noting that the left-hand sides of these equations approach unity as $\sigma_0 \rightarrow \infty$ while the right-hand sides are constant only if average output per worker per hour is constant—that is, only if marginal per hour product and thus total work hours are constant.   Geometrically, the result obtains because the marginal productivities at points *A* and *B* in Figure 1.1 are the same and the indifference curves are parallel straight lines.   To justify such indifference curves, Sen assumes that there is a constant marginal utility to income over the relevant region and that there is a constant marginal utility to leisure (disutility to work) independent of the level of income.   If, however, the marginal utility to income increases as income level falls (as seems particularly likely at low-income levels) or the marginal utility to leisure decreases as leisure increases, the indifference curves are not straight lines but convex to the origin (our $\sigma_0 < \infty$).

A second corollary leads to the same result as Corollary 1.

Corollary 2:   If the elasticity of factor substitution between labor and land σ is zero, then, again, work hours per worker decline proportionately to the increase in new family members (again, point *B* in Figure 1.1).

To show this result, merely substitute $\sigma = 0$ in (1.9).   Then the right-hand side is only constant if total work hours are constant—work hours per worker decline proportionately.

The following result is merely a restatement of a direct implication of the proposition.

Corollary 3:   If the elasticity of indifferent substitution between leisure and income σ_0 equals the elasticity of factor substitution between labor

---

[1] Actually, Sen argues in terms of withdrawing members from a farm because he is (presumably) interested in the planning implications of increasing industrial employment.   All the above results are unchanged mutatis mutandis.

and land σ, work hours per worker are constant (point C in Figure 1.1).

We can now return to the purpose of this discussion: the theoretical distinction between the classical, or surplus-labor, description of low-income agriculture and the neoclassical description. Thus, the strict form of the classical description (that the marginal product of a laborer is zero) is implied by an elasticity of indifferent substitution between leisure and income approaching infinity (Corollary 1) or an elasticity of factor substitution between labor and land equal to zero (Corollary 2). The strict form of the neoclassical description (that no theoretical distinction between laborers and man-hours is necessary) is implied by an elasticity of indifferent substitution between leisure and income equal

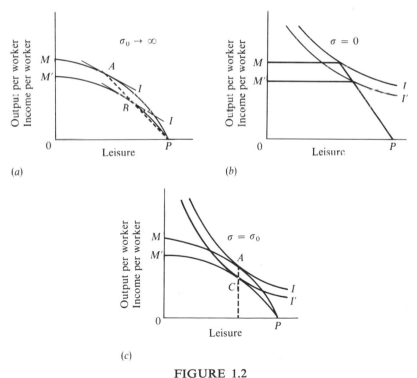

(a)

(b)

(c)

FIGURE 1.2

Corollaries 1 to 3.   (a) Corollary 1, surplus labor; (b) Corollary 2, surplus labor; (c) Corollary 3, neoclassical

to the elasticity of factor substitution between labor and land (Corollary 3). A middle position between these two descriptions would therefore assert that the elasticity of indifferent substitution is greater than the elasticity of factor substitution, but both are greater than zero and do not approach infinity; then, work hours decrease when a new member is added to a farm, but not proportionately, so that total work hours increase. (For convenience, the three corollaries are graphed in Figure 1.2.)

A basic assumption of much of this book is that the elasticity of farm output, with respect to farm *laborers*, is greater than zero and may be less than, equal to, or greater than the *man-hour* elasticity as described by the proposition above. In other words, we assume that the elasticity of indifferent substitution σ_0 is substantially less than infinity and the elasticity of factor substitution σ is substantially larger than zero, so that neither Corollary 1 nor Corollary 2 is believed to be a close approximation to reality. Thus, this book does not subscribe to the strict form of the surplus-labor, or classical, school. If we had to choose one of the corollaries as being the closest approximation to reality, we would choose Corollary 3; but we suspect that reality is somewhere between the classical and neoclassical descriptions of low-income agriculture (that is, $0 < \sigma < \sigma_0 < \infty$).

This first section has only considered a very simply economic structure of the farm. In the next section, our basic proposition is re-examined with respect to different economic structures in agriculture, changes in the farm economy, and nonhomothetic indifferent curves.

1.2 Extensions of the Proposition

MARKETED OUTPUT AND PURCHASED INPUTS

On most farms, some or all of the output is sold or traded, depending upon the income level and the crop produced. In this case, merely reinterpret output, above, as income and, as Sen (1966, p. 428) notes, "the product should be divided in such a manner between direct consumption and exchange in the market that the relevant marginal rate of indifferent substitution between the two commodities equals their price ratio."

Sen also indicates that any use of purchased factor inputs at fixed prices does not affect his results. In his case, labor is purchased from within the family (by varying work hours) at a constant real price; thus the competitive equilibrium for the farm (including *total* work hours) is invariant to the number of family members.   In our case, labor hours are not offered at constant price (real cost); rather, the arrival of a new worker lowers the real price of total labor hours.   In other words, the farm is a monopsonistic buyer of (its own) labor and a competitive buyer of purchased inputs.   The result, then, assuming that at constant purchased input utilization our production function is still appropriate, is that the new equilibrium work hours H' is greater than predicted by our proposition: If purchased input utilizations were constant after the arrival of a new worker, their marginal productivities would be above their prices (as total work hours increase); therefore, these input utilizations are higher than their previous levels.   Consequently, new work hours per worker are higher than predicted by our proposition.

The Addition of Nonworking Family Members

Next, suppose that the new family member is a nonworker (a newborn child or an old relative) and that all farm output is still shared equally, but that work-hour decisions are based only on the indifference curves of the working members.   Then, Equation (1.4) is multiplied by n/n' to yield per-family-member marginal product.   Equation (1.9) is thus derived as

$$\beta\left(\frac{y'}{nH'}\right)^{1-\rho}\frac{n}{n'} = \frac{b}{c}\left(\frac{y'/n'}{H_0 - H'}\right)^{1-\rho_0}$$

$$= \frac{b}{c}\left(\frac{y'/n}{H_0 - H'}\right)^{1-\rho_0}\left(\frac{n}{n'}\right)^{1-\rho_0}$$

so that

(1.11) $$\left(\frac{H'}{H_0 - H'}\right)^{\sigma/\sigma_0} = k\left(\frac{n}{n'}\right)^{(\sigma_0-1)\sigma/\sigma_0}\left(\frac{y'}{nH'}\right)^{1-\sigma/\sigma_0}$$

If the elasticity of indifferent substitution σ_0 is unity, this equation reduces to Equation (1.8).   If $\sigma_0 < 1$, work hours per worker increase; if $\sigma_0 > 1$, work hours decrease.   Therefore, assuming $\sigma > 0$, the addition of a nonworking family member implies the following change in equilibrium work hours:

(1.12) $$H'\begin{Bmatrix}>\\=\\<\end{Bmatrix}H \quad \text{accordingly as} \quad \sigma_0\begin{Bmatrix}<\\=\\>\end{Bmatrix}1$$

Of course, if and when a new member does start working his share, then the proposition holds relative to the farm-work structure before he came on the farm.

EXOGENOUS FACTORS AFFECTING THE WORK-HOUR DECISION

Technical change on the farm will generally occur independent of the arrival of new family members and, therefore, is conceptually distinct (unless the arrival of new members encourages technical change either because the new members are aware of new techniques or because income per family member is suffering a decline).   If the technical change is neutral (the interested reader can examine nonneutral change), then it is formally equivalent to a reduction in nonworking family members—each member receives more output for the same work input.   Thus, using the results of the previous subsection and again assuming $\sigma > 0$, equilibrium hours of work move as

$$(1.13) \qquad H' \begin{Bmatrix} < \\ = \\ > \end{Bmatrix} H \qquad \text{accordingly as} \qquad \sigma_0 \begin{Bmatrix} < \\ = \\ > \end{Bmatrix} 1$$

In other words, if the elasticity of indifferent substitution between leisure and income is unity, equilibrium work hours do not change when neutral technical change occurs.   If the elasticity is less than unity, equilibrium work hours decrease; if it is greater than unity, equilibrium work hours increase.

Changes in output or input prices facing the farm are generally independent of considerations over arrivals of new family members except when the agricultural sector as an aggregate is being examined. On the one hand, changes in output price do not affect work hours if no output is sold (a subsistence farm); on the other hand, changes in output price affect work hours exactly as does neutral technical change if all of the output is sold (production of a cash crop).   If some of the farm's output is sold and some consumed, the problem is more complex because an indifference curve between consumption of the produced crop and consumption of purchased goods is needed; the interested reader should see Sen (1966, pp. 436–438) for a suggested approach to this problem.

Increases in purchased input prices lead to decreased utilization of these inputs and therefore to decreased marginal productivity of labor hours—work hours decrease. Decreases in purchased input prices have the opposite effect—work hours increase.

EXISTENCE OF A LABOR MARKET

To this point we have discussed what is often called *peasant agriculture* —labor is performed on family farms only so that farmers do not hire labor or work off the farm. Empirically, this is unrealistic because virtually all agricultural economies have some sort of labor market. Unfortunately for analytic purposes, the form of any agricultural labor market varies widely among countries and regions of countries. Hopefully, the discussion here, together with the discussion of surplus labor and land tenure in Chapter 8, covers the important cases.

To study the labor market, it is perhaps best to examine the agricultural sector as a whole. However, we discuss formally only the extreme case in which landlords do not work but earn the profits from the farm while all workers are landless and receive an income equal to their number of hours worked times their wage. Those cases in which landlords also work are more complicated but should lead to results somewhere between those of the present analysis and the results obtained in Section 1.1.

In the first instance, suppose that the labor market is competitive with respect to both the hourly wage rate and the number of hours worked. Then, all workers choose the number of hours worked that equates the wage with the marginal rate of substitution between income and leisure. In this case, an increase in the labor/land ratio, as rural population grows ceteris paribus, decreases the marginal product of an hour's work and thus the wage rate. Therefore, using the conceptual framework of Section 1.1, except that the income relevant for the indifference curve is not average per-worker product y/n but rather hours worked per worker times the wage [that is, $H\beta[y/(nH)]^{1-\rho}$, using Equation (1.3)], we obtain the same results as for relation (1.12). In other words, the results are equivalent to an increase in nonworking family members in the case of the "peasant" economy: Work hours are unaffected by changing agricultural population and thus changing wages only if the elasticity of indifferent substitution is unity.

Second, suppose that the market for hired labor requires a worker to work a full work day or a full work week (or whatever), but that the wage rate is still competitively determined. This problem is a bit more complex and depends upon the time units relevant for measuring the indifference curve between leisure and work. If the farm workers are willing to work full time for a short period of time and then have leisure, the time units for the indifference curve are greater than for the working requirement (i.e., leisure and income may be measured on a monthly or, less likely, yearly basis). In this case, we obtain the same results as in the previous paragraph.

If, however, the employment requirement is in time units greater than or equal to the units for the indifference curve, then workers are faced with a binary choice: to work or not to work. When a worker has savings from the last time he worked, has support from relatives, or also works on a family farm, the choice is a real one and depends, of course, on whether such work raises or lowers total utility. (It is therefore possible that, to induce more work, landowners of large farms have to pay a higher wage than the marginal productivity on small farms if the landless worker class plus the supply forthcoming from small farms is too small to satisfy labor demand on large farms.[1]) When a worker has no resources (e.g., is landless), then he must work at the required hours. Either case is equivalent to institutionally determined work hours in developed countries.

Suppose that the earnings per worker that would result either from a competitive market in hourly wages and hours worked or from wages only is below a subsistence level or below institutionally determined minimum standards. One possibility is that land area and known agricultural technology are inadequate to support the rural population even if everyone receives the average agricultural product. This possibility does not seem to be at all prevalent—yet. More frequently, the distribution of land acreage per farm is enormously skewed, as in Latin America, so that a competitive wage with a large number of landless workers (and/or many very small farms) would be below subsistence. In such cases, earnings per worker may stabilize at a subsistence level while hours of work are competitively determined (and could be brought to an institutional limit or to a level approaching zero marginal productivity of labor[2]). Thus, additions of new workers to the labor

---

[1] At this level of abstraction, it would be in the interest of landowners of large farms, collectively, to permit workers to choose the number of hours worked.

[2] This is the only case of marginal productivity per work hour approaching zero that we can conceive. However, Viner (1957) notes:

When I was in Brazil, I heard of complaints by plantation owners in districts in which there was also peasant and squatter agriculture of "shortage of hands" (*falta de mao*). I don't see how this can be reconciled with the

force increase work hours per worker because competition for jobs raises the workload demanded by big landowners. If work hours are institutionally fixed or reach their physical limit, total agricultural work hours rise according to the increase in the number of agricultural workers or additional workers are unemployed.[1]

NONHOMOTHETIC INDIFFERENCE CURVES

Finally, examine the proposition with respect to nonhomothetic indifference curves by considering three possibilities. First, the average number of work hours per farm worker may not institutionally be a variable if either the local community dictates the amount of work hours performed per worker or if, more likely, family traditions dictate the level of work hours. In this case, the leisure-income indifference curve is a vertical line (through A and C in Figure 1.1).

Second, in a dynamic setting, consumers appear to want to maintain past consumption levels in the face of adversity [see, particularly, Duesenberry (1949)]. This behavior is, in fact, most likely to occur

---

prevalence of zero marginal productivity of labor, whether on the plantations or for self-employed agricultural labor. [From the extract in Meier (1970, p. 153).]

[1] The possibility that some workers are involuntarily unemployed led Stephen Marglin (1966, pp. 60–61) to assert:

The "classical" surplus-labor hypothesis stands or falls on the premise that *no invisible hand guarantees full employment*. Instead, the classical theory assumes exogenous determination of the industrial wage rate and posits a wage too high to permit full employment in an enterprise economy in which employers hire additional workers until the marginal productivity falls to the wage. Exogenous determination of the industrial wage rate is the root cause of the gap between the wage and the social opportunity cost of adding to industrial employment: the social opportunity cost is the productivity of the wholly unemployed worker or the productivity of the partially unemployed agriculturalist, depending on which pool of workers is the relevant one for industry. In contrast to the classical wage hypothesis, the neoclassical hypothesis is that *full employment is guaranteed* by the invisible hand of a flexible wage rate, with an assist by government (if necessary) to ensure adequate aggregate demand. The neoclassical hypothesis permits of no gap between the industrial wage and the social opportunity cost of industrial employment. Hence accounting prices and market prices are identical. (Italics added.)

Note, though, that, insofar as this remark refers to urban unemployment, an upward sloping supply curve of labor to industry and such unemployment are not inconsistent (see Chapter 3).

at low (perhaps close to subsistence) levels of income.   Then, the indifference curve is horizontal through the initial point A, and, if attainable, new equilibrium work hours are point D.   This argument, however, is not reversible; a decrease in the number of family members, leading to a higher marginal productivity of remaining members, would lead to a traditional leisure-income choice.

Third, Berry and Soligo (1968) show that if leisure is an inferior good (decreases in real income—utility—at a constant marginal productivity of work hours lead to higher consumption of leisure), then point B, the Sen result, could obtain even though the indifference curves are not straight lines.   Furthermore, it is even possible that *total* work hours on the farm decline (a point to the right of B) if leisure is sufficiently inferior.[1]

1.3   Methodological Implications

A considerable amount of space has been devoted to discussing the leisure-income choice in agriculture.   We have seen that work hours per worker are more rigid, behaviorally, than suggested by the strict version of the classical description of agriculture but more flexible than suggested by the strict version of the neoclassical description.   In particular, rising labor/land ratios in agriculture can increase, decrease, or leave constant the work hours per worker, depending upon the leisure-income choice and the economic characteristics of the farm.   The implication, in any case, is that the supply curve of labor to industry is not horizontal because the number of workers in agriculture generally does affect agricultural output and wages; even under a labor market leading to fixed subsistence wages, agricultural output and hourly wages are not fixed.

Throughout the remainder of this book, no distinction is made between the marginal productivity of a man-hour in agriculture and the marginal productivity of a laborer; all discussion refers to the marginal productivity of laborers.   We ask the reader to break this down into its components—the marginal productivity of a man-hour and the change in work hours—as he sees fit, given the remarks made in this chapter.   For a point of reference, we note here a set of assumptions, other than institutionally determined hours of work, that implies no change in work hours with respect to changes in the labor/land ratio,

---

[1] Is there a difference between leisure and Irish potatoes?

that is, assumptions that allow one to ignore the distinction between laborers and man-hours.

AGGREGATING ASSUMPTIONS

(1) All farm workers have the same homothetic indifference curves between leisure and income.

(2) All farms have the same homothetic production function in labor hours and land (no purchased inputs) with constant returns to scale.

(3) (*a*) The distribution of the proportion of workers to non-workers is constant across families, *or* the elasticity of indifferent substitution between leisure and income equals unity; and (*b*) if the farms are peasant owned and worked, the distribution of farms according to labor/land ratio is constant.

(4) All farms face the same output price.

BEHAVIORAL ASSUMPTIONS

(5) No technical change occurs, *or* the elasticity of indifferent substitution equals unity.

(6) No output is sold, *or* no output-price change occurs, *or* all output is sold and the elasticity of indifferent substitution equals unity.

(7) Laborers maximize utility, and (*a*) if labor is performed only on family farms where work is shared equally among workers and output is shared equally among family members, then the elasticity of factor substitution between labor and land in production equals the elasticity of indifferent substitution (Corollary 3); but (*b*) if large farms profit-maximize, all work is performed by hired labor, and the labor market is competitive in hourly wage rates and hours of work (or competitive in wage rates only and the time unit for the leisure-income choice is greater than for work-hour contracts), then the elasticity of indifferent substitution equals unity.

Note that if the elasticity of indifferent substitution equals unity, assumptions 3(*a*), 5, and 7(*b*) are all satisfied, and if additionally all farm output is sold, assumption 6 is also satisfied.

PART TWO

THE CLOSED ECONOMY

Chapter Two

A DUAL ECONOMY MODEL

Many developing countries are still at a very low level of per-capita income, with a large percentage of their populations engaged in agriculture. Food is produced by labor-intensive methods, and increases in farm output are due to a more labor-intensive use of land and those improvements in productive techniques which require small expenditures by the farm owner (such as improvements in seed, small-scale irrigation projects, and clearing of marginal land). Farmers use only small amounts of physical capital on the farm in the form of plows, hand tools, and structures.

Industry is usually concentrated in large urban enclaves which become centers for the migration of farmers out of rural areas. However, large urban unemployment may be observed as farmers leave the rural areas in hopes of a better future in the city even if they cannot find immediate employment there. The industrial sector uses both capital and labor as inputs to the production process, while growth in industrial output depends upon investment in new capital, increases in the employment of labor, and technological improvements in the means of production.

This type of economy is faced with a number of difficulties inhibiting economic growth. First, it must increase its output of agricultural products at a sufficient rate to feed a rapidly growing population. But

29

these economies are not in a position to capitalize the farm; labor and technical improvements must be relied upon for more food.   Second, the economy must induce farmers to market food surpluses to urban areas, perhaps in exchange for manufacturing products.   To obtain this marketable surplus, the terms of trade must be favorable to agriculture and efficient marketing facilities must exist, or else direct taxation of the peasants may be required.   Third, the large populations in urban areas must be able to find employment; if they do not, their productive abilities are left unutilized while they consume scarce resources.   Finally, the economy needs to generate enough savings to allow a substantial growth in industrial investment and thus in industrial capital and output.   Many times this savings requirement suggests taxation on producers and/or workers, but, in any case, it requires a reinvestment of the earnings on existing capital stock.

This chapter formulates a basic dual economy model for countries which are characterized by these problems and which are closed to international trade.   The model is built in order to capture many, but not all, of the essential elements of a closed dual economy and in order to provide a framework for discussion of development problems examined in the rest of the book.

The model is formulated by first studying the supply of outputs in the two sectors, agriculture and manufacturing, through an examination of the technical conditions of production.   Then the demand for investment goods is derived and assumed to be satisfied by secondary sector output.   Next labor supply and equilibrium in the labor market are obtained.   Finally, the demand for food is ascertained in order to close the model (the demand for secondary-sector consumption goods is given implicitly).

Although most of the issues raised in this introduction are included in this first model, some are not.   For example, the problem of urban unemployment is not considered until Chapter 3, where it is examined in a partial-equilibrium context.   There it is shown that a stable wage-rate differential between rural and urban areas can lead to a stable long-run nonzero unemployment rate.   Here it will become evident that such a stable unemployment rate does not affect any of the conclusions of our model.   In addition, the model does not introduce an explicit role for the government; for example, taxation or investment in rural infrastructure is not an available instrument.   Nevertheless, the conclusions from the model help indicate appropriate government action (or inaction) to aid development.

2.1 Production

As determinants of the level of agricultural crop production, Johnston and Cownie (1969, p. 571) have listed five variables in addition to the variety of seed planted, the level of application of chemical fertilizers, and other current inputs. They are: "(1) human labor, considering both the stock represented by the farm labor force and the flow of labor inputs; (2) nonhuman power inputs; (3) the quantity and quality of land inputs as determined by the total cultivated area and the crop intensity; (4) water availability, with attention to timing as well as quantity; and (5) farming practices." Current inputs, water availability, and farming practices are all absorbed in the constant term of our aggregate agricultural production function; any improvements in these inputs are incorporated in a technical change variable. Human labor, represented by the number of people in agriculture L_1, is included in the function. Cropped area for the whole country is assumed fixed, or else growing at a fixed rate (including abandonment of fallow land and increased double-cropping) and included in the technical change variable.

Capital in agriculture is a much more difficult problem. To the extent that capital consists of nonhuman power inputs which are livestock, we can assume that it remains in fixed proportion with human inputs (livestock are primarily used by human laborers to pull farm implements). Furthermore, mechanized equipment is seldom used in traditional agriculture, and farm implements are often produced on the farm. However, the agricultural sector also includes capital infrastructure.

In this chapter we assume that growth of capital stock in agriculture, as represented particularly by improvements in capital infrastructure, can also be included in the exogenous technical change variable. Essentially, therefore, we are assuming that there are no important intersectoral flows of capital between the primary and secondary sectors so that increases in agricultural capital stock are produced primarily through resources available in the primary sector. Although there is certainly an important element of truth in this assumption in a descriptive model of growth, for planning purposes intersectoral capital flows would be crucial.[1]

---

[1] Thus, Sanjit Bose and Avinash K. Dixit (1972), in their study of development planning, focus on capital by assuming fixed capital/output ratios in agriculture and manufacturing.

To summarize, the agricultural production function is formulated in terms of one variable input, labor, which exhibits decreasing returns to scale β_1, and technical change b_1, which also includes increases in land acreage and capital stock (see Chapter 8).   Thus,

$$(2.1) \qquad\qquad Y_1 = e^{b_1 t} L_1^{\beta_1} \qquad 0 < \beta_1 < 1$$

where Y_1 is a quantity index of agricultural output with appropriate units of measurement and t is time in years from the initial year.   As explained in Chapter 1, this agricultural production function implies that the marginal product of a laborer (not only labor hours) is not equal to zero.

The industrial, or secondary sector, production function relates output Y_2 to the standard variable inputs of capital K_2 and labor L_2 and to shifts in the production function due to technological improvements.[1] However, an important consideration is the form of the production function as described by the elasticity of substitution between inputs. There is very little work available on this elasticity using data from underdeveloped economies.   An important reason is that estimation of the elasticity is sensitive to the data chosen, and data available in these countries are usually less reliable than data from developed economies. However, as Lloyd Reynolds (1969, p. 95) has noted, "If the real wage level is rising rapidly employers will respond in the normal fashion by capital-labour substitution and other measures.   The sight of employers striving energetically to save labour in the midst of a general labour surplus is common in the less developed countries."

Furthermore, the work of Arrow et al. (1961, pp. 234–238) and Fuchs (1963) containing cross-country estimates of the elasticity of substitution suggest an elasticity in the neighborhood of unity.   Their data include observations from underdeveloped countries.   Additionally, Sankar (1970) studied Indian manufacturing and could reject unity in only one out of fifteen industries, while Katz (1969, pp. 47–50) studied Argentine

---

[1] Incidentally, if industrial capital is thought of as consisting of two types of capital, structures and equipment, it may still be possible to describe the industrial production function in terms of a single capital good.   Suppose that in developing countries structures are built with a very labor-intensive technology and that there are no significant improvements in this technology over time. The price of structures will then rise with the wage rate for labor.   Thus structures in the industrial production function can be aggregated with labor so that labor L_2 refers to labor directly required in industrial production as well as labor indirectly required in building structures.   Capital K_2 then refers to capital in equipment only.

manufacturing and obtained estimates not significantly different from one at 5 percent for most two-digit industries. For developed economies, the studies for United States manufacturing of Griliches (1967, pp. 285–297) and of Zarembka (1970a) and Zarembka and Chernicoff (1971) accept the hypothesis that the elasticity equals unity. (Nevertheless, it is clear that the value of this elasticity is controversial within the profession.[1])

In summary, available empirical evidence can support an assumption that the elasticity of substitution for industry equals 1. Furthermore, we do not believe that the most important problems of development are described by the curvature of the production isoquant so that convenience should, in part, determine any assumed value. Therefore, the secondary sector production function is a Cobb–Douglas function

$$(2.2) \qquad Y_2 = e^{b_2 t} K_2^{1-\beta_2} L_2^{\beta_2} \qquad 0 < \beta_2 < 1$$

with appropriate units of measurement, where b_2 is the annual rate of technical change and β_2 is the elasticity of output with respect to labor. Note that constant returns to scale are assumed: Such an assumption should be a good approximation, and estimates of production functions generally have great difficulty distinguishing between nonconstant returns to scale and the rate of technical change.

2.2   Capital and Labor Markets

The impact of the assumption that the elasticity of factor substitution in industry equals unity is its influence on the savings rate. Thus, given that labor is paid the value of its marginal product either because the manufacturing sector consists of profit-maximizing competitive firms or because the sector is owned by the government, then the share of manufacturing output going to capital is exactly equal to the elasticity of output with respect to capital $1 - \beta_2$ and the share of output going to labor is the labor elasticity β_2. Therefore, assuming that a constant fraction s_k of the capital share and another constant fraction s_ℓ of the labor share are saved, the demand for investment goods I_2 is

$$I_2 = s_k(1 - \beta_2) Y_2 + s_\ell \beta_2 Y_2 = s Y_2$$

where s is $s_k(1 - \beta_2) + s_\ell \beta_2$.

---

[1] For one example, an elasticity estimate significantly greater than unity for aggregate United States manufacturing in 1957 has been reported in Ramsey and Zarembka (1971).

When the elasticity of substitution departs from unity, the shares and thus savings rate are affected by factor prices; for example, if the elasticity is less than unity, the labor share rises and the capital share falls as the industrial wage rises (if $s_k > s_\ell$, the savings rate thus falls). It is the near constancy of the shares that has partly supported the widespread use of the Cobb–Douglas function.

As to the value of the fraction s, it should be noted that this fraction may have *any* stable value without influencing the solution of the model obtained in Section 2.4. In other words, it is the constancy of the fraction that is important here, not its value. In any case, Williamson (1968, p. 209) has investigated personal saving in Asian countries and has concluded that "the marginal propensity to save out of nonlabor income exceeds by far that of labor income." Also, Furtado (1970, pp. 65–66) reports evidence for Latin America that the savings levels of workers are very low (see Table 2.1).[1] Thus, an assumption that the return to labor is only consumed so that $s_\ell = 0$ may be a reasonable approximation to behavior (see also Chapter 4). For convenience, we also assume that the entire capital share is reinvested so that $s_k = 1$. Therefore,

$$(2.3) \qquad\qquad I_2 = (1 - \beta_2) Y_2$$

Given the demand for gross investment I_2 and assuming a supply of investment goods from the secondary sector is available to meet this demand, then the change in capital stock of the industrial sector $\dot{K}_2$ is determined by netting out depreciation from investment. The usual assumption is that depreciation is a constant fraction δ of existing capital stock so that

$$(2.4) \qquad\qquad \dot{K}_2 = I_2 - \delta K_2 \qquad 0 < \delta < 1$$

To discuss the utilization of the labor factor input in the two sectors, first consider the total population of the country. On the one hand, the medical revolution has already made its most significant impact in most developing countries so that the death rate has been brought from high levels of 30 or 40 per thousand to as low as 10 to 15 per thousand, even though the low levels of income suggest poor health conditions. On the other hand, the birth rate has remained at its high previous

---

[1] Saving by landowners is considered in the export economy of Chapters 5 and 6. In this closed-economy chapter, landowners, as laborers, are regarded as having lower income and so save little.

TABLE 2.1
Allocation of Personal Income in Latin America (in Percent)

Group	Percent of Total Population	Average Yearly Income (Dollars)	Taxes and Social Insurance Contributions	Savings	Consumption	Total
Rural workers	50	120	13.0	−3.0	90.0	100
Urban workers	45	400	20.0	3.5	76.5	100
Higher income brackets and small entrepreneurs	3	1750	16.5	9.5	74.0	100
Big landowners and entrepreneurs	2	3500	21.0	21.0	58.0	100
Total population			18.4	6.6	75.0	100

SOURCE: Furtado, Celso (1970). *Economic Development of Latin America.* Cambridge, Cambridge University Press, pp. 65–66 (as drawn from ECLA, *The Economic Development of Latin America in the Post-War Period, 1964*). Furtado notes (p. 65) that "since the data for Venezuela and Mexico—countries in which income is particularly highly concentrated—carried considerable weight in the preparation of this scheme and since data for Argentina were not available at the time, the figures must be taken as representing the Latin American mode rather than the Latin American average."

levels of 35 to 45 per thousand because members of the extended family can best ensure at least a subsistence income by having many children who may be able to earn an income.   However, economic variables do not seem to play a significant role in changing either birth or death rates at these low levels of income [see Giesbrecht (1971), for a recent discussion of the importance of noneconomic influences on birth rates].

These remarks suggest that the rate of population growth may be quite high while at the same time exogenous to the level of economic development.   Thus, if we label the population growth rate ϵ and if we arbitrarily index the initial population as having a unit value, then the equation for total population L can be written

(2.5) $$L = e^{\epsilon t}$$

This total supply of labor is divided between two sectors, the primary and the secondary, so that

(2.6) $$L_2 = L - L_1$$

In each sector it is assumed that a constant fraction of the sector's population is unemployed (including children and unemployed and underemployed men and women), which allows us to write production functions ignoring unemployment—its effects are absorbed in the constant terms of the production functions.

To describe the allocation of workers between the sectors, a rather simple mechanism is posited in this chapter: Migration is assumed to ensure that the rural wage remains some constant fraction of the urban wage.   The constant fraction μ is less than 1 and reflects the belief that farm workers require some premium over their agricultural wage to induce them to incur the transport costs of moving to a perhaps less well-known and more risky urban area.   The constancy of the fraction is an approximation, and its value may change as the economy moves away from low income.   Furthermore, it would not be surprising if the fraction were close to 1 if account were taken of the higher cost of food in urban areas due to transportation costs and of the fact that a smaller number of family members are able to find work in cities (i.e., the usual formulation of wages in terms of employment, not sectoral population, overstates the difference in urban-rural per-capita income).

In calculating agricultural wages, farm workers may take their wages as either their marginal product or their average product.   If the typical worker who migrates is landless or sells or rents land that he owns, his wage is his marginal product $\beta_1 Y_1 / L_1$.   If the migrant owns land but loses it when he moves (e.g., it is typical to pass land on to relatives), or if he worked on a family farm, then he takes his wage as the return to labor input and the implicit rent on land; in other words, any farm net revenue per worker is the opportunity cost of moving to an urban area, so that wages are simply average agricultural product Y_1/L_1. In either rural case, urban wages are equal to the marginal product of industrial labor $\beta_2 Y_2/L_2$. Thus, if q_1 is the price of food in terms of manufacturing products, then

$$(2.7) \qquad \frac{q_1 \beta_1 Y_1}{L_1} = \frac{\mu \beta_2 Y_2}{L_2} \qquad 0 < \mu \leq 1$$

where $\mu \leq \beta_1$ if the typical migrant owns agricultural land that he does not sell upon moving. Note, also, that if the economy has surplus agricultural labor in the sense that the marginal product is less than the wage, then μ is smaller. Again, as for Equation (2.3), it is the constancy of the fraction that is important for our purposes here, not its value.

2.3 Marketable Surplus of Food

To close the dual economy model, we must introduce an explanation for the trade of the surplus agricultural product in the rural areas for the manufactured products of the urban areas. First, the consumption of food in rural areas depends upon the consumption levels of two separate groups: those who are landless L_1' and those who live on the farm as a part of a farm family L_1'' ($L_1' + L_1'' = L_1$). The average income level of the former group is their wage rate, equal to the marginal product of farm labor $\beta_1 Y_1/L_1$; the average income of the latter group is the average product per farm net of wage payments to landless labor, or $(Y_1 - L_1' \beta_1 Y_1/L_1)/L_1''$. Therefore, if food consumption depends upon real income (defined in terms of purchasing power over food) and upon the relative food price q_1, then food consumption is

$$L_1' f_1\left(\frac{\beta_1 Y_1}{L_1}, q_1\right) + L_1'' f_1\left(\frac{Y_1 - L_1' \beta_1 Y_1/L_1}{L_1''}, q_1\right)$$

where f_1 is the rural consumption function for food.

In the secondary, urban, sector food consumption is also formulated as depending upon real income (defined, again, in terms of purchasing power over food) and upon the relative food price. Thus, if only capital income is invested [see the remarks preceding Equation (2.3)], then urban food demand is

$$L_2 f_2 \left(\frac{\beta_2 Y_2}{L_2 q_1}, q_1 \right)$$

where f_2 is the food consumption function in urban areas.

Note that income in both sectors is measured in terms of the purchasing power over food because the mathematics is simplified without greatly distorting reality. As indicated by the empirical evidence in Chapter 10, at low-income levels food consists of the major part of a household budget (see Table 10.3) while the remainder is spent on industrial goods and services. Our assumption is only a distortion to the extent that the income effects of a price change of other goods are ignored. This distortion is small, particularly if, in a dual economy model, services are not included in the definition of secondary sector outputs. However, by defining real income as the purchasing power over food, growth in income is underestimated whenever costs of food are rising relative to those of manufactured goods.

The marketed surplus of the primary sector is its sectoral output minus its own consumption. In equilibrium between the primary and secondary sectors, the supply of food to the urban areas must be equated to the food demand in the cities; that is,

$$Y_1 - L_1' f_1 \left(\frac{\beta_1 Y_1}{L_1'}, q_1 \right) - L_1'' f_1 \left(\frac{Y_1 - L_1' \beta_1 Y_1 / L_1'}{L_1''}, q_1 \right) = L_2 f_2 \left(\frac{\beta_2 Y_2}{L_2 q_1}, q_1 \right)$$

Using Equation (2.7), this equation becomes

$$Y_1 - L_1' f_1 \left(\frac{\beta_1 Y_1}{L_1'}, q_1 \right) - L_1'' f_1 \left\{ \frac{[1 + (1 - \beta_1) L_1' / L_1''] Y_1}{L_1}, q_1 \right\}$$

$$= L_2 f_2 \left(\frac{\mu^{-1} \beta_1 Y_1}{L_1}, q_1 \right)$$

Now, assuming that the consumption functions for the sectors are the same so that subscripts can be dropped, we specify a functional form for f. It will be assumed that the implicit demand function for manufactured goods is such that the consumption function for food has a constant elasticity in both income α_1 and relative price $-\eta_1$. (Of course, the function for manufactured products does not, in general, have constant elasticities in this case.) The marketable surplus equation then becomes

$$Y_1 - L_1' c \beta_1{}^{\alpha_1} \left(\frac{Y_1}{L_1}\right)^{\alpha_1} q_1{}^{-\eta_1} - L_1'' c \left(1 + \frac{(1-\beta_1)L_1'}{L_1''}\right)^{\alpha_1} \left(\frac{Y_1}{L_1}\right)^{\alpha_1} q_1{}^{-\eta_1}$$

$$= L_2 c \left(\mu^{-1} \frac{\beta_1 Y_1}{L_1}\right)^{\alpha_1} q_1{}^{-\eta_1}$$

where c is the constant in the consumption function.   In other words,

(2.8) $$Y_1 - L_1 c' \left(\frac{Y_1}{L_1}\right)^{\alpha_1} q_1{}^{-\eta_1} = L_2 c \left(\frac{\beta_1}{\mu}\right)^{\alpha_1} \left(\frac{Y_1}{L_1}\right)^{\alpha_1} q_1{}^{-\eta_1}$$

where

$$c' = \left\{ \frac{L_1'}{L_1} \beta_1{}^{\alpha_1} + \frac{L_1''}{L_1} \left[1 + \frac{(1-\beta_1)L_1'}{L_1''} \right]^{\alpha_1} \right\} c$$

If, as we shall assume, the distribution between landless workers and landowners is constant (so that L_1'/L_1 and L_1''/L_1 are constant), then c' is constant.   Also, incomes to landless workers and landowners grow proportionately.   If there are no landless workers so that $L_1'/L_1 = 0$ and $L_1''/L_1 = 1$, then c' is equal to c.   In general, $c' \leq c$, but c_1' must be greater than $\beta_1{}^{\alpha_1} c$.

Finally, Equation (2.8) can be rewritten

$$Y_1 - (L_1 + L_2) c_1 \left(\frac{Y_1}{L_1}\right)^{\alpha_1} q_1{}^{-\eta_1} = 0$$

or

(2.9) $$\frac{Y_1}{L} = c_1 \left(\frac{Y_1}{L_1}\right)^{\alpha_1} q_1{}^{-\eta_1}$$

where

$$c_1 = c' \left[1 - \frac{L_2}{L} \left(1 - \frac{(\beta_1/\mu)^{\alpha_1}}{c'/c} \right) \right]$$

If $c'/c = (\beta_1/\mu)^{\alpha_1}$, then $c_1 = c'$ and is constant.   In any case, c_1 can be treated as a constant because secondary sector population is small relative to total population.

The specification of the model for the dual economy is now complete. We shall see that a special case of this specification is the dual economy model of Dale Jorgenson (1961).   In any case, the closed model here contains eight equations in the eight unknowns L, Y_1, L_1, Y_2, L_2, K_2, I_2, and q_1. Implicit in the model, which by Walras' law need not be made explicit, is that consumption of secondary sector goods is the difference between secondary sector output Y_2 and investment I_2. The solution of the model is a logical consequence of our economic formulations and is undertaken in the next section. The reader who is not interested in the mathematics should skip to Table 2.2, where the solution is provided.

Before turning to the solution of the model, however, we should mention that in many developing countries a large portion of manufacturing is the processing of foods; however, our model ignores the flow of raw material from the primary to the secondary sector. These processed foods generally have a higher income elasticity of demand than subsistence foods (as evidenced in Chapter 10 by a higher-income elasticity for total food than for cereals only) and become an important part of the consumer's budget at higher-income levels. A model incorporating this addition (important for some higher-income countries, as in Latin America) would therefore disaggregate the secondary sector to include a food-processing sector.

The results of such a model would differ from our dual economy model to the extent that the production functions and demand elasticities in the two secondary sectors differ and that a portion of primary output is an interindustry flow to the food-processing sector. To account for the interindustry flow, the model here could be modified by separating unprocessed food consumption C_1 from primary production Y_1 so that $C_1 = Y_1 - \iota Y_2$, where ι is the interindustry coefficient between the primary and food-processing sectors multiplied by the proportion of food-processing output in total secondary sector output. However, now real income cannot be defined in terms of purchasing power over only directly consumed primary output but must at least include purchasing power over processed food and should also include manufactured goods (because these economies typically have higher-income levels). In sum, such a model would be considerably more complicated than ours.

2.4 Solution of the Model

The solution for the endogenous variables of the model in this chapter is not a simple matter, and an assumption about the capital/output ratio in industry will be helpful in simplifying it. As a first step toward solution, the primary production relation (2.1) and the wage-rate relation (2.7) are substituted into Equation (2.9) to eliminate the unknowns Y_1 and q_1. Thus, we obtain

$$e^{b_1 t}\frac{L_1{}^{\beta_1}}{L} = c_1(e^{b_1 t}L_1{}^{\beta_1-1})^{\alpha_1+\eta_1}\left(\frac{\mu\beta_2 Y_2}{L_2}\right)^{-\eta_1}$$

or, taking natural logarithms and differentiating with respect to time,

$$[\beta_1(1-\alpha_1-\eta_1)+\alpha_1+\eta_1]\frac{\dot{L}_1}{L_1} = \frac{\dot{L}}{L} - (1-\alpha_1-\eta_1)b_1 - \eta_1\left(\frac{\dot{Y}_2}{Y_2}-\frac{\dot{L}_2}{L_2}\right)$$

Now,

$$\frac{\dot{L}_1}{L_1} = \frac{\dot{L}-\dot{L}_2}{L_1} = \frac{\dot{L}}{L}\frac{L}{L_1} - \frac{\dot{L}_2}{L_2}\frac{L_2}{L_1} = \epsilon\left(1+\frac{L_2}{L_1}\right) - \frac{\dot{L}_2}{L_2}\frac{L_2}{L_1}$$

so that

$$(2.10) \quad [\beta_1(1-\alpha_1-\eta_1)+\alpha_1+\eta_1]\left[\epsilon\left(1+\frac{L_2}{L_1}\right)-\frac{\dot{L}_2}{L_2}\frac{L_2}{L_1}\right]$$

$$= \epsilon - (1-\alpha_1-\eta_1)b_1 - \eta_1\left(\frac{\dot{Y}_2}{Y_2}-\frac{\dot{L}_2}{L_2}\right)$$

This equation is solved for $\dot{L}_2/L_2$. For this purpose, obtain an expression for $\dot{Y}_2/Y_2 - \dot{L}_2/L_2$. First, note that by (2.2)

$$\frac{\dot{Y}_2}{Y_2} - \frac{\dot{L}_2}{L_2} = b_2 + (1-\beta_2)\frac{\dot{K}_2}{K_2} - (1-\beta_2)\frac{\dot{L}_2}{L_2}$$

or, using (2.3),

$$(2.11) \quad \frac{\dot{Y}_2}{Y_2} - \frac{\dot{L}_2}{L_2} = b_2 + (1-\beta_2)^2\frac{Y_2}{K_2} - (1-\beta_2)\delta - (1-\beta_2)\frac{\dot{L}_2}{L_2}$$

This expression could be substituted into (2.10) to obtain a complicated solution for $\dot{L}_2/L_2$ in terms of the parameters of the model, the ratio of urban to rural populations, and some given capital/output ratio. In fact, such a solution is provided in Appendix B. However, a simpler and more easily understood solution can be derived by making a convenient assumption about the value of the capital/output ratio. Such an assumption allows us to focus attention on the structural characteristics of the model rather than on the initial conditions (which differ from country to country).

In Appendix A, using standard growth-theory techniques, it is demonstrated that, given the rate of growth of urban employment $\dot{L}_2/L_2$ and a constant savings rate equal to $1 - \beta_2$, the long-run capital/output ratio in industry is a constant given by

$$(2.12) \qquad \frac{K_2}{Y_2} = \frac{1 - \beta_2}{b_2/\beta_2 + \delta + \dot{L}_2/L_2}$$

Furthermore, it is demonstrated that a gap between an initial capital/output ratio and this asymptotic ratio closes at the rate $b_2 + \beta_2 \delta + \beta_2(\dot{L}_2/L_2)$ annually. (Appendix A also shows that the asymptotic capital/output ratio varies directly with the savings rate; therefore, in the long run, the savings rate does not affect the rate of industrial output growth.) Using this value for the capital/output ratio, Equation (2.11) simplifies considerably to give

$$(2.13) \qquad \frac{\dot{Y}_2}{Y_2} - \frac{\dot{L}_2}{L_2} = \frac{b_2}{\beta_2}$$

that is, secondary sector labor productivity grows at the rate of labor augmenting technical change.

To evaluate the efficacy of taking $\dot{L}_2/L_2$ as given and deriving (2.12), three observations can be noted. First, Appendix B, in addition to providing the exact solution of the model, shows how the solution provided here can be reinterpreted to allow for an initial value of the capital/output ratio that departs from the value given by (2.12). In particular, only a reinterpretation of b_2/β_2 is needed. Second, an interpretation of our assumed value of the capital/output is that the secondary sector is sufficiently capitalized so that it is no longer dominated by low initial values of the capital/output ratio. For example, Dixit (1970, p. 23, figure 1) has shown in a similar context that after some time period (his t^*) the difference between the growth rate of capital stock and that of labor force is approximately labor augmenting technical change, which implies our (2.13). Finally, if, in fact, $\eta_1 = 0$, then our approximation plays no role in the solution for $\dot{L}_2/L_2$ or for $\dot{Y}_1/Y_1$, $\dot{L}_1/L_1$ and growth of real wages.

Given Equation (2.13), Equation (2.10) can now be solved with a number of manipulations to give

$$(2.14) \quad \frac{\dot{L}_2}{L_2} = \epsilon + \frac{\dot{L}_1}{L_1} \left\{ \frac{\eta_1(b_2/\beta_2) + [b_1 - (1 - \beta_1)\epsilon](1 - \alpha_1 - \eta_1)}{1 - (1 - \beta_1)(1 - \alpha_1 - \eta_1)} \right\}$$

This equation is the fundamental equation from which growth paths of other variables can be obtained.   Thus, using (2.13),

(2.15) $$\frac{\dot{Y}_2}{Y_2} = \frac{\dot{K}_2}{K_2} = \frac{\dot{I}_2}{I_2} = \frac{b_2}{\beta_2} + \frac{\dot{L}_2}{L_2}$$

And, because

$$\frac{\dot{L}_1}{L_1} = \epsilon\left[1 + \frac{L_2}{L_1}\right] - \frac{\dot{L}_2}{L_2}\frac{L_2}{L_1}$$

then

(2.16) $$\frac{\dot{L}_1}{L_1} = \epsilon - \frac{\eta_1(b_2/\beta_2) + [b_1 - (1 - \beta_1)\epsilon](1 - \alpha_1 - \eta_1)}{1 - (1 - \beta_1)(1 - \alpha_1 - \eta_1)}$$

Also,

(2.17) $$\frac{\dot{Y}_1}{Y_1} = b_1 + \beta_1\frac{\dot{L}_1}{L_1}$$

and

(2.18) $$\frac{\dot{q}_1}{q_1} = \frac{\dot{Y}_2}{Y_2} - \frac{\dot{L}_2}{L_2} - \left(\frac{\dot{Y}_1}{Y_1} - \frac{\dot{L}_1}{L_1}\right)$$

$$= \frac{b_2}{\beta_2} - b_1 + (1 - \beta_1)\frac{\dot{L}_1}{L_1}$$

$$= \frac{b_2}{\beta_2} - \frac{(1 - \beta_1)\eta_1(b_2/\beta_2) + [b_1 - (1 - \beta_1)\epsilon]}{1 - (1 - \beta_1)(1 - \alpha_1 - \eta_1)}$$

We have now solved the model; Table 2.2 summarizes it and the solution.

2.5   Analysis of the Dual Economy

Viability

Given the solution of the dual economy model in Table 2.2, a most important initial consideration is whether the economy, with its existing structure, shows rising per-capita output.   If it does, we label such an economy as viable because starvation is not a consequence in the longer run.   If it does not, what are the crucial constraints that prevent its growth, and can the system be restructured, say, by the government, to allow the economy to grow?

To study the question of viability, we should begin by noting that there are several, but not independent, ways to explicitly define a viable

TABLE 2.2
Specification and Solution of the Dual Economy Model

Equations

(2.5) $\qquad L = e^{\epsilon t}$

(2.1) $\qquad Y_1 = e^{b_1 t} L_1^{\beta_1}$ $\qquad 0 < \beta_1 < 1$

(2.9) $\qquad \dfrac{Y_1}{L} = c_1 \left(\dfrac{Y_1}{L_1}\right)^{\alpha_1} q_1^{-\eta_1}$ $\qquad 0 \leq \alpha_1, \eta_1 \leq 1$

(2.2) $\qquad Y_2 = e^{b_2 t} K_2^{1-\beta_2} L_2^{\beta_2}$ $\qquad 0 < \beta_2 < 1$

(2.3) $\qquad I_2 = (1 - \beta_2) Y_2$

(2.4) $\qquad \dot{K}_2 = I_2 - \delta K_2$ $\qquad 0 < \delta < 1$

(2.6) $\qquad L_2 = L - L_1$

(2.7) $\qquad \dfrac{q_1 \beta_1 Y_1}{L_1} = \dfrac{\mu \beta_2 Y_2}{L_2}$ $\qquad 0 < \mu \leq 1$

Endogenous Variables

$$
\begin{array}{ccc}
 & Y_1 & Y_2 \\
L & L_1 & L_2 \\
 & q_1 & K_2 \\
 & & I_2
\end{array}
$$

Solution

(2.16) $\qquad \dfrac{\dot{L}_1}{L_1} = \epsilon - \dfrac{\eta_1(b_2/\beta_2) + [b_1 - (1 - \beta_1)\epsilon](1 - \alpha_1 - \eta_1)}{1 - (1 - \beta_1)(1 - \alpha_1 - \eta_1)}$

(2.17) $\qquad \dfrac{\dot{Y}_1}{Y_1} = b_1 + \beta_1 \dfrac{\dot{L}_1}{L_1}$

(2.14) $\qquad \dfrac{\dot{L}_2}{L_2} = \epsilon + \dfrac{L_1}{L_2} \left\{ \dfrac{\eta_1(b_2/\beta_2) + [b_1 - (1 - \beta_1)\epsilon](1 - \alpha_1 - \eta_1)}{1 - (1 - \beta_1)(1 - \alpha_1 - \eta_1)} \right\}$

(2.15) $\qquad \dfrac{\dot{Y}_2}{Y_2} = \dfrac{\dot{K}_2}{K_2} = \dfrac{\dot{I}_2}{I_2} = \dfrac{b_2}{\beta_2} + \dfrac{\dot{L}_2}{L_2}$

(2.18) $\qquad \dfrac{\dot{q}_1}{q_1} = \dfrac{b_2}{\beta_2} - \dfrac{(1 - \beta_1)\eta_1(b_2/\beta_2) + [b_1 - (1 - \beta_1)\epsilon]}{1 - (1 - \beta_1)(1 - \alpha_1 - \eta_1)}$

economy. First, an economy can be defined as viable if per-capita agricultural output tends to rise. Because food is a basic necessity for existence and current per-capita food output is low, this may seem to be a minimum requirement. However, what should be at issue is not whether the economy actually does show rising food output per capita, but whether it *could* do so without declines of manufacturing per-capita output; that is, demand for food must also be considered.

Second, an economy can be defined as viable if the labor force grows faster in urban areas than in rural; that is, L_2/L_1 rises. A rise in L_2/L_1 might imply that the society can afford to draw workers away from agriculture because it could have chosen to employ these laborers in obtaining more of the basic necessity—food. In any case, a rapidly rising industrial employment is a goal in many developing countries.

Third, viability may mean a sustainable rise in per-capita disposable income calculated in terms of food, where "disposable" refers to income that is consumed, not saved and invested (i.e., all income here except income to capital). This definition leaves the actual determination of the consumption bundle up to the consumer but allows him the purchasing power to have more agricultural goods (and, because it will be seen that terms of trade move in favor of agriculture in virtually all cases, more manufacturing goods as well).

Finally, an economy may be defined as viable if industrial output grows faster than population. Such a definition is only concerned with industrialization, and the Stalin years in the Soviet Union would be a classic example.

The last definition is rejected out of hand because the will of the consumers plays no direct role in the question of viability. The first definition is not used here because examining per-capita food output alone does not carry a logical (although perhaps an empirical) implication about consumer welfare. The second definition is rejected for a similar reason. Viability is then defined by growth in real per-capita disposable income, or, more simply, real *consumer* income (where the consumers in this model are landowners, landless rural workers, and urban workers). In many cases, the satisfaction of this condition also satisfies the other definitions for viability.

Addressing the issue of viability with our definition, note first that a change in consumer income in terms of agricultural products is the same for landowners, landless rural workers, and urban workers because income to landowners and landless rural workers grows proportionately [see the remarks following Equation (2.8)] and because of the assumed constancy in the ratio of the wages to labor in agriculture and manufacturing [see Equation (2.7)]. Therefore, the economy is viable if $\dot{Y}_1/Y_1 - \dot{L}_1/L_1 > 0$, that is, if

$$\frac{\dot{Y}_1}{Y_1} - \frac{\dot{L}_1}{L_1} = b_1 - (1 - \beta_1)\frac{\dot{L}_1}{L_1} > 0$$

or, using the solution for $\dot{L}_1/L_1$,

(2.19) $\quad \dfrac{\dot{Y}_1}{Y_1} - \dfrac{\dot{L}_1}{L_1} = \dfrac{[b_1 - (1 - \beta_1)\epsilon] + (1 - \beta_1)\eta_1(b_2/\beta_2)}{1 - (1 - \beta_1)(1 - \alpha_1 - \eta_1)} > 0$

Thus, viability obtains when

(2.20) $\qquad\qquad\qquad \dfrac{b_1 - (1 - \beta_1)\epsilon}{1 - \beta_1} + \eta_1 \dfrac{b_2}{\beta_2} > 0$

where use has been made of the implication that $1 - (1 - \beta_1) \times (1 - \alpha_1 - \eta_1) > 0$, given the stated restrictions on the parameter values.

The first term of the viability condition (2.20) essentially asks the economic question whether, ignoring demand, the rate of primary technological change is fast enough so that consumer income rises even if there is no migration to the cities. The second term takes account of the possibility that the increase in the price of food may, in fact, induce a rise in income (through discouraging food consumption) although the technology of the primary sector alone does not encourage it. In other words, the second term allows for $\dot{L}_1/L_1 < b_1/(1 - \beta_1)$ even though the rate of population growth is greater than $b_1/(1 - \beta_1)$. The first term may be positive or negative, and the second term must be nonnegative; thus, the first term must be negative in a nonviable economy but need not be positive in a viable economy.

These remarks on viability can be extended somewhat further, however. Suppose that the price elasticity of food demand η_1 is zero (it is argued in Section 2.6 that this is likely). Then the viability expression (2.20) simplifies to

$$b_1 - (1 - \beta_1)\epsilon > 0$$

or

(2.21) $\qquad\qquad\qquad\qquad \dfrac{b_1}{1 - \beta_1} > \epsilon$

This inequality provides a more useful expression for ascertaining whether a dual economy exhibits growing real consumer income because empirically the price elasticity of food demand is close to zero.[1] The

---

[1] In Zarembka (1970c, p. 117) it is argued that the viability expression (2.21) obtains because "as an empirical proposition it is observed that as real wages rise in terms of food people do not *decrease* their consumption of food even if manu-

inequality is the same expression as Dale Jorgenson's (1961, pp. 316–317) condition for viability of a low-income economy even though Jorgenson assumes a zero income elasticity of food demand as well as a zero price elasticity.   Thus, viability does not hinge upon the nature of the income elasticity of food demand (which, of course, is only relevant when the economy does not show stable per-capita income). In fact, it is technology in the primary sector that must permit agricultural output to grow faster than population.   As an example, if the rate of primary technical change is 1.5 percent and the labor elasticity is 0.5, then the rate of population growth has an upper bound of 3.0 percent if the economy is to be viable.   In sum, the nature of the primary sector production function is a very important constraint on the economy.

When the economy is not viable, only two policy instruments adopted by the government can alter the problem.   First, the government can encourage higher rates of growth in labor productivity in the primary sector, principally through irrigation projects, new seeds, and improved planting, cultivating, harvesting, and marketing techniques (i.e., increasing b_1).   Second, the government can reduce the growth in population by encouraging birth-control methods through dissemination of information and use of incentives.   Thus, to achieve a viable economy, the government can focus only on agricultural productivity or population growth.

VERBAL DESCRIPTION

Assuming that viability of the model obtains, its behavior can be verbally stated.   Because real consumer income is defined by purchasing power over food, the growth of real income is given by $\dot{Y}_1/Y_1 - \dot{L}_1/L_1 = b_1 - (1 - \beta_1)\dot{L}_1/L_1$.   But, as can be ascertained from Equation (2.16), conditions for an absolute decline in the primary labor force

_____

facturing goods prices fall," which is shown to imply (2.21).   However, this empirical observation is probably valid only because the price elasticity of food demand is close to zero or because most empirical data do not refer to an economy exhibiting very slow growth in real consumer income.   Thus, the argument here that, simply, the price elasticity is close to zero is a preferable and more direct justification for obtaining (2.21) from (2.20).   The reader may notice other differences in emphasis between the dual economy model presented here and the one depicted in Zarembka (1970c).

are very difficult to satisfy in this model.   Thus, real consumer income
rises more slowly than the rate of technological change in the primary
sector and often much more slowly.[1]   In any case, per-capita demand
for primary products is rising.   However, because the secondary sector
is capitalized, labor productivity grows more rapidly there than in the
primary sector; the price of food rises (the terms of trade move in
favor of agriculture) at the rate given by the secondary sector productivity growth less that of the primary sector.   This rise in the price of
food products decreases food demand in the urban sector but further
increases the marketed supply from the rural sector above the increases
due just to productivity advances; trade can be balanced between the
sectors at the higher real income.

At the same time that there is growth in real income, there is migration from the rural to urban areas at the rate $\epsilon - \dot{L}_1/L_1$ [see Equation
(2.16)]: Labor productivity rises faster in the capitalized secondary
sector than in the primary sector, and so agricultural laborers are
attracted to the secondary sector to the extent that wage equilibrium is
maintained with the primary sector.   The faster the rise in food prices,
as reflected primarily in the productivity conditions in agriculture, the
less migration the secondary sector absorbs.   Investment in the
secondary sector continues as a constant fraction of output as the
owners of the secondary sector capital stock (private or government)
reinvest their earnings.

A noteworthy characteristic of the model which agrees with the experience of developing countries is that, as long as viability obtains,
there is an increasing percentage of total population in the secondary
sector.   (In fact, the ratio of secondary sector population to total
population approaches unity in the very long run.)   Thus, the model
is a nonproportional growth model.   Note, however, that when food
ceases to be a substantial portion of the consumer's budget at higher
incomes, the model must be modified so that real consumer income is
no longer defined as purchasing power over food.

Important observations from our low-income economy model can be
summarized by saying that primary sector technical change is very important in determining a rise in real consumer income, that agricultural
prices can be expected to rise, and that there is a systematic transformation of population from agriculture to industry.

---

[1] Income in terms of the secondary sector products grows by the rate of labor
augmenting technical change b_2/β_2 [see Equation (2.15)].

IMPLICATIONS FOR THE MARKETABLE-SURPLUS PROBLEM

Turning specifically to the marketable surplus of food, we first recall that this surplus is the difference between production of food and rural consumption; that is, it is the food surplus available for urban consumption. Referring back to Equation (2.8), the most obvious variable in our model that equates the surplus with urban demand is food prices; if the demand exceeds the surplus, then food prices rise so that the surplus rises (rural consumption decreases) and urban demand falls. However, in addition, equilibrium can be obtained through a lowering of wages and a concomitant increase in food output by maintaining more laborers in agriculture.

As far as the often-cited marketable surplus "problem" is concerned, economists do not seem to have clearly defined the problem. One definition could be that the marketable surplus problem is synonymous with the question of viability. If this is believed appropriate, then a marketable surplus problem exists only when Equation (2.21) is not satisfied, in which case the policy recommendations (suggested above) to achieve viability are relevant.

However, a more appropriate definition seems to be that the marketable surplus problem refers to a difficulty, not an impossibility, of obtaining food surpluses from rural areas for urban areas. With this notion, the growth rate of the economy (although perhaps positive in terms of real income) may be low due primarily to a low rate of technical change in agriculture b_1 combined with high income, low price elasticities of food demand, and a high population growth rate. In this case, the policy recommendations are to improve technological conditions in agriculture, lower the rate of population growth, and, if possible, lower the income elasticity and raise the price elasticity of food demand.

BALANCED GROWTH

Beginning with Ragnar Nurkse (1953), a controversy has arisen in development economics over the issue of whether "balanced" or "unbalanced" growth is preferable to accelerate development. Nurkse argues that balanced growth between agriculture and industry and between industrial sectors is necessary because a "big push" of growth in many sectors creates the necessary demand for expanded outputs and because such growth is accompanied by externalities. Albert Hirschman (1958), on the other hand, argues that unbalanced growth is preferable because vertical linkages are most important and because the tensions created by unbalanced growth spur further growth. Although we are not interested here in the merits of two sides in the controversy, the concept of balanced growth is useful for better understanding the dual economy.

One possible definition of balanced growth is that the growth rates of sectoral outputs correspond to the growth rates of sectoral output demands as determined by the income elasticities of demand. [This definition is used in the empirical work on balanced growth of Swamy (1967) and Yotopoulos and Lau (1970).] The dual to this definition is another definition which states that balanced growth obtains if relative sectoral prices are constant; that is, balanced growth obtains if supply and demand shifts in each sector lead to the same proportionate rise in nominal prices so that relative prices are constant.

The latter definition is particularly useful in the context of the dual economy model because it allows an easy analysis of the interaction of factors that lead to balanced growth. Above, we saw that the change in relative food price is given by Equation (2.18). Thus, to achieve balanced growth, the rate of technical change b_1 (broadly defined to include increases in land and capital) must be raised to a level, say, b_1^*, that leaves relative food prices constant. Solving (2.18) for b_1^*, we have

$$(2.22) \qquad b_1^* = [1 - (1 - \beta_1)(1 - \alpha_1)]\frac{b_2}{\beta_2} + (1 - \beta_1)\epsilon$$

for constant relative prices.

As can be expected, balanced growth is harder to achieve the higher the rate of population growth and the higher the rate of labor augmenting technical change in the secondary sector. Furthermore, a high income elasticity of food demand makes balanced growth somewhat more difficult (the influence is not large because real income is not rising fast). However, a high marginal product of agricultural labor (that is, a high β_1) increases the possibility of balanced growth as long as $(1 - \alpha_1)b_2/\beta_2 < \epsilon$. In general, though, balanced growth between the agricultural and manufacturing sectors is difficult to achieve because agriculture, as opposed to manufacturing, is subject to decreasing returns (land is fixed) and because little farm income is reinvested in farm capital. These factors are only partially compensated for by a lower income elasticity of food demand than of manufactured-good demand.

2.6   Two Special Cases

There are two important special cases of the dual economy model which are worth receiving particular attention: first, the case of zero price elasticity of demand for food products (and thus also for manufactured products) and, second, the case of zero price and income elasticities for food.

The price elasticity of demand for food can be expected to be close to zero because manufacturing products are poor substitutes for food. If, in fact, the price elasticity equals zero ($\eta_1 = 0$), then increases in the price of food do not increase food surpluses in the primary sector and do not decrease the demand in the cities.   Therefore, only labor productivity advances in the rural sector can provide the marketed surplus. As long as the economy is viable, such advances do occur.   Nevertheless, the growth rates of real consumer income and of the secondary sector variables may be less than when $\eta_1 > 0$ if less migration is possible from the primary sector.   For example, as a special case of Equation (2.19) the growth in real income is now given by

$$(2.23) \qquad \frac{\dot{Y}_1}{Y_1} - \frac{\dot{L}_1}{L_1} = \frac{b_1 - (1 - \beta_1)\epsilon}{1 - (1 - \beta_1)(1 - \alpha_1)}$$

This equation can be shown to be less than Equation (2.19) whenever food prices are rising [see Equation (2.18) with $\eta_1 = 0$].[1]

This case in which $\eta_1 = 0$ is important both because it is empirically realistic and because it simplifies the model rather considerably.   Thus, from (2.23), we can see an important property of the model when $\eta_1 = 0$; the growth of real consumer income depends only upon primary sector parameters and the rate of population growth.   In other words, the growth rate of rural consumer income in terms of food determines the growth of urban consumer income (i.e., urban wages) in terms of food. In fact, the primary sector is a closed system in output and labor; any released labor migrates to the city to augment the industrial labor force.[2]   This mathematical result is due to defining real income as the

---

[1] It also might be noticed here that if, contrary to empirical evidence, the food income elasticity equals unity ($\alpha_1 = 1$) when $\eta_1 = 0$, then $\dot{L}_2/L_2 = \dot{L}_1/L_1 = \epsilon$; there is no migration from the rural to urban areas.   This result follows from defining consumer income in the consumption function in terms of food so that $\dot{Y}_1/Y_1 - \dot{L}/L = \dot{Y}_1/Y_1 - \dot{L}_1/L_1$; primary labor force must grow with population.

[2] In Chapters 3 and 5, we make use of the assumption that $\eta_1 = 0$ to simplify the solution of more complex models.

purchasing power over food but is plausible, given that food consumes such a large proportion of the family budget at low-income levels. In sum, our mathematical result only points out the growing belief that agriculture is the most important constraint on economic growth of developing countries.

The second special case assumes that both the price and income elasticities of demand for food equal zero in Equation (2.9). This case is unrealistic in that the income elasticity of food demand in developing countries is generally greater than one-half, although less than unity (see Chapter 10). However, this special case is the model of Dale Jorgenson (1961) because the other seven equations of the present model are the same as Jorgenson's. A detailed description of such an economy is presented in his article. Here we note that the growth rate of real consumer income now becomes

$$(2.24) \qquad \frac{\dot{Y}_1}{Y_1} - \frac{\dot{L}_1}{L_1} = \frac{b_1 - (1 - \beta_1)\epsilon}{\beta_1}$$

and

$$(2.25) \qquad \frac{\dot{Y}_2}{Y_2} = \frac{\dot{K}_2}{K_2} = \frac{\dot{I}_2}{I_2} = \frac{b_2}{\beta_2} + \epsilon + \frac{L_1}{L_2}\frac{b_1 - (1 - \beta_1)\epsilon}{\beta_1}$$

in which the appropriate solution for $\dot{L}_2/L_2$ has been employed.

This form of the solution to Jorgenson's model is preferable to that provided by Jorgenson (1961, p. 332) in that his solution is given by an infinite series or can be examined at its asymptote (when $L_1/L_2 \to 0$). Here, Equation (2.24) is an exact solution. Furthermore, given the ratio of rural to urban populations L_1/L_2 at a point in time, Equation (2.25) is generally close to exact; the exact solution is given in Appendix B.[1]

---

[1] These solutions do not even depend upon our minor approximation to obtain Equation (2.9) because $\alpha_1 = 0$ implies that (2.9) is exact.

Chapter Three

URBAN UNEMPLOYMENT
AND A LABOR-INTENSIVE
SERVICE SECTOR

Two important relationships in the previous chapter that tie the behavior of the agricultural sector to that of the manufacturing sector are the two labor market equations. One of these, Equation (2.7), indicates equilibrium in that market by positing a constant relative wage between rural and urban areas; that is, "migration is assumed to ensure that the rural wage remains some constant fraction of the urban wage." Turner and Jackson (1970, p. 848) suggest that the rural-urban wage gap may be widening in developing countries so that our μ in Equation (2.7) may not be a constant. Although not studied here, the phenomenon, if confirmed, requires further causal investigation.

The second labor market equation, Equation (2.6), allocates population between the agricultural and manufacturing sectors under the presumption that sectoral unemployment rates remain fixed. However, the connection between migration and urban unemployment is unexplored. The first two sections of this chapter are devoted to showing how equilibrium in the labor market can exist concomitantly with urban unemployment.

Finally, a weakness of both of these equations is that employment is presumed to take place in either agriculture or manufacturing when, in fact, service sector employment is an important source of jobs in developing countries. Furthermore, it is empirically weak to argue that production in the service sectors is sufficiently capitalized to be aggregated along with manufacturing. Therefore, the last section of this chapter extends the model of Chapter 2 to include a labor-intensive sector service. By doing so, we are able not only to introduce the possibility of service sector employment but also to disaggregate urban output between secondary sector goods and services.

3.1   Income as a Determinant of Migration

The high labor-migration rate from rural to urban areas leads to some of the most pressing problems faced by developing countries: The high rate often implies high urban unemployment or underemployment, development of urban slums, and important psychological problems that threaten the social structure. The common explanations for the migration are the urban attractions of the "bright lights," greater opportunity for social advancement, a better educational system, and higher wages. Nevertheless, if rural laborers are aware of the high level of unemployment in the cities, why do they emigrate? And if there is an excess supply of labor in the cities, why does not the urban wage fall relative to the rural wage?

Four empirical studies of labor migration in underdeveloped countries have been published recently, all using census data on characteristics of migrants. Beals, Levy, and Moses (1967) studied internal migration in Ghana and concluded that migration is responsive to income differentials and that geographic distance—as a surrogate for differences in culture, social organization, and language, as well as for transport cost —is a strong deterrent to migration. Also, regions of large population are attractive to migrants, but educational level does not seem to directly affect migration.

The major findings of G. S. Sahota (1968) in a study of Brazil were again that internal migration is highly responsive to earning differentials and that distance is a strong deterrent to migration. (However, he found that pecuniary costs of moving are more important than cultural and social differences.) Further, Sahota found evidence that education is important to migration, even abstracting from its influence on other variables, and that urbanization and industrialization as well as population density turn out to be related to migration. In sum, he asserts that "economic costs and returns appear, on the whole, to dominate the behavior of migrants, though some evidence of the non-economic 'push' and 'pull' factors is not denied," or, again, "there is a strong conformity of the migration function to the neo-classical costs-and-returns approach" (p. 243).

Third, M. J. Greenwood (1969) analyzed migration in Egypt and similarly concluded that "distance acts as an important impediment to migration" and that "migration is away from low-wage and toward high-wage regions" (p. 290). His conclusions concerning urbanization, population density, and education were much the same as those of Sahota. Finally, T. P. Schultz (1971) in studying Colombia also found that migration responds to market forces of wage differentials and employment opportunities and that distance to the city and schooling influence migration in the expected direction. He found, additionally, that migration in Colombia increased with the frequency of rural violence ("politically motivated homicide," which totaled around 200,000 deaths during the fifties!).

Each of these studies refers to long-term migration since each is based upon data from separate censuses. The basic finding of all is that economic factors do play an important role in determining migration. In this section and the next, two such economic factors are discussed: income and employment opportunities. Thus, we examine the long-run (nonseasonal) decision to move from a rural area to an urban area when rural wages are lower than urban wages but urban employment is not assured.

First, by staying in a rural area, a potential migrant is aware that he will earn an average annual wage, say, w_r, which he is reasonably certain of obtaining, either because he lives on a family farm or because he knows his employment opportunities in agriculture. This wage leads to a flow of utility $u(w_r)$ so that, given that he discounts future utility[1] at the rate λ and that he has a time horizon n, his total utility at time t from remaining in agriculture is given by

$$U_r(t) = \int_t^{t+n} e^{-\lambda(t'-t)} u(w_r) \, dt'$$

where $U_r(t)$ is total utility from remaining in agriculture. Integrating this equation leads to

(3.1)
$$U_r(t) = \frac{u(w_r)}{\lambda} (1 - e^{-n\lambda})$$

---

[1] Discounting utility is more carefully discussed in Chapter 4.

The wage rate for employed urban workers shows a considerable amount of variation, depending upon a worker's job, his level of skills, and unionization. However, the migrants coming from rural areas are generally rather homogeneous with respect to skills for urban jobs (but not necessarily with respect to the ease of obtaining a job); in most cases, the only skills they have are those learned on the farm, most of which are inapplicable to urban jobs. Thus, each of the migrants can be expected to receive about the same wage upon finding employment.

The newly arrived migrant has three possibilities open to him in the city: First, he may obtain a steady job, given his skills, at an average wage rate w_u. Second, he may remain unemployed, at least for a time, and have to live on relief or be supported by relatives. Third, he may become underemployed in the sense of being able to find only low-paying short-term jobs in the service sector. For simplicity, the second two possibilities are aggregated in the sense that a potential migrant believes that if he cannot get a job in the city at a wage w_u, he can at least get some income from tertiary sector jobs, relatives, or relief. This alternative income, in real terms, is called *underemployment income* and is labeled w_s. It is presumed to be less than rural income.

The ease of obtaining a steady urban job is not homogeneous with respect to the migrants. In particular, one important means of matching urban job vacancies with employable workers is "contacts." Thus, many migrants leave the rural area knowing they will obtain a good urban job or that they have friends or relatives in the city who can help them obtain a job. However, a central assumption here is that not all jobs are filled by contacts, so that migrants without contacts do have some chance of obtaining good employment. Thus, we derive urban expected wages for these migrants. For migrants who can get help finding an urban job, their urban expected total utility over a time horizon n would simply be Equation (3.1) with w_u replacing w_r.

For migrants without union contacts, urban expected income is expected wages, where the latter, at a point in time, is taken as the probability of having a steady job times its wage w_u *plus* the probability of other income times its level w_s. Therefore, if $J(t)$ is labeled the probability of having a steady urban job so that $1 - J(t)$ is the probability of not having such a job, then

$$(3.2) \qquad U_u(t) = \int_t^{t+n} J(t')e^{-\lambda(t'-t)}u(w_u)\, dt'$$

$$+ \int_t^{t+n} [1 - J(t')]e^{-\lambda(t'-t)}u(w_s)\, dt'$$

where $U_u(t)$ is total expected urban utility over time horizon n from migrating at time t.

This formulation of urban expected utility is related to a model of labor migration and urban unemployment proposed by M. P. Todaro (1969). He first suggested the concept of taking account of expected urban employment as well as wages.[1] The expected-wage formulation here, however, also introduces alternative urban income sources other than employment at wage w_u. Additionally, it focuses on expected utility rather than on expected income.[2]

The probability of having an urban job at time t', $J(t')$, can be obtained as follows: The probability of getting a job at time t', $J'(t') = dJ(t')/dt'$, equals the probability of getting a job if unemployed $j(t')$ times the probability of being unemployed. In other words,

$$J'(t') = j(t')[1 - J(t')]$$

or

$$-\frac{J'(t')}{1 - J(t')} = -j(t')$$

so that, by integrating from t to t' with $J(t' = t) = 0$,

$$\ln [1 - J(t')] = -\int_t^{t'} j(t'') \, dt''$$

Thus,

$$J(t') = 1 - \exp\left\{-\int_t^{t'} j(t'') \, dt''\right\}$$

where $J(t' = t) = 0$.

$j(t')$ is the density function for the probability that an unemployed urban worker obtains a job at time t'. If it were assumed that all unemployed workers are homogeneous with respect to skills and ability, that all have similar information (or lack of it) about job vacancies, and that all make the same effort to find jobs, then it would be reasonable to assume that each unemployed worker has an equal probability of finding an urban job. In fact, we shall make this strong assumption because it simplifies the discussion greatly; $j(t')$ is then the same for

---

[1] See Zarembka (1970b) for some comments on the Todaro model, including a correction of the mathematical solution.
[2] Note that expected utility cannot be taken as the utility of expected income unless the income elasticity of utility is 1.

everyone and does not depend upon the time the worker migrated to the urban area. Thus, $j(t')$ is constant and equal to $j(t' = t)$ so that

$$(3.3) \qquad\qquad J(t') = 1 - e^{-[j(t)](t'-t)}$$

It is, in fact, more likely, first, that the initial period after migration is a learning experience in which the migrant discovers the better avenues for obtaining a job and, second, that if the migrant is continually unable to find a job, he may become discouraged and not search so hard. In the latter case, he may then effectively join the chronic unemployed, as observed in so many developing countries, or he may return to the rural area when he has enough money for the transportation costs. In any case, instead of $j(t')$ being constant, it may rise initially and then fall.

Substituting (3.3) into (3.2) gives

$$U_u(t) = \int_t^{t+n} e^{-\lambda(t'-t)} u(w_u)\, dt' - \int_t^{t+n} e^{-[\lambda + j(t)](t'-t)} u(w_u)\, dt'$$

$$+ \int_t^{t+n} e^{-[\lambda + j(t)](t'-t)} u(w_s)\, dt'$$

$$= \frac{u(w_u)}{\lambda}(1 - e^{-n\lambda}) - \frac{u(w_u)}{\lambda + j(t)}(1 - e^{-n[\lambda + j(t)]})$$

$$+ \frac{u(w_s)}{\lambda + j(t)}(1 - e^{-n[\lambda + j(t)]})$$

so that

$$(3.4) \quad U_u(t) = \frac{u(w_u)}{\lambda}(1 - e^{-n\lambda}) - \frac{u(w_u) - u(w_s)}{\lambda + j(t)}(1 - e^{-n[\lambda + j(t)]})$$

3.2   Labor Market Equilibrium and Urban Unemployment

Equilibrium in the rural-urban labor market obtains when there is no tendency for changes in wages or in the probability of obtaining employment for those who are unemployed. The preceding discussion refers basically to one phenomenon, the decision to migrate, so that both relative wages and the probability of employment cannot be ascertained. Our interest here is in the probability of employment so that relative wages are taken as given. In particular, urban wages w_u for jobs requiring the same skills are taken to be higher than rural wages, perhaps owing to minimum wage laws, even apart from higher costs of urban living. Also, when the migrant is not employed in a steady urban job, urban income is assumed to be less than rural income (otherwise, there would always be an income incentive to migrate, regardless of urban employment possibilities).

Assuming that there are substantial numbers of migrants who move primarily for reasons of higher incomes, labor market equilibrium obtains when the opportunity cost of migrating, Equation (3.1), equals the expected return to migrating, Equation (3.4), less transportation costs. If we ignore transportation costs (they may be one cause for higher urban wages, but they do not basically affect our remarks here), then equating (3.1) and (3.4) gives

$$\frac{u(w_u) - u(w_r)}{\lambda} (1 - e^{-n\lambda}) = \frac{u(w_u) - u(w_s)}{\lambda + j(t)} (1 - e^{-n[\lambda + j(t)]})$$

or

$$\frac{1 - e^{-n[\lambda + j(t)]}}{\lambda + j(t)} = \frac{u(w_u) - u(w_r)}{u(w_u) - u(w_s)} \frac{1 - e^{-n\lambda}}{\lambda}$$

If λ is not large and we choose units of measurement for utility such that $u(w_s) = 0$, then as an approximation we have

$$\frac{1 - e^{-n[\lambda + j(t)]}}{n[\lambda + j(t)]} = 1 - \frac{u(w_r)}{u(w_u)}$$

Thus,

(3.5) $$1 - \frac{1 - e^{-n[\lambda + j(t)]}}{n[\lambda + j(t)]} = \frac{u(w_r)}{u(w_u)}$$

where it should be remembered that $u(\cdot)$ is defined such that $u(w_s) = 0$ (implying also that w_s does not change in the discussion below).

Equation (3.5) gives an implicit expression for the probability density $j(t)$ that an unemployed urban worker finds a job when the labor market is in equilibrium, given the relative level of utility from rural and urban incomes when employed. An analytic solution for the equilibrium level of $j(t)$ is apparently impossible to obtain. However, in Figure 3.1 the solution is graphed against values for $u(w_r)/u(w_u)$, given alternative values of the time horizon n. Notice, first, that lower values of $u(w_r)/u(w_u)$, say, due to higher urban wages w_u, imply lower equilibrium values for the probability of obtaining an urban job. In other words, higher urban wages lead to migration being more attractive, but the larger flow of migrants makes it more difficult to find a job. Second, notice that a longer time horizon, for given wage levels, implies a lower

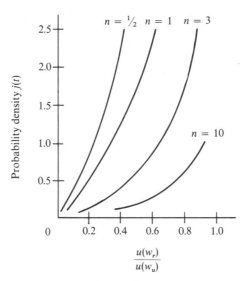

FIGURE 3.1
Probability density of obtaining an urban job in equilibrium, Equation (3.5),
for alternative values of $u(w_r)/u(w_u)$. (Drawn on the assumption that
$\lambda = 0$.   For $\lambda > 0$, reduce $j(t)$ by the same amount)

probability of obtaining a job in equilibrium.   That is, a longer time
horizon implies that migrants are less concerned with short-term employment (that they have greater ability to maintain themselves when
unemployed) so that migration is again more attractive.   However,
although this influence of time horizon on equilibrium employment
opportunities is quite substantial, we have little knowledge of a realistic
value for n or whether time horizons vary substantially among migrants.
    We are now prepared to move one step further by relating the prob-
ability of obtaining an urban job, when unemployed, to the urban
unemployment rate.   M. P. Todaro (1969, p. 143) suggests that the
probability of obtaining an urban job is related to the rate of job
creation in the urban areas relative to total unemployed.   Thus, if L_2 is
the total urban population which is employed at any one time, and P
is the urban labor force participation (so that $P - L_2$ is the unemployed
or underemployed), then

(3.6) $$j(t) = \frac{\xi L_2}{P - L_2}$$

where ξ is the rate of job openings available to urban unemployed (i.e., the increase in labor demand *plus* the attrition of employed workers due to death, retirement, quits, and firings *less* those employed workers who merely transfer jobs and those migrants who obtain jobs through friends). Equation (3.6) can be rewritten

$$j(t) = \frac{\xi L_2/P}{1 - L_2/P}$$

or

(3.7) $$1 - \frac{L_2}{P} = \frac{\xi}{\xi + j(t)}$$

in which $1 - L_2/P$ is the rate of urban unemployment. [Of course, a higher probability of obtaining an urban job $j(t)$ is consistent with a lower unemployment rate.]

An important conclusion from Equation (3.7) is that the unemployment rate is *directly* related to the rate of job openings ξ, not inversely! In other words, a constant probability of obtaining an urban job is consistent with a higher rate of job openings only if the unemployment rate rises. Thus, a governmental policy of directly increasing employment in the urban areas can actually have the opposite effect; the increase in the job openings temporarily raises the urban/rural expected wage ratio and causes more migration. This increase in migration is so large as to increase the unemployment rate. In the new equilibrium, with wage rates the same as before, the probability of finding employment after migration must be the same; but the number of job openings per unit of time and the unemployment rate will be higher.

For an empirical example, in 1964 unemployment in Kenya rose when urban employment opportunities increased under basically *ceteris paribus* conditions [see Todaro (1969, pp. 140–141)]. In this case, the government and private industry agreed to increase employment by 15 percent, while labor unions agreed to refrain from seeking new wage increases. But the improved prospect of urban jobs so increased migration that unemployment rose.

Finally, in a recent article, Turner and Jackson (1970) provide very interesting evidence (for countries with sufficient data) that the average real-wage-rate growth in the manufacturing sector of developing countries is about the same magnitude as for developed countries ($3\frac{1}{2}$ percent), while they suggest (p. 848) that the gap between urban and rural wages in developing countries has been widening. They also report (p. 848) that, for an average of 14 developing countries, the growth rate of known unemployed has been about $8\frac{1}{2}$ percent annually since the late fifties. This evidence is consistent with the model here: A rising urban relative wage w_u increases migration to the city, decreases the probability of finding a job [Equation (3.5) and Figure 3.1], and increases the unemployment rate [Equation (3.7)].

3.3   Introduction of a Labor-Intensive Service Sector

An important limitation of a dual economy structuring of a less developed country is that a labor-intensive service sector is not given an explicit role. This sector, consisting of personal services, trade, and government activities, is often a larger portion of gross domestic product than industry and is an important method by which laborers move from agricultural to industrial occupations. Furthermore, this sector differs from manufacturing and capital-intensive services (such as transportation, housing, and utilities) by having a much lower wage rate in addition to having only labor as the principal factor of production. In this section we explicitly introduce the role of this service, or tertiary, sector into the model formulated in Chapter 2 to better characterize the economy of developing countries. To accomplish this, we build directly upon the dual economy model.

A THREE-SECTOR MODEL

Our equations for the primary and secondary sectors, as well as for total population, are virtually the same in the three-sector model as in Chapter 2, with the very convenient exception that all price elasticities of food demand are presumed zero. Therefore, instead of Equation (2.9), we now have

$$(3.8) \qquad \frac{Y_1}{L} = c_1 \left(\frac{Y_1}{L_1} \right)^{\alpha_1} \qquad 0 \leqq \alpha_1 \leqq 1$$

in which real consumer income is still defined in terms of food. In addition, the secondary sector is defined to include only those goods produced with relatively large amounts of capital. Therefore, Equation (2.6), which allocates total population, must be modified to account for tertiary sector employment L_3:

$$(3.9) \qquad L_2 = L - L_1 - L_3$$

In the tertiary sector, production Y_3 is presumed to depend only upon labor as a variable factor of production. If we assume that any other factor increases proportionately with labor, then constant returns to labor can be assumed and

$$(3.10) \qquad\qquad Y_3 = e^{b_3 t} L_3$$

with appropriately defined units of measurement for output, where b_3 is exogenous technical change. Consumption of tertiary sector goods is equal to tertiary production and is specified to depend upon real consumer income (defined, as always, in terms of food) and upon its own relative price q_3 (tertiary sector price relative to secondary sector price taken as the numéraire). Therefore,

$$(3.11) \qquad\qquad \frac{Y_3}{L} = c_3 \left(\frac{Y_1}{L_1}\right)^{\alpha_3} q_3^{-\eta_3}$$

where α_3 is the income elasticity of demand, $-\eta_3$ is the price elasticity, and c_3 is a constant. As in Chapter 2, secondary sector consumption is defined implicitly by the consumption functions for food and services and by the secondary sector investment equation.

The real wage rate in the tertiary sector is just equal to average product $q_3 Y_3 / L_3$. This wage rate is observed to be less than the secondary sector wage rate in developing countries, perhaps owing to low skill levels. Turner and Jackson (1970, p. 829, footnote 1) summarize two studies of developing countries, indicating that wage increases in all nonagricultural sectors taken together are about the same as in manufacturing sectors alone. Thus, we can express the relationship between tertiary and secondary sector wages by

$$(3.12) \qquad\qquad \frac{q_3 Y_3}{L_3} = \frac{\mu' \beta_2 Y_2}{L_2} \qquad 0 < \mu' \leqq 1$$

where μ' is some constant not greater than 1.

SOLUTION

The solution of the model is not as complex as the number of equations suggests primarily because we have blocked the model recursively by assuming the price elasticities of food demand to be zero. In other words, given these zero price elasticities, the agricultural sector responds

TABLE 3.1
Specification and Solution of the Three-sector Model

Equations

(2.5)	$L = e^{\epsilon t}$	
(2.1)	$Y_1 = e^{b_1 t} L_1^{\beta_1}$	$0 < \beta_1 < 1$
(3.8)	$\dfrac{Y_1}{L} = c_1 \left(\dfrac{Y_1}{L_1} \right)^{\alpha_1}$	$0 \leq \alpha_1 \leq 1$
(2.2)	$Y_2 = e^{b_2 t} K_2^{1 - \beta_2} L_2^{\beta_2}$	$0 < \beta_2 < 1$
(2.3)	$I_2 = (1 - \beta_2) Y_2$	
(2.4)	$\dot{K}_2 = I_2 - \delta K_2$	$0 < \delta < 1$
(3.9)	$L_2 = L - L_1 - L_3$	
(2.7)	$\dfrac{q_1 \beta_1 Y_1}{L_1} = \dfrac{\mu \beta_2 Y_2}{L_2}$	$0 < \mu \leq 1$
(3.10)	$Y_3 = e^{b_3 t} L_3$	
(3.11)	$\dfrac{Y_3}{L} = c_3 \left(\dfrac{Y_1}{L_1} \right)^{\alpha_3} q_3^{-\eta_3}$	
(3.12)	$\dfrac{q_3 Y_3}{L_3} = \dfrac{\mu' \beta_2 Y_2}{L_2}$	$0 < \mu' \leq 1$

Endogenous Variables

	Y_1	Y_2	Y_3
L	L_1	L_2	L_3
	q_1	K_2	q_3
		I_2	

independently of the two other sectors and determines the growth of real wages. Thus, growth of primary employment is given by Equation (2.16) with $\eta_1 = 0$;

$$(3.13) \qquad \frac{\dot{L}_1}{L_1} = \epsilon - \frac{[b_1 - (1 - \beta_1)\epsilon](1 - \alpha_1)}{1 - (1 - \beta_1)(1 - \alpha_1)}$$

and, of course,

$$(3.14) \qquad \frac{\dot{Y}_1}{Y_1} = b_1 + \beta_1 \frac{\dot{L}_1}{L_1}$$

Solution

(3.13) $\dfrac{\dot{L}_1}{L_1} = \epsilon - \dfrac{[b_1 - (1 - \beta_1)\epsilon](1 - \alpha_1)}{1 - (1 - \beta_1)(1 - \alpha_1)}$

(3.14) $\dfrac{\dot{Y}_1}{Y_1} = b_1 + \beta_1 \dfrac{\dot{L}_1}{L_1}$

(3.21) $\dfrac{\dot{L}_2}{L_2} = \epsilon + \dfrac{L_1}{L_2} \dfrac{[b_1 - (1 - \beta_1)\epsilon](1 - \alpha_1)}{1 - (1 - \beta_1)(1 - \alpha_1)}$

$\qquad\qquad - \dfrac{L_3}{L_2}\left[\alpha_3 \dfrac{b_1 - (1 - \beta_1)\epsilon}{1 - (1 - \beta_1)(1 - \alpha_1)} - \eta_3\left(\dfrac{b_2}{\beta_2} - b_3\right) - b_3\right]$

(3.16) $\dfrac{\dot{Y}_2}{Y_2} = \dfrac{\dot{K}_2}{K_2} = \dfrac{\dot{I}_2}{I_2} = \dfrac{b_2}{\beta_2} + \dfrac{\dot{L}_2}{L_2}$

(3.17) $\dfrac{\dot{q}_1}{q_1} = \dfrac{b_2}{\beta_2} - \dfrac{b_1 - (1 - \beta_1)\epsilon}{1 - (1 - \beta_1)(1 - \alpha_1)}$

(3.20) $\dfrac{\dot{L}_3}{L_3} = \epsilon + \alpha_3 \dfrac{b_1 - (1 - \beta_1)\epsilon}{1 - (1 - \beta_1)(1 - \alpha_1)} - \eta_0\left(\dfrac{b_2}{\beta_2} - b_3\right) - b_3$

(3.19) $\dfrac{\dot{Y}_3}{Y_3} = b_3 + \dfrac{\dot{L}_3}{L_3}$

(3.18) $\dfrac{\dot{q}_3}{q_3} = \dfrac{b_2}{\beta_2} - b_3$

Furthermore, the growth of real consumer income is accordingly just Equation (2.23):

(3.15) $$\dfrac{\dot{Y}_1}{Y_1} - \dfrac{\dot{L}_1}{L_1} = \dfrac{b_1 - (1 - \beta_1)\epsilon}{1 - (1 - \beta_1)(1 - \alpha_1)}$$

As in Chapter 2, we hypothesize that the secondary sector capital/output ratio is such that secondary sector labor productivity grows at the rate of labor augmenting technical change b_2/β_2. Therefore,

(3.16) $$\dfrac{\dot{Y}_2}{Y_2} = \dfrac{\dot{K}_2}{K_2} = \dfrac{\dot{I}_2}{I_2} = \dfrac{b_2}{\beta_2} + \dfrac{\dot{L}_2}{L_2}$$

Furthermore, using (2.7), the change in the price of food, which does not affect the economic structure, is given by

(3.17)
$$\frac{\dot{q}_1}{q_1} = \frac{b_2}{\beta_2} - \frac{b_1 - (1 - \beta_1)\epsilon}{1 - (1 - \beta_1)(1 - \alpha_1)}$$

Also, because tertiary sector labor productivity grows by the rate of technical change in that sector, then using (3.12)

(3.18)
$$\frac{\dot{q}_3}{q_3} = \frac{b_2}{\beta_2} - b_3$$

Because we now have solutions for the growth of real consumer income (3.15) and for tertiary sector relative price (3.18), by Equation (3.11) the growth of tertiary sector output is

$$\frac{\dot{Y}_3}{Y_3} = \epsilon + \alpha_3 \frac{b_1 - (1 - \beta_1)\epsilon}{1 - (1 - \beta_1)(1 - \alpha_1)} - \eta_3\left(\frac{b_2}{\beta_2} - b_3\right)$$

However, using (3.10), growth of tertiary sector output is also

(3.19)
$$\frac{\dot{Y}_3}{Y_3} = b_3 + \frac{\dot{L}_3}{L_3}$$

Therefore, using these two equations, tertiary sector growth of employment is

(3.20)
$$\frac{\dot{L}_3}{L_3} = \epsilon + \alpha_3 \frac{b_1 - (1 - \beta_1)\epsilon}{1 - (1 - \beta_1)(1 - \alpha_1)} - \eta_3\left(\frac{b_2}{\beta_2} - b_3\right) - b_3$$

Finally, the growth of secondary sector employment is given by

$$\frac{\dot{L}_2}{L_2} = \frac{\dot{L} - \dot{L}_1 - \dot{L}_3}{L_2} = \frac{\dot{L}}{L}\frac{L}{L_2} - \frac{\dot{L}_1}{L_1}\frac{L_1}{L_2} - \frac{\dot{L}_3}{L_3}\frac{L_3}{L_2}$$

$$= \epsilon + \frac{L_1}{L_2}\left(\epsilon - \frac{\dot{L}_1}{L_1}\right) + \frac{L_3}{L_2}\left(\epsilon - \frac{\dot{L}_3}{L_3}\right)$$

or

(3.21)
$$\frac{\dot{L}_2}{L_2} = \epsilon + \frac{L_1}{L_2}\frac{[b_1 - (1 - \beta_1)\epsilon](1 - \alpha_1)}{1 - (1 - \beta_1)(1 - \alpha_1)}$$

$$- \frac{L_3}{L_2}\left[\alpha_3 \frac{b_1 - (1 - \beta_1)\epsilon}{1 - (1 - \beta_1)(1 - \alpha_1)} - \eta_3\left(\frac{b_2}{\beta_2} - b_3\right) - b_3\right]$$

Implications of Introducing the Service Sector

The implications of the three-sector model are in many ways quite similar to the dual economy model and may, in part, explain why dual economy models are so much more popular. First, of course, the primary sector and the price of food behave exactly as in Chapter 2 when the price elasticity of food demand there is zero; most important, the primary sector determines the growth of real consumer income.

Given the growth of real income, the rate of growth of tertiary sector output is the rate of population growth *plus* the rate of growth in tertiary demand due to rising income *minus* the change in demand due to relative price change. The higher the rate of population growth and the higher the income elasticity of demand for services, the higher the growth rate of tertiary output. The price effect is assuredly negative because the relative price of services rises (empirically, secondary sector labor augmenting technical change exceeds technical change in the tertiary sector). However, if the price elasticity of demand $-\eta_3$ is not large, the effect of changing relative price will not be large.

The behavior of the secondary sector differs somewhat from that described by a dual economy structure. Because we have used the same method of solving for secondary sector variables here as in Chapter 2, we need to examine only the growth rate of secondary sector labor force. Comparing Equation (3.21) with Equation (2.14), note that the first two terms of (3.21) are algebraically the same as Equation (2.14). However, there is a difference: In Chapter 2 the secondary sector consists of all nonagricultural sectors, while in our present discussion it includes only the capitalized sectors. Thus, because L_2 is smaller, the term L_1/L_2 is greater in our current solution; and, if the last term of (3.21) could be ignored, the rate of growth of secondary sector employment (and output, capital stock, and investment) is greater.

The last term of (3.21) is negative whenever

$$\alpha_3 \frac{b_1 - (1 - \beta_1)\epsilon}{1 - (1 - \beta_1)(1 - \alpha_1)} - \eta_3\left(\frac{b_2}{\beta_2} - b_3\right) - b_3 > 0$$

that is, whenever tertiary sector labor force grows faster than the rate of population growth [see Equation (3.20)]. This may or may not occur. For example, if the income elasticity of demand for services α_3 is 1.0 and real consumer income is rising by 1.0 percent annually and if $\eta_3 = 0$, then the last term of (3.21) is negative only when tertiary sector technical change is less than 1.0 percent. Otherwise, the term is positive and secondary sector employment grows even faster than predicted by the first two terms.   In any case, no general statement can be made without some knowledge of the parameter values of the model.

   This section has not led to any unexpected results.   However, it does show how a labor-intensive tertiary sector can be explicitly included in a model of economic development, and it does show the role of each parameter.   Thus, when the tertiary sector is not included in a development model, such as in Chapter 5, we can now obtain some idea of the importance of the omission.

Chapter Four

TOWARD A THEORY OF SAVINGS

One of the most difficult problems in economics is to explain total savings of a country; yet, savings, particularly those channeled into physical capital, are crucially important for economic growth. Because the problem is so complex, most analytic work in both development and growth theory assumes that a constant fraction (perhaps zero) of worker income is saved and that another constant fraction (perhaps unity) of capital income is saved. These assumptions are made in Chapter 2 and in Section 3.3 of Chapter 3 where they imply that, given a Cobb–Douglas production function in manufacturing, a constant proportion of secondary sector output is saved and reinvested.

A theory of aggregate savings is necessarily complex because it must first study intertemporal choice for the consumer. That choice depends upon the consumer's preferences, the level and the uncertainty of his income, the size of his family and the desire to leave inheritance, and the return to savings. After the consumer's intertemporal choice is examined, the taxation policy of the government must be introduced, individual consumer savings must be aggregated together, international financial movements may have to be considered, and the demand for investment funds, as it helps to determine the rate of return on savings, needs to be provided. Only if it is assumed that the government uses its power of taxation and expenditures to adjust the savings rate to a predetermined level can a characterization of savings be substantially simplified.   But the latter is rarely relevant in practice.

In this chapter we shall not attempt to develop a complete theory of savings because such a theory would provide subject matter for another book.   What we hope to achieve, however, is the stimulation of further exploration by providing a theoretical framework for intertemporal choice of the consumer.   We begin by examining the determinants of the subjective rate of discount, a discussion which is necessarily on an abstract level.   Then a model of intertemporal choice is developed and related to the situation of low-income countries.   That model is extended in Section 4.3 by introducing two important characteristics for developing economies: the work-hour choice and income uncertainty. Finally, the implications for savings theory applied to developing countries are discussed.   We believe that the remarks here help explain the low level of savings observed both in agriculture and among urban labor by integrating the survival and profit motives into one model.

Finally, it should be noted that this chapter is the most difficult in the book, both conceptually and mathematically.   It is conceptually difficult because we are essentially imagining how a consumer might value present consumption vis-à-vis future consumption; it is mathematically difficult because the calculus of dynamic programming is required.   However, the mathematical problems are relegated to Appendix C, and the reader may skip this chapter, in any case, and not lose the train of the argument in other chapters.

4.1   The Subjective Rate of Discount

The subjective rate of discount in economics refers to the time rate of change by which a consumer (or society as a whole) discounts future utility relative to present utility.   In particular, the subjective rate of discount can be defined as (the negative of) the rate of change in the *marginal* utility of consumption expenditures, holding "real" expenditures constant.   In other words, if c is consumption expenditures and $u_t(c)$ is utility as a function of time t, then the subjective rate of discount is given by $-[du_t'(c)/dt]/u_t'(c)$ where c is time invariant.   Note that, although this rate of discount may depend upon the level of consumption, that level over time is held constant.   Thus, the importance of the timing of utility is isolated from any possible change over time in consumption level.   In any case, the recent procedure has been to assume this subjective discount rate constant, say, λ, so that utility over time may be written $e^{-\lambda t}u(c)$.

Irving Fisher (1930, p. 62) defined *impatience* as "the (percentage) excess of the present marginal want [utility] for one more unit of *present* goods over the *present* marginal want for one more unit of *future* goods." Thus, he did not hold expenditures constant over time so that his rate of discount depends upon the shape of the consumption stream.   In fact, he showed that, using a capital market, the consumer adjusts consumption relative to income so that the consumer's rate of impatience exactly equals the interest rate on lending or borrowing.   However, under our definition, the subjective rate of discount is *not* necessarily equal to the interest rate.

Our definition of the subjective rate of discount ignores the composition of consumption both in the present and in the future (as well as inflation).   Fisher (1930, p. 76) simplifies in the same way: "For practical purposes, however, we may ordinarily neglect the characteristic of income [expenditure] called composition; for ordinarily any variation in the mere composition of family budgets will very seldom be sufficient to have any appreciable effect on the rate of interest."

According to John Rae (1905), the most important determinant of the value of the subjective rate of discount is the shortness and uncertainty of life itself.   A rather long quote from him is useful for our purposes (pp. 53–54):

> A pleasure to be enjoyed, or a pain to be endured, fifty or a hundred
> years hence, would be considered deserving the same attention as if it
> were to befall us fifty or a hundred minutes hence, and the sacrifice of
> a smaller present good, for a greater future good, would be readily
> made, to whatever period that futurity might extend.   But life, and
> the power to enjoy it, are the most uncertain of all things, and we are
> not guided altogether by reason.   We know not the period when
> death may come upon us, but we know that it may come in a few days,
> and must come in a few years.   Why then be providing goods that
> cannot be enjoyed until times, which, though not very remote, may
> never come to us, or until times still more remote, and which we are
> convinced we shall never see?   If life, too, is of uncertain duration
> and the time that death comes between us and all our possessions
> unknown, the approaches of old age are at least certain, and are dull-
> ing, day by day, the relish of every pleasure.

For Böhm-Bawerk (1912), however, uncertain longevity is only one of several factors influencing the rate of discount.   He argued that the first cause of a systematic higher valuation of present over future goods is the "difference between the relation of supply to demand as it exists at one point in time and that relation as it exists at another point in time" (pp. 265–266, the original is italicized).   Irving Fisher (1930, pp. 72–75) clarified this cause by writing that impatience depends upon the level as well as the time shape of expenditures.   Because our definition of the rate of discount abstracts from the time shape of expenditures, only its level is relevant here.   This factor, for Fisher, is primarily important at low-income levels and is "partly rational, because of the importance, by supplying present needs, of keeping up the continuity of life and thus maintaining the ability to cope with the future; and partly irrational, because the pressure of present needs blinds a person to the needs of the future" (p. 72).   In any case, in addition to the level of expenditures, Fisher also mentioned the degree of its uncertainty as a possible influence on impatience.

Böhm-Bawerk's second cause for the lesser valuation of future utility is a combination of three factors: "(a) erroneous valuation by reason of fragmentary imagery of future wants; (b) lack of will power; and (c) consideration of the uncertainty of life" [Böhm-Bawerk (1912, p. 271)]. To these three, Fisher added three other personal characteristics: habits determined by cultural surroundings and past personal experiences, the desire to provide inheritance for relations, and "fashion" [Fisher (1930, pp. 80–91)].

In this chapter the uncertainty in the length of life is the first of two determinants of the value of the subjective rate of discount.   This uncertainty itself has two components: First, the lower the level of consumption expenditures, the higher the probability of dying due to both inadequate food consumption and inadequate medical care; second, the older the consumer, the higher the probability of dying independent of the consumption level.   The first component is essentially the rational influence of poverty mentioned by Fisher (the irrational influence is not explicitly included, but could be).   The second component has been suggested by Rae, by Böhm-Bawerk (as part of his second cause), and by Fisher (in his listing of personal factors).

Our second determinant of the rate of discount might be called personal *maturity*.   Modern psychology theory often defines maturity as the ability to postpone gratification until the future.   It is clear that a baby lacks this ability altogether and may be said to have a rate of discount approaching infinity.   As a person ages he begins to perceive more and more clearly that sometimes a sacrifice in the present may

have higher rewards in the future.   But a person's maturity level at a
given age is determined by both his personal makeup and life experiences.   In our model, the influence of maturity is assumed to be
exogenous, according to the age of the individual; it is possible that
economic variables play some minor role (for example, low or fluctuating consumption, implying hardship, may lead to higher maturity and
a lower discounting of the future), but they can probably be safely
ignored.

This second determinant of the rate of discount would certainly
include Böhm-Bawerk's fragmentary imagery of future wants, which is
Fisher's "foresight," as well as lack of will power mentioned by both
Böhm-Bawerk and Fisher.   Additionally, it may also include other
influences not strictly called maturity, such as habits and fashion mentioned by Fisher.   The key factor is that this determinant is basically
exogenous to economic models, and the degree of its influence can only
be ascertained by making use of psychological and sociological theory.

The two other determinants of impatience mentioned by Fisher, the
bequest motive and income uncertainty, deserve attention.   The desire
to provide inheritance for relations is not discussed here because it is
believed that this influence is not strong at low-income levels.   The
uncertainty in the level of income does not fall under our definition of
the subjective rate of discount because we hold expenditures constant.
However, the influence of uncertainty is important for savings and is
examined in Section 4.3.

4.2   A Simple Model of Intertemporal Consumer Behavior

To set up a model of intertemporal consumer behavior, the consumer
shall be described as attempting to maximize the total utility of the consumption stream over his life cycle.   Thus, first let $u_t(c(t))$ represent
the instantaneous utility *expected in the present* derived from the rate
of consumer expenditures $c(t)$ at future time t.   Then, assuming that
the utility function is additive in a conceptual sense (it will not be so in
a mathematical sense), the consumer seeks to maximize

$$(4.1) \qquad U(a) = \int_a^\infty u_t(c(t))\, dt$$

where a is the consumer's present age, t is his age in the future, and
$U(a)$ is total lifetime utility expected in the present.

Now, in Section 4.1 it is argued that there are two reasons why the consumer may value a given level of future expenditures lower than the same level of present expenditures, that is, why $u_t(\cdot)$ may be decreasing over time: uncertain longevity and the level of the consumer's maturity. Thus, we may describe $u_t(c(t))$ by three components: the utility derived from consumption which is independent of discounting, say, $u(c(t))$; the discounting due to the uncertain longevity; and the discounting due to level of maturity. Then, Equation (4.1) can be written

$$(4.2) \qquad\qquad U(a) = \int_a^\infty \ell(t) e^{-mt} u(c(t)) \, dt$$

where $\ell(t)$ is the probability of being alive at time t and m is the constant rate of discounting due to level of maturity [which could decline as the consumer ages (as a increases)]. Note that the multiplicative term $\ell(t)$ implies that if the consumer is alive at a point in future time, the expected utility is $e^{-mt} u(c(t))$; but if he is dead, the utility is zero. Thus, any choice of utility function $u(c(t))$ should keep in mind the indexing of utility, if dead, as zero.

The probability of being alive at time t is dependent upon the probability of dying at each point in time between the present a and the future t. But the probability of dying at time t is the product of the probability of being alive at time t and the probability of dying if alive. Therefore,

$$(4.3) \qquad\qquad \dot{\ell}(t) = -\ell(t)[d(t) + f(c(t))]$$

where $d(t)$ is the probability of dying independent of the level of consumption and $f(c(t))$ is the increased probability of dying owing to low consumption levels. Thus, the subjective rate of discount at time t equals $\dot{\ell}(t)/\ell(t) + m$, which equals $d(t) + f(c(t)) + m$. Note that this rate of discount cannot be determined independent of the consumer's consumption level; however, $d(t)$ is assumed to be a known function of time and $f(c(t))$, a known function of consumption.

The consumer's problem is to maximize expected total utility at age a. However, he faces an income and debt constraint. *Given that the consumer is alive at future time t*, let $S(t)$ be savings (or debt, if negative) and let r be the annual rate of return on savings (investment). Also, let $y^*(t)$ be the expected income, if alive, independent of the return on savings, at time t. Then the change in savings $\dot{S}(t)$ is given by

$$(4.4) \qquad\qquad \dot{S}(t) = y^*(t) + rS(t) - c(t)$$

Therefore, savings at future time t, if the consumer is alive at time t, is the solution of the above linear differential equation, or

$$(4.5) \quad S(t) = \left\{ \int_a^t [y^*(t') - c(t')]e^{-r(t'-a)} \, dt' + S(a) \right\} e^{r(t-a)}$$

where $S(a)$ is the given initial savings.

The role of debt (negative savings) is very important for our problem. If the consumer were unconstrained in his level of debt, then he would have unlimited borrowing—and thus consuming—capabilities. In particular, he could plan to remain in debt and thus default at time of death (assuming that relatives would not be obligated for the debt). However, the individual faces an institutional constraint in any economic environment that prohibits him from borrowing, at any point in time, more than he can be expected to pay back. A debt constraint itself can be formulated in many ways, depending upon the institutions relevant to the consumer. In point of fact, however, an individual has very limited opportunities in developing countries to borrow against future earnings without collateral. Thus, the debt constraint will be taken as the requirement that net savings is nonnegative (net debt is nonpositive). Therefore,

$$(4.6) \qquad\qquad S(t) \geq 0 \qquad \text{for all } t$$

Having discussed the formulation of the problem, we now restate it. At age a, the problem for the consumer is to find that planned consumption stream, say, $c^*(t)$, together with planned savings stream, say, $S^*(t)$, that maximizes his total expected utility, given his expected income stream. In undertaking the solution of the problem, the consumer discounts the future and has a debt constraint that prohibits net debt. As he ages, the consumer reformulates the same problem but now with the knowledge of his actual income stream in the interval and with the certainty that he has lived through the interval. Thus, the time path of actual consumption differs from that of planned consumption at age a, $c^*(t)$.[1]

---

[1] The only other formal analysis known to us that explicitly considers uncertain death is that of Yaari (1965). Basically, he considers a consumer model with constant discounting but an uncertain time horizon (lifetime); the derivative of his distribution function on time horizon should therefore be our $d(t)$. In any case, unlike our own, his distribution function on time horizon is independent of consumption levels.

Turning now to the factors which affect the consumer's consumption and savings decision, first consider the expected income stream $y^*(t)$. This variable refers to expected income per unit of time for each time period in the future, *given* that the individual is alive.   It depends upon the individual's earning potential in his economic environment and upon its expected time path, including retirement plans.   However, until the next section of this chapter, we ignore any elements of uncertainty in this expected income, which can be important in developing countries, so that $y^*(t)$ is treated as a nonrandom variable.

The interest rate r reflects the rate of return on investments out of savings, on savings deposits, and/or on direct lending.   It is taken to be independent of savings levels.   Very often wealthy persons have better investment opportunities than poor people, so that it might be expected that independence is not totally justified.   Nevertheless, it is possible to adjust this rate to different individuals according to their initial wealth position $S(a)$.   In any case, r is here taken as fixed (nonrandom) and known to the consumer.

A person's subjective rate of discount depends upon his estimate of the probability of remaining alive and upon his level of maturity.   The consumer can be expected to have some idea of his probability of dying at different ages due to accidents or diseases unrelated to personal consumption levels $d(t)$.   He can also be expected to understand the relationship between personal expenditure levels on food, housing, clothing, and medical needs and the probability of his remaining alive $f(c)$.   This latter relationship $f(c)$ is the most important concept to which attention is drawn in this chapter.

Harvey Leibenstein (1957), in part, has emphasized the relationship in developing countries between consumption or income levels and mortality, particularly in regard to the effect on the rate of population growth.   For example, he says (p. 57):

> Does the rate of population growth always increase as average income grows?   This assertion is universally true only for the early stages of development and is not necessarily true for advanced countries.   It depends on the related generalization that the high fertility rates found in backward economies have a high degree of stability and will persist unless subjected to very considerable shocks.   This being the case, the mortality rate will then be the crucial variable that determines the rate of population growth.   As indicated, we would visualize the mortality rate as the result of two types of effects.   One we might call the autonomous effect—the effect on mortality that takes

place apart from and regardless of changes in income and consumption. Such factors as the medical and public health discoveries previously alluded to are of this nature. The other is the income effect for which we visualize a direct connection between the level of consumption and the related levels of nutrition, sanitation, health, and mortality. Clearly, as mortality rates drop with income increases, population will grow.

Furthermore, Leibenstein provides some empirical evidence on the historical (mainly before World War II) relationship between life expectancy at birth and per capita income for countries that are now at a higher level of income (p. 241):

> We correlated life expectancy [at birth] with per capita income. . . . Although the evidence suggests that there is some connection between life expectancy and the level of per capita income, the relation is certainly not a unique or perfect one. This is to be expected. Sanitary habits, the state of medical knowledge, and hygienic and other discoveries do play their part. Furthermore, out of a given income the amount spent on nutrition, public health, and other factors that determine the health and vitality of the group can, in principle, vary to a considerable degree. Nevertheless, the size of the correlation coefficient ($r = 0.71$) suggests that the historical relationship between the two variables is not without significance.

He adds, however, "Of what significance this 'historical relationship' is for present-day backward economies is most difficult to say. At best it is probably suggestive only of what the orders of magnitude were in the past" (p. 241, footnote 13).

For our purposes of ascertaining the probability of dying at different ages independent of, as well as dependent upon, personal consumption levels [that is, $d(t)$ and $f(c)$], the Leibenstein analysis has some deficiencies. First, his stated relationship between mortality, or life expectancy, and per-capita income levels is not age-specific, while infant mortality is substantially influenced by per-capita income. Thus, with the Leibenstein data we are unable to ascertain directly the relationship between consumption and mortality at older ages—ages when the consumer makes his own choice between consumption and savings. To overcome this difficulty somewhat, Table 4.1 presents the age-specific national averages of the probability of dying within one year in the United States and seven developing countries for ages above five years. Note that the age-specific rates are generally higher in the developing

TABLE 4.1

Age-specific Death Rates for Males in the United States and Some Developing Countries (in Percent)

AGE	U.S., 1966	ARGENTINA, 1963	MEXICO, 1966	BRAZIL, STATE OF GUANABARA, 1950	U.A.R., 1960	PHILLIPINES, 1965	THAILAND, 1960	INDIA RURAL SAMPLE SURVEY, 1958–1959
5–9	0.05	0.08	0.22	0.23	0.24	0.26	0.33	} 0.56
10–14	0.05	0.08	0.13	0.17	0.21	0.12	0.21	
15–19	0.15	0.13	0.19	0.34	0.23	0.14	0.21	} 0.35
20–24	0.20	0.20	0.30	} 0.61	0.27	0.23	0.28	
25–29	0.19	0.21	0.39		0.34	0.30	0.31	} 0.42
30–34	0.22	0.26	0.47	} 0.90	0.41	0.35	0.39	
35–39	0.31	0.34	0.69		0.50	0.46	0.54	} 0.58
40–44	0.47	0.52	0.77	} 1.41	0.66	0.52	0.72	
45–49	0.75	0.81	0.95		0.84	0.73	0.99	} 1.28
50–54	1.22	1.29	1.21	} 2.64	1.51	0.94	1.30	
55–59	1.92	1.93	1.76		1.68	1.18	1.69	} 3.22
60–64	2.82	2.95	2.46	} 5.18	2.74	2.00	2.51	
65–69	4.30	3.96	3.80		4.81	2.41	3.31	n.a.
All ages	1.10	1.01	1.02	1.45	1.76	0.79	0.92	1.96

SOURCE: United Nations (1968). *Demographic Yearbook, 1967.* New York, United Nations, pp. 412, 415, 416, 418–420. Data are for the United States and those developing countries having more than 20 million people, except (owing to inadequate data) Ethiopia, Nigeria, Burma, China (mainland), Indonesia, Iran, Republic of Korea, Pakistan, Turkey, and North Vietnam.

countries than in the United States until about age fifty, then often are lower. This result may be due to a stronger constitution of those able to survive poorer health conditions to older age.

A second difficulty with the Leibenstein analysis, as well as with the data in Table 4.1, is that they are based on aggregate concepts; but aggregate data on consumption levels and death rates do not adequately reflect income distribution. Thus, for our microeconomic concept, microeconomic data are needed to separate out the influence of individuals' food, clothing, housing, and medical expenditures on their probability of dying. The only microeconomic data available that are at all useful are the well-known facts that the income elasticity of food demand at low income is well above zero—closer to unity—and that it declines as income rises (see Chapter 10 below); thus, people in low-income circumstances have a demonstrated need for more food. Furthermore, the income elasticities of demand for housing, clothing, and health services are even higher. Although a component of the increasing demand for food, housing, and clothing is only "taste" changes, another important component aids in sustaining life.

In summary, the relation $f(c)$ between the probability of dying and expenditure levels, as well as the relation $d(t)$, require an integration of information from both nutritional experts and from data on death rates in different economic circumstances. It is expected that $f(c)$ is quite high until a threshold of consumption expenditures is reached and then falls as consumption level continues to rise.

THE OPTIMAL PROGRAM

The key to analyzing the full implications of the problem here is to obtain a fairly general solution. In the language of optimal control theory:

$U(a)$ is the functional to be maximized at age a where

(4.2) $$U(a) = \int_a^\infty \ell(t)e^{-mt}u(c(t))\, dt$$

$c(t)$ is the control variable
$\ell(t)$ is a state variable and obeys the law

(4.3) $$\dot{\ell}(t) = -\ell(t)[d(t) + f(c(t))]$$

$S(t)$ is a state variable, is greater than or equal to zero by (4.6), and obeys the law

(4.4) $$\dot{S}(t) = y^*(t) + rS(t) - c(t)$$

$d(t)$ is a known function of age t
$f(c(t))$ is a known function of $c(t)$
$y^*(t)$ is a known function of age t.

Unfortunately, an explicit analytic solution to this problem cannot be obtained basically because utility at any future point in time depends upon the time path of consumption up to that point (through the influence on ℓ) so that utility is not additive: Appendix C sets up the Pontryagin solution to this problem.   When the inequality constraint on savings is not binding, that solution involves solving a nonlinear, third-order differential equation in c.   Furthermore, it is important for our problem to know when the constraint is binding and savings are zero.   The problem could be solved on a computer using Bellman's dynamic programming technique after assuming specific functional forms for $u(c)$ and $f(c)$.   Alternative solutions for other functional forms could also be obtained.   However, a Bellman solution awaits more empirical information on the function $f(c)$.

In any case, we expect the solution to the problem to show that at low-income levels the inequality constraint is *virtually always* binding (consumption equals income and savings are zero) because the need to consume in order to maintain life itself dominates the intertemporal decision.   That is, a small increase in the probability of dying at age a due to lower consumption decreases planned total lifetime utility very considerably because the probability of being alive is decreased for *every* point in future time.

This factor of the influence of consumption levels on the probability of remaining alive is also expected to be important at somewhat higher income levels.   In fact, we believe this factor to be more important for savings than what Fisher calls "habit."   Only at "comfortable" living standards would we expect the influence of consumption levels on the probability of life to be negligible.   Then, the subjective rate of discount is almost entirely determined by $d(t)$ and m, and savings may take place to earn the rate of return r or to provide for retirement or unemployment.   But note that the discount rate increases as a person ages, particularly past fifty.

In summary, this model of intertemporal consumer behavior seems to provide a theoretical procedure to integrate the so-called "survival motivation" that is dominant at low-income levels and the profit motive that is dominant at high-income levels. At low-income levels the need to consume to maintain life leads to consuming all of income; at high-income levels the need for survival has been as well provided for as possible and the rate of return on savings (investment) is the most important determinant of savings, as long as the consumer does not anticipate retirement or unemployment in the near future. Thus, low-income peasant farmers and workers may be maximizing in a well-defined sense even though they are not saving.

4.3   Two Extensions by Reconsidering Income

The model in Section 4.2 treats income as both exogenous and non-random. This characteristic is particularly unrealistic in low-income countries because work hours and thus income are often under some control by the worker and because considerable uncertainty in future income is typical. The simple model is therefore reexamined, first, for work-hour choice and, second, for uncertainty.

THE WORK-HOUR CHOICE

Most landless agricultural workers in developing economies and many urban workers, particularly in the service sector, have a wide range of choice in determining their hours of work (or, equivalently, days of work per week) but earn an hourly wage (or a daily wage) that is independent of their work hours. In other words, their income is not exogenous but rather is a part of the consumer decision problem through choice of work hours. In this case, the expected income $y^*[t,H(t)]$ is the hourly wage times the hours of work:

$$(4.7) \qquad y^*[t,H(t)] = w^*(t)H(t)$$

where $w^*(t)$ is the exogenous time path of the hourly wage the worker expects to receive (which may well be constant) and $H(t)$ is the time path of work hours (which is under the worker's control).

In other circumstances, such as family work on a private farm (as discussed in Chapter 1) and small-scale retail trade, income is subject to decreasing returns from work input, but work hours nevertheless are under the consumer's control. Then, $y^*[t,H(t)]$ takes a more general

form in which $\partial y*[t,H(t)]/\partial H(t) > 0$ and $\partial^2 y*[t,H(t)]/\partial H(t)^2 \leqq 0$.
For example, in the case of a privately operated family farm without
technical progress, $y*[t,H(t)]$ may be the average per-worker product
given by Equation (1.2) of Chapter 1.

In any case, the number of work hours $H(t)$ is an additional decision
variable for the consumer which affects his utility. Thus, the objective
function (4.2) must be reformulated as

$$(4.8) \qquad U(a) = \int_a^\infty \ell(t)e^{-mt}u[c(t),H(t)]\, dt$$

where $u[c(t),H(t)]$ is the utility function if the consumer is alive, as
determined by the consumption level and by hours of work, in which
$\partial u/\partial c(t) > 0$ and, presumably, $\partial u/\partial H(t) < 0$. [In Equation (1.5)
utility is assumed homothetic in consumption and leisure.] The opti-
mal problem now is to maximize (4.8) subject to (4.3), (4.6), and

$$(4.9) \qquad \dot{S}(t) = y*[t,H(t)] + rS(t) - c(t)$$

with the time paths of consumption and work hours as control variables.

In Appendix C the Pontryagin procedure for solving this problem is
set up. That problem is the same as for Section 4.2 except that an
additional differential equation is introduced for the work-hour choice.
The equation, which obtains whether or not the consumer is constrained
by the zero debt constraint, is, dropping time subscripts,

$$(4.10) \qquad \frac{\partial u(c,H)}{\partial c}\frac{\partial y*(t,H)}{\partial H} + \frac{\partial u(c,H)}{\partial H} = p_1\frac{df(c)}{dc}\frac{\partial y*(t,H)}{\partial H}$$

where p_1 is the imputed price of the influence of consumption level on
the probability of dying. The first term on the left is the marginal
utility of consumption *times* the marginal productivity of work hours
[equal to $w*$ if Equation (4.7) obtains], while the second term is the
marginal utility of work (which is negative). If $\partial c = \partial y*$, the sum is
therefore the marginal total utility of work.

In a static model, such as in Chapter 1, the influence of consumption
level on the probability of remaining alive is ignored so that $df(c)/dc = 0$.
Thus, for the case in which the consumer consumes all his earnings,
Equation (4.10) simply says that a worker chooses his work hours so
that the marginal total utility of work is zero. However, when the influence of consumption on the probability of dying is introduced in the

dynamic problem [where the probability of dying decreases as consumption rises, that is, $df(c)/dc < 0$], Equation (4.10) says that the worker works beyond the point where the static marginal utility of work is zero as long as the marginal productivity of work is positive. The static marginal utility is now negative but is compensated for by the increased probability of remaining alive. In sum, at low levels of income where $df(c)/dc$ is nonnegligible, the dynamic problem suggests harder work than does the static problem. (Appendix C also discusses the time path of the marginal disutility of work, but it need not concern us here.)

INCOME UNCERTAINTY

At the end of Section 4.2, it is suggested that no savings take place at low-income levels because the survival motive dominates the profit motive. This result, however, abstracts from an important characteristic of much of income earnings in developing countries—the uncertainty in the level of that income. Furthermore, this uncertainty has a very important asymmetry attached to it: An income higher than expected can lead to extra consumption or savings, but an income lower than expected, when savings are zero, *forces* the consumer to consume less and thus decrease his chance of survival. Therefore, there is, in fact, some small savings in low-income circumstances to protect partly against such drops in income.

The precise influence of uncertainty on savings is quite difficult to ascertain, but some general comments can be made on the form of the savings (rather than on its level). First, private farmers have savings embodied in the land they own. However, borrowing against these savings is very costly because moneylenders in rural areas are known for charging high interest rates and for making frequent conscious efforts to *keep* a farmer in debt once he is in debt. Thus, it is preferable for the farmer to rely upon other forms of savings. These savings may be those embodied in cattle, which can be eaten or easily sold, or those embodied in jewelry, which can also be easily sold. Note, though, it is not the rate of return on such savings that is important but rather the negotiability of the savings assets in time of emergency.

In spite of these remarks, an even more secure asset against very low-income levels is the extended family system. For it is rare that many members of an extended family all suffer declines in income at once (except, say, in general droughts). Thus, the extended family is a rational response to protect survival against sudden drops in income.

Furthermore, not only is an extended family useful in protecting survival on the family farm, but it is even more important for landless agricultural workers and urban workers. These workers generally have no savings embodied in land and thus can only rely on savings in durables such as jewelry (which, unfortunately, can be stolen) and on the extended family. If these remarks are correct, an increase in the *certainty* of income, rather than just its level, could decrease the economic motivation for an extended family. This increased certainty of income could then lower the desire for an extended family and could indirectly lower birth rates.

The implication of all these statements is that any savings that do take place at low-income levels emphasize the security of the savings assets. And generally the most secure assets are not assets that are also used directly as capital in production processes; rather they are jewelry and an extended family. In sum, uncertainty in income seems to increase the need for an extended-family system but does not increase savings invested in productive assets.

4.4   Implications for Savings in Developing Countries

First and most important, this chapter has suggested that savings in productive assets are unlikely to occur among low-income farm families, landless agricultural laborers, and urban workers because at low-income levels the survival motive dominates the profit motive. Thus, the theory here is consistent with Table 2.1 of Chapter 2, which shows very small average savings among these groups. Second this chapter has shown that work hours per worker are greater in the dynamic low-income setting than predicted in the static setting because workers choose to work harder to increase consumption and thus the chance for survival.

In summary, a theory of savings for low-income countries may be able to ignore voluntary savings within peasant agriculture [which is not to say that farmers do not try to increase output (see Chapter 8)] and by both rural and urban laborers. Savings theory, therefore, must move to introduce governmental taxation policy and the determinants of rates of return on investments for the higher-income groups (see, again, Table 2.1). Governmental taxation policy is an important topic in planning theory [see, for example, Bose and Dixit (1972)]. For savings in higher-income groups, a model such as the one developed here would have to be extended to obtain the level of savings at different income levels both when the rate of return on investment is either known with certainty or is uncertain and when there is also a demand to leave bequests.   Additionally, savings embodied in consumer durables may need to be included.   Finally, noneconomic considerations such as the desire for power through control of wealth may have to be considered for a complete theory of savings.   In short, all the theoretical topics at issue for savings in developed countries are probably equally relevant for the upper-income groups of developing countries.

Part Three

THE OPEN ECONOMY

Chapter Five

LUXURY IMPORTS IN AN OPEN ECONOMY MODEL

The role of international trade in economic development has been an absorbing topic probably because the role of trade can differ considerably from country to country as well as over time for any one country. Thus, on the export side, the role of trade can be discussed from the point of view of the commodity sold (e.g., agricultural, minerals, petroleum, or manufactured goods), the ownership of the foreign exchange earned (domestic or foreign and plantation owner or small farmer), the resources required for export production (e.g., "vent-for-surplus" or resource-using), and the linkages between the export sector and other domestic sectors (e.g., the development of infrastructure needed for exporting). On the import side, trade and development can be discussed according to whether imports are food, raw materials, capital machinery, or luxury consumer goods.

Obviously, we are not able to consider all of the cases, and so choices must be made. First, we choose to study only agricultural exports because they are still predominant in the developing world. Thus, in Table 5.1 we provide a list of those developing countries that have received at least one-half of their export earnings from a single product. As can be seen, about two out of every three of these countries export an agricultural product; one out of six, petroleum (all in the Middle

TABLE 5.1
Developing Countries with Given Product as the Principal Export

PRODUCT	NUMBER OF COUNTRIES	COUNTRIES
Agricultural		
Coffee	7	Angola, Brazil, Colombia, El Salvador, Ethiopia, Rwanda, Uganda
Cotton and cotton seeds	5	Chad, Nicaragua, Sudan, Syria, UAR
Bananas	3	Ecuador, Honduras, Panama
Groundnuts and groundnut oil	3	Gambia, Niger, Senegal
Sugar	3	Cuba, Dominican Republic, Réunion
Live animals	2	Somalia, Upper Volta
Rice	2	Burma, Cambodia
Cloves	1	Zanzibar
Cocoa	1	Ghana
Jute and jute products	1	Pakistan
Palm nuts, kernels, and oil	1	Dahomey
Rubber	1	Republic of Vietnam
Saw and veneer logs	1	Sabah
Tea	1	Ceylon
Wool	1	Uruguay
Total agricultural	33	
Other		
Petroleum	9	Algeria, Brunei, Iran, Iraq, Kuwait, Libya, Saudi Arabia, Southern Yemen (refined petroleum), Venezuela
Copper	3	Chile, Democratic Rep. of the Congo, Zambia
Diamonds	2	Central African Republic, Sierra Leone
Iron ore	2	Liberia, Mauritania
Tin	1	Bolivia
Total other	17	

SOURCE: United Nations (1969 and 1970). *Yearbook of International Trade Statistics, 1967 and 1968. New York, United Nations.* Countries listed are those from Africa, Asia, Latin America, and the Middle East (excluding Japan, Hong Kong, and Singapore) that received at least half of their export earnings from one product or directly related products in at least one of the years 1964 to 1968. There are 34 countries not satisfying this criterion, although most were primary exporters: Afghanistan, Argentina, Cameroon, China (Taiwan), Congo (Brazzaville), Costa Rica, Gabon, Guatemala, India, Indonesia, Israel, Ivory Coast, Jordan, Kenya, Korea (Republic of), Lebanon, Madagascar, Malawi, Sarawak, West Malaysia, Mali, Mexico, Morocco, Mozambique, Nigeria, Paraguay, Peru, Phillipines, South Africa, Southern Rhodesia, Tanzania, Thailand, Togo, Tunisia.

East except Brunei and Venezuela); and one out of six, a metal or diamonds. In addition, some other developing countries export mainly two agricultural products. [In any case, for analyzing exports produced outside the agricultural sector, the reader should consult Bardhan (1970, part I)].

Second, domestic rather than foreign ownership of export earnings is assumed because, again, this is the predominant pattern today. In this chapter these domestic owners are thought to be middle- to large-scale farmers. In Chapter 6 the possibility of governmental taxes on exports or imports is introduced. Third, the discussion here presumes that exports are resource-using. Such a presumption is consistent with our results in Chapter 1 suggesting that surplus labor in agriculture is a limiting case of a more general description of laborer behavior. Finally, linkages from the export sector to the rest of the economy are generally ignored, not so much in the belief that they are unimportant, but because they are difficult to discuss analytically. For agricultural exporting economies, any important linkages are more often forward, for example, to an export-processing sector.

In summary, on the export side, the models of this chapter and the next presume a resource-using, agricultural exporting economy, with no important linkages from the export sector but with foreign exchange earnings returned to the domestic economy. On the import side, two cases are highlighted: in this chapter, luxury consumption imports; in the next, capital imports. Luxury consumption imports is chosen as one case because it has been historically relevant [see Levin (1960, particularly chapter 4)], because it is the simplest analytically, and, most importantly, because it indicates how a "wastage" of foreign exchange earnings from producing a resource-using export can hamper, not aid, economic growth. Capital goods imports, instead of raw material imports, is chosen as the second case only because economists are (somewhat!) more confident of the theoretical role of capital in the aggregate production function than of raw materials. Food imports is discussed briefly in Section 5.4.

The basic structure of the model in this chapter is to divide the agricultural sector into an export sector and a food sector, with land and labor under each crop as variable factors of production and other factors, discussed in Chapter 8, taken as exogenous. The secondary sector is the same as in Chapter 2. Imports are consumer goods substitutable in consumption with domestically produced secondary sector goods.

In Chapter 2 the closed economy model refers basically to a sub-sistence economy in which the major portion of consumer expenditures is for food for both landless workers and landowners. Thus, real consumer income could there be defined as purchasing power over food. In economies with a substantial export sector, however, this character-ization is unrepresentative. In particular, ownership of land often leads to much higher income levels than those· obtained by landless workers. Furthermore, a substantial portion of this income to land ownership is spent on manufactured goods (either domestically pro-duced or imported). To capture this characteristic, real income to land ownership is defined in this chapter as purchasing power over *manu-factured* goods, not food as in Chapter 2. (No serious analytic problem would arise if only real income to land ownership in the export sector is so defined while income to land in the food sector is defined as purchasing power over food.) However, real wages, rural or urban, are again defined as purchasing power over food. Influences on changes in labor and land real income of changes in terms of trade for exports relative to imports are then studied (thus, income distribution rather than total income is the focus). Saving by landowners is initially ignored but is later introduced into export agriculture.

The most important conclusion is that, on the one hand, a rising growth rate in terms of trade (or, equivalently, export technology) *lowers*—or, at best, leaves constant—the rate of growth of real wages in both the short and long runs; on the other hand, the rate of growth in income to land ownership *rises* but only in the short run. The result depends upon (1) food, which faces rising prices, being a large proportion of consumer expenses at lower-income levels, and (2) a reduced rate of growth of secondary sector employment (owing to a higher growth rate of wages in terms of manufactured goods) and thus of secondary sector output and savings.

5.1   The Structure of an Agricultural Export Economy

To undertake an investigation of an open economy exporting an agricultural product, we first study the properties of production in the food and the export sectors to determine within agriculture the structure of land use, the allocation of labor, and the relative output price. Then we complete the agricultural sector and turn to the secondary sector. Throughout the chapter, the food sector refers to that portion of agricultural output used for domestic food consumption (even if the product that is exported, e.g., rice, is also the basic food good).

To begin, label acreage in the food crop A_1 and label acreage in the export crop A_x, so that total cultivated land is allocated between them, that is, so that

$$(5.1) \qquad\qquad A_x = 1 - A_1$$

where total acreage is indexed by unity. Now, in the general case for this chapter, the production function for the food crop can be written

$$(5.2) \qquad Y_1 = e^{b_1 t} L_1^{\beta_1} A_1^{\gamma_1} \qquad 0 < \beta_1 + \gamma_1 \leqq 1$$

and the production function for the export crop,

$$(5.3) \qquad Y_x = e^{b_x t} L_x^{\beta_x} A_x^{\gamma_x} \qquad 0 < \beta_x + \gamma_x \leqq 1$$

where Y is output with appropriate units of measurement, L is labor, b is the rate of technical change (including the sources of growth discussed in Chapter 8, such as growth in aggregate acreage under crops), β is the elasticity of output with respect to labor, and γ is the elasticity of output with respect to land. The elasticity of factor substitution is assumed to be 1, while decreasing returns to scale are permitted as land acreage is shifted between crops.

We now posit that, at least in the longer run, the value of the marginal product of an acre of land in alternative uses must be equal. In most of Africa and Asia, such an assumption is reasonably realistic; in much of Latin America, the assumption would not be realistic if the *latifundia* there do not profit-maximize (see Chapter 8, Section 8.2).[1] In any case, if q_1 is the domestic price of the food product and q_x is the domestic price of the export crop both relative to secondary sector prices, land is then allocated by

$$(5.4) \qquad\qquad \frac{q_1 \gamma_1 Y_1}{A_1} = \frac{q_x \gamma_x Y_x}{A_x}$$

We also suppose that labor in agriculture is allocated by the marginal productivity condition so that

$$(5.5) \qquad\qquad \frac{q_1 \beta_1 Y_1}{L_1} = \frac{q_x \beta_x Y_x}{L_x}$$

[1] In this latter case, it is possible to treat the land under exports and under food as fixed, so that the production functions ignore land. However, the growth of real wages, for example, is then determined completely by the food sector if, as is assumed in this chapter, the demand function for food has a zero price elasticity.

If wages (or, for that matter, the rental prices of land) differ by a constant proportion between the food and export sectors, results of this chapter are unaffected.

With these equations we can draw a useful implication for characterizing the agricultural sector; in particular, we can derive the change in the domestic price ratio between the export crop and the food crop. Thus, using production relations (5.2) and (5.3), Equation (5.4) becomes

$$q_1\gamma_1 e^{b_1 t}\left(\frac{L_1}{A_1}\right)^{\beta_1} A_1^{\beta_1+\gamma_1-1} = q_x\gamma_x e^{b_x t}\left(\frac{L_x}{A_x}\right)^{\beta_x} A_x^{\beta_x+\gamma_x-1}$$

On the other hand, if we divide (5.4) by (5.5), then

$$\frac{L_1}{A_1} = \frac{\beta_1}{\beta_x}\frac{\gamma_x}{\gamma_1}\frac{L_x}{A_x}$$

Therefore, substituting this expression into the previous one and carrying out some algebraic manipulations, we obtain

(5.6)
$$\frac{q_1}{q_x} = e^{(b_x-b_1)t}\left(\frac{\beta_x}{\beta_1}\right)^{\beta_1}\left(\frac{\gamma_x}{\gamma_1}\right)^{1-\beta_1}\left(\frac{L_x}{A_x}\right)^{\beta_x-\beta_1}\frac{A_1^{1-\beta_1-\gamma_1}}{A_x^{1-\beta_x-\gamma_x}}$$

For mathematical simplicity, assume for the remainder of this chapter that $\beta_1 = \beta_x$ and $\gamma_1 = \gamma_x$. (Thus, a convex production set obtains when $\beta_1 + \beta_x = \gamma_1 + \gamma_x < 1$. A footnote to Section 5.3 briefly examines the convexity case of $\beta_1 + \beta_x = \gamma_1 + \gamma_x = 1$ but $\beta_1 \neq \beta_x$.) Equations (5.3) to (5.5) then become

(5.3′)
$$Y_x = e^{b_x t}L_x^{\beta_1}A_x^{\gamma_1}$$

(5.4′)
$$\frac{q_1 Y_1}{A_1} = \frac{q_x Y_x}{A_x}$$

(5.5′)
$$\frac{q_1 Y_1}{L_1} = \frac{q_x Y_x}{L_x}$$

and Equation (5.6) becomes

(5.6′)
$$\frac{q_1}{q_x} = e^{(b_x-b_1)t}\left(\frac{A_1}{A_x}\right)^{1-\beta_1-\gamma_1}$$

Therefore, the price of the food crop rises relative to that of the export crop when the rate of technical change in export agriculture exceeds that in food agriculture or when land is allocated to food production away from the export crop.

Now consider two types of exports: one that is substitutable in production with the domestic food crop and one that is not.

CASE I: SUBSTITUTES. If the same crop is exported and used for the dominant domestic food crop (e.g., rice in Southeast Asia), then the export crop and the food crop are substitutes in production in the most obvious sense. However, other crops can also be considered substitutable, as indicated in the examples listed in Table 7.1. In both of these cases, there are no decreasing returns to scale to shifting between crops so that $\beta_1 + \gamma_1 = 1$. Then the production functions (5.2) and (5.3) become

$$(5.7) \qquad Y_1 = e^{b_1 t} L_1^{\beta_1} A_1^{1-\beta_1} \qquad 0 < \beta_1 < 1$$

$$(5.8) \qquad Y_x = e^{b_x t} L_x^{\beta_1} A_x^{1-\beta_1} \qquad 0 < \beta_1 < 1$$

Note that the rates of technical change are still permitted to differ because different crops may differ in their response to changing production conditions. However, if the export and food crops are the same, then, of course, $b_1 = b_x$. In any case, the relative price equation here becomes

$$(5.9) \qquad \frac{q_1}{q_x} = e^{(b_x - b_1)t}$$

CASE II: NONSUBSTITUTES. For an export crop that is not easily substitutable in production with food because land highly productive in the export crop is not necessarily highly productive in the food crop (e.g., bananas or coffee as exports and wheat or corn as cereals), the production functions are given by (5.2) and (5.3') and the relative price equation by (5.6').

In Figure 5.1 the static transformation curves for these two cases are shown. For substitutes in production, the two crops are basically the same good on the production side with the exception that the slope of the linear transformation line will change over time if the rates of technical change differ.

To complete the primary sector of our model, first specify that domestic food consumption per capita depends upon real wages defined as purchasing power over food, that is, equivalent to Equation (2.9)

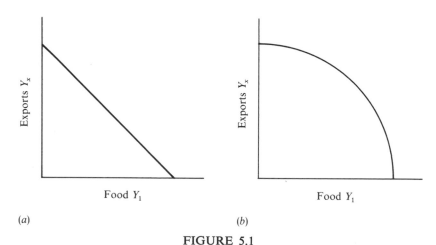

FIGURE 5.1

Transformation curves between the export and food crops. (a) Substitutes in production; (b) nonsubstitutes in production

except that, as in Section 3.3, the price elasticity of demand is assumed zero. Thus,

$$(5.10) \qquad \frac{Y_1}{L} = c_1 \left(\frac{Y_1}{L_1}\right)^{\alpha_1} \qquad 0 \leqq \alpha_1 \leqq 1$$

If the relative price between agricultural and manufacturing goods does not change, for example, when q_x is fixed and $b_1 = b_x$, then the neglect of the relative price effect on consumption cannot affect any results. Nevertheless, note that, as in Chapter 2, defining real wages as purchasing power over food implies that food is assumed to be a large portion of the consumer budget at low-income levels (the level of wages).

Second, in the next three sections of this chapter we assume that the country does not influence its terms of trade on the international market by the quantity it exports, but that the terms may be changing exogenously. Suppose that the rate of change in the exogenous terms of trade $\dot{q}_x/q_x$ is labeled τ. Suppose, further, that there are no tariffs or export taxes (these are discussed in Chapter 6). Then, Equation (5.6) becomes

$$(5.11) \qquad q_1 = q_x(0)e^{(\tau + b_x - b_1)t}\left(\frac{A_1}{A_x}\right)^{1 - \beta_1 - \gamma_1}$$

and (5.9) becomes

(5.12) $$q_1 = q_x(0)e^{(\tau + b_x - b_1)t}$$

where $q_x(0)$ is the initial level of the export (and therefore food) price.

Export earnings are $q_x Y_x$ if no appreciable portion of the export crop is consumed domestically (otherwise, exports should be thought of as net exports), if there is no inventory accumulation, and if any processing of the export crop before exportation is ignored. Imports, on the other hand, are assumed to be manufactured goods—either consumer goods or capital goods—and are aggregated with the secondary sector and so have a unit price. Then, the balance-of-payments equation is

(5.13) $$M_2 = q_x Y_x$$

where M_2 is secondary sector imports. The important consumers of these imports are landowners, as labor income is spent mainly on food and capital income is invested (as will be discussed).

To close the model, the total population is given by Equation (2.5) in Chapter 2. Also, the secondary sector production function is Equation (2.2), while secondary sector employment is

(5.14) $$L_2 = L - L_1 - L_x$$

The allocation of labor between the food, export, and secondary sector labor forces is determined by (5.5′) and by Equation (2.7). As in Chapter 2, the change in capital stock is given by the difference between investment and depreciation [Equation (2.4)]. Finally, for investment, assume that, as in Equation (2.3) for the closed economy, domestic manufacturing production is able to supply the demand for gross investment given by capital's share of secondary sector output $(1 - \beta_2) Y_2$. Any constant fraction of output, however, again would not change conclusions. (In any case, with regard to the "two-gap" literature the savings gap is dominant.)

5.2 Exports Substitutable in Production with Food

There are essentially two types of agricultural export economies that are considered in this chapter: First, the economies considered in this section are those exporting a crop substitutable in production with the domestic food crop. For these economies, production functions (5.7) and (5.8) obtain, as does the agricultural price equation (5.12). Thus, the model is solved first and summarized in Table 5.2, and then implications are drawn.   Second, the economies considered in Section 5.3 are those exporting a crop which is not directly substitutable in production for the food crop.   In Section 5.4 we consider the effects of a downward-sloping foreign demand curve.

SOLUTION OF THE OPEN ECONOMY MODEL

The solution of the model of this section is similar to the solution in Chapter 2 with the important constraint that the domestic relative price of the export agricultural good to secondary sector goods q_x is determined by the international market.   First, given the constant investment assumption of (2.3), we saw in Chapter 2 that, in the longer run (the short run is examined later in this section), secondary sector labor productivity grows by b_2/β_2, the rate of labor augmenting technical change.   Therefore, the solutions for $\dot{Y}_2/Y_2$, $\dot{K}_2/K_2$, and $\dot{I}_2/I_2$ are given by (2.15).

Given that secondary sector labor productivity growth is given by b_2/β_2, growth of real wages in all sectors [see Equations (2.7) and (5.5')] is given by b_2/β_2 less the growth of food prices $\tau + b_x - b_1$ [see Equation (5.12)], or

$$(5.15) \qquad \frac{\dot{w}_1}{w_1} = \frac{b_2}{\beta_2} + b_1 - b_x - \tau$$

where w_1 is defined as real wages (the subscript 1 suggesting that real wages are defined in terms of food).   Therefore, from (5.10)

$$(5.16) \qquad \frac{\dot{Y}_1}{Y_1} = \epsilon + \alpha_1 \frac{\dot{w}_1}{w_1},$$

and, because $\dot{L}_1/L_1 = \dot{Y}_1/Y_1 - \dot{w}_1/w_1$,

$$(5.17) \qquad \frac{\dot{L}_1}{L_1} = \epsilon - (1 - \alpha_1) \frac{\dot{w}_1}{w_1}$$

To ascertain the change in land distribution under crops, use the food production function (5.7) to obtain

$$\frac{\dot{A}_1}{A_1} = \frac{1}{1 - \beta_1} \left[\frac{\dot{Y}_1}{Y_1} - b_1 - \beta_1 \frac{\dot{L}_1}{L_1} \right]$$

$$= \frac{1}{1 - \beta_1} \left[\epsilon + \alpha_1 \frac{\dot{w}_1}{w_1} - b_1 - \beta_1 \left(\epsilon - (1 - \alpha_1) \frac{\dot{w}_1}{w_1} \right) \right]$$

$$= \frac{1}{1 - \beta_1} \left[(1 - \beta_1)\epsilon + (1 - \beta_1)\alpha_1 \frac{\dot{w}_1}{w_1} - b_1 + \beta_1 \frac{\dot{w}_1}{w_1} \right]$$

or

$$(5.18) \quad \frac{\dot{A}_1}{A_1} = \frac{[1 - (1 - \beta_1)(1 - \alpha_1)](\dot{w}_1/w_1) - [b_1 - (1 - \beta_1)\epsilon]}{1 - \beta_1}$$

Therefore, also,

$$(5.19) \quad \frac{\dot{A}_x}{A_x} = -\frac{A_1}{A_x}\frac{\dot{A}_1}{A_1} = -\frac{L_1}{L_x}\frac{\dot{A}_1}{A_1}$$

Also, from (5.5') and (2.7), and from the export production function (5.8),

$$\frac{\dot{Y}_x}{Y_x} - \frac{\dot{L}_x}{L_x} = \frac{b_2}{\beta_2} - \tau = b_x + (1 - \beta_1)\left(\frac{\dot{A}_x}{A_x} - \frac{\dot{L}_x}{L_x}\right)$$

Therefore,

$$\frac{\dot{L}_x}{L_x} = -\frac{b_2/\beta_2 - b_x - \tau}{1 - \beta_1} + \frac{\dot{A}_x}{A_x}$$

or

$$(5.20) \quad \frac{\dot{L}_x}{L_x} = \frac{b_1 - \dot{w}_1/w_1}{1 - \beta_1} - \frac{L_1}{L_x}\frac{\dot{A}_1}{A_1}$$

Also,

$$\frac{\dot{Y}_x}{Y_x} = \frac{b_2}{\beta_2} - \tau + \frac{b_1 - \dot{w}_1/w_1}{1 - \beta_1} - \frac{L_1}{L_x}\frac{\dot{A}_1}{A_1}$$

$$= \frac{\dot{w}_1}{w_1} - b_1 + b_x + \frac{b_1 - \dot{w}_1/w_1}{1 - \beta_1} - \frac{L_1}{L_x}\frac{\dot{A}_1}{A_1}$$

or

$$(5.21) \quad \frac{\dot{Y}_x}{Y_x} = b_x + \frac{\beta_1}{1 - \beta_1}(b_1 - \dot{w}_1/w_1) - \frac{L_1}{L_x}\frac{\dot{A}_1}{A_1}$$

Thus,

$$(5.22) \quad \frac{\dot{M}_2}{M_2} = \tau + \frac{\dot{Y}_x}{Y_x}$$

TABLE 5.2
Specification and Solution of the Open Economy Model of Section 5.2

Equations

(2.5) $\qquad\qquad L = e^{\epsilon t}$

(5.7) $\qquad\qquad Y_1 = e^{b_1 t} L_1^{\beta_1} A_1^{1-\beta_1} \qquad 0 < \beta_1 < 1$

(5.10) $\qquad\qquad \dfrac{Y_1}{L} = c_1 \left(\dfrac{Y_1}{L_1}\right)^{\alpha_1} \qquad 0 \leqq \alpha_1 \leqq 1$

(5.8) $\qquad\qquad Y_x = e^{b_x t} L_x^{\beta_1} A_x^{1-\beta_1} \qquad 0 < \beta_1 < 1$

(5.5') $\qquad\qquad \dfrac{q_1 Y_1}{L_1} = \dfrac{q_x Y_x}{L_x}$

(5.12) $\qquad\qquad q_1 = q_x(0) e^{(\tau + b_x - b_1)t}$

(5.1) $\qquad\qquad A_x = 1 - A_1$

(2.2) $\qquad\qquad Y_2 = e^{b_2 t} K_2^{1-\beta_2} L_2^{\beta_2} \qquad 0 < \beta_2 < 1$

(2.3) $\qquad\qquad I_2 = (1 - \beta_2) Y_2$

(2.4) $\qquad\qquad \dot{K}_2 = I_2 - \delta K_2 \qquad 0 < \delta < 1$

(5.14) $\qquad\qquad L_2 = L - L_1 - L_x$

(2.7) $\qquad\qquad \dfrac{q_1 \beta_1 Y_1}{L_1} = \dfrac{\mu \beta_2 Y_2}{L_2} \qquad 0 < \mu \leqq 1$

(5.13) $\qquad\qquad M_2 = q_x Y_x$

Endogenous Variables

$$
\begin{array}{cccc}
 & Y_1 & Y_x & Y_2 \\
L & L_1 & L_x & L_2 \\
 & A_1 & A_x & K_2 \\
 & q_1 & & I_2 \\
 & & & M_2
\end{array}
$$

Finally,

$$
\frac{\dot{L}_2}{L_2} = \frac{\dot{L}}{L}\frac{L}{L_2} - \frac{\dot{L}_1}{L_1}\frac{L_1}{L_2} - \frac{\dot{L}_x}{L_x}\frac{L_x}{L_2}
$$

$$
= \epsilon + \frac{L_1}{L_2}\left(\epsilon - \frac{\dot{L}_1}{L_1}\right) + \frac{L_x}{L_2}\left(\epsilon - \frac{\dot{L}_x}{L_x}\right)
$$

$$
= \epsilon + \frac{L_1}{L_2}(1 - \alpha_1)\frac{\dot{w}_1}{w_1}
$$

$$
+ \frac{L_x}{L_2}\left\{\frac{\dot{w}_1/w_1 - [b_1 - (1-\beta_1)\epsilon]}{1 - \beta_1} + \frac{L_1}{L_x}\frac{\dot{A}_1}{A_1}\right\}
$$

Solution

(5.17) $\qquad \dfrac{\dot{L}_1}{L_1} = \epsilon - (1 - \alpha_1)\dfrac{\dot{w}_1}{w_1}$

(5.18) $\qquad \dfrac{\dot{A}_1}{A_1} = \dfrac{[1 - (1 - \beta_1)(1 - \alpha_1)](\dot{w}_1/w_1) - [b_1 - (1 - \beta_1)\epsilon]}{1 - \beta_1}$

(5.16) $\qquad \dfrac{\dot{Y}_1}{Y_1} = \epsilon + \alpha_1\dfrac{\dot{w}_1}{w_1}$

(5.20) $\qquad \dfrac{\dot{L}_x}{L_x} = \dfrac{b_1 - \dot{w}_1/w_1}{1 - \beta_1} - \dfrac{L_1}{L_x}\dfrac{\dot{A}_1}{A_1}$

(5.19) $\qquad \dfrac{\dot{A}_x}{A_x} = -\dfrac{L_1}{L_x}\dfrac{\dot{A}_1}{A_1}$

(5.21) $\qquad \dfrac{\dot{Y}_x}{Y_x} = b_x + \dfrac{\beta_1}{1 - \beta_1}\left(b_1 - \dfrac{\dot{w}_1}{w_1}\right) - \dfrac{L_1}{L_x}\dfrac{\dot{A}_1}{A_1}$

(5.22) $\qquad \dfrac{\dot{M}_2}{M_2} = \tau + \dfrac{\dot{Y}_x}{Y_x}$

(5.23) $\qquad \dfrac{\dot{L}_2}{L_2} = \epsilon + \dfrac{L_1 + L_x}{L_2}\dfrac{\dot{w}_1/w_1 - [b_1 - (1 - \beta_1)\epsilon]}{1 - \beta_1}$

(2.15) $\qquad \dfrac{\dot{Y}_2}{Y_2} = \dfrac{\dot{K}_2}{K_2} = \dfrac{\dot{I}_2}{I_2} = \dfrac{b_2}{\beta_2} + \dfrac{\dot{L}_2}{L_2}$

(5.12) $\qquad \dfrac{\dot{q}_1}{q_1} = \tau + b_x - b_1$

where

(5.15) $\qquad \dfrac{\dot{w}_1}{w_1} = \dfrac{b_2}{\beta_2} + b_1 - b_x - \tau$

or, using Equation (5.18),

(5.23) $\qquad \dfrac{\dot{L}_2}{L_2} = \epsilon + \dfrac{L_1 + L_x}{L_2}\left\{\dfrac{\dot{w}_1/w_1 - [b_1 - (1 - \beta_1)\epsilon]}{1 - \beta_1}\right\}$

The model and its solution are summarized in Table 5.2. Note that all solutions, except (2.15), are defined in terms of $\dot{w}_1/w_1$, the growth rate of real wages, so that if the capital/output ratio in the secondary sector is not at its asymptotic level and therefore secondary sector labor productivity growth is not given by b_2/β_2, only a reinterpretation of $\dot{w}_1/w_1$ is needed (see Appendix B).

IMPLICATIONS

The implications of this model of an open economy are studied by discussing the growth of real wages and of real income to landowner-ship. A considerable amount of space is devoted to this discussion because subsequent sections do not change the basic results here.

The growth of real wages is given by Equation (5.15):

$$\frac{\dot{w}_1}{w_1} = \frac{b_2}{\beta_2} + b_1 - b_x - \tau$$

An important conclusion emerges: Improving terms of trade in the export sector (or technological change in the export sector, which amounts to the same) *decreases* real-wage-rate growth in the long run. In part, the result follows from defining real wages in terms of the food crop so that a lowering relative price of domestic manufactured goods and of imports, implied by improving terms of trade, does not affect real-wage-rate growth. However, more surprisingly, growth in income to landownership in terms of manufacturing goods *remains* at the rate of labor augmenting technical change b_2/β_2 in the long run.

To explain our result it may be best to start with the short-run effects of improving terms of trade and then move to the long-run result. In the short run, improving terms of trade for the export crop relative to manufacturing goods implies that exporting is relatively more profitable for landowners. This increases the demand for land in that sector at the expense of the food sector until food prices rise proportionately to the rise in export prices. Concomitantly, however, the demand for labor in agriculture as a whole rises at the expense of manufacturing. (Nominal wages rise in all sectors but, as we shall see, not by as much as the rise in food prices.) Therefore, the marginal product of labor in agriculture in terms of its own output is lower. Thus, real wages—wages in terms of food—decline in all sectors.

Finally, because nominal income to landownership rises with nominal (not real) wages as long as the ratio of landowners to landless workers remains constant, income to landowners in purchasing power over manufactures rises. Because secondary sector output falls, the in-creased landowner income is being used on imports. Thus, imports are driving out domestic manufacturing production.

In the long run, the analysis is similar to the short run, except to realize that the initial more rapidly rising manufacturing wages in terms of their own output decrease the demand for labor in manufacturing.

Thus, manufacturing output is rising more slowly so that income to capital and the resulting investment are rising more slowly. Furthermore, the secondary sector returns to steady growth, given that a constant fraction of output is saved and reinvested, when the capital/output ratio returns to constancy and labor productivity and wages in terms of secondary sector goods again grow at the rate of labor augmenting technical change b_2/β_2. In the long run, then, real income to landowners is growing at the same rate b_2/β_2, and real wages are growing at the rate given by (5.15)—even lower than in the short run.

In summary, improving terms of trade on the international market implies lower secondary sector employment growth and therefore lower capital-stock growth and lower real-wage-rate growth. Income to landownership is only rising more rapidly in the short run. Figure 5.2 shows the growth rate of real wages and of real income to landowners in both the short and long runs.[1]

A question that may arise for an agricultural exporting economy is the conditions under which land area is *not* shifting over time toward or away from the export or food crop. In this model, the change in land area under food is given by (5.18). This expression is equal to zero when

$$\frac{\dot{w}_1}{w_1} = \frac{b_1 - (1 - \beta_1)\epsilon}{1 - (1 - \beta_1)(1 - \alpha_1)}$$

which is exactly the expression (2.24) for the growth of real wages (or, in Chapter 2, also real consumer income) in a closed economy (when

---

[1] The growth rate of real wages in the short run is obtained as follows: Let Δ refer to changes so that $\Delta\dot{w}_1/w_1$ is the change in real-wage-rate growth. Now, from Equation (2.11) the change in secondary sector labor productivity growth in the short run is $-(1 - \beta_2)\Delta\dot{L}_2/L_2$, so that the change in the real-wage-rate growth in the short run from a change in the growth rate of terms of trade is $-\Delta\tau - (1 - \beta_2)\Delta\dot{L}_2/L_2$. But, from Equation (5.23),

$$\Delta\frac{\dot{w}_1}{w_1} = -\Delta\tau - (1 - \beta_2)\Delta\frac{\dot{L}_2}{L_2}$$

$$= -\Delta\tau - \frac{1 - \beta_2}{1 - \beta_1}\frac{L_1 + L_x}{L_2}\Delta\frac{\dot{w}_1}{w_1}$$

or

$$\Delta\frac{\dot{w}_1}{w_1} = \frac{-\Delta\tau}{1 + [(L_1 + L_x)/L_2](1 - \beta_2)/(1 - \beta_1)}$$

Thus, even in the short run, growth of real wages is a negative function of variation in terms-of-trade growth, although to a lesser extent.

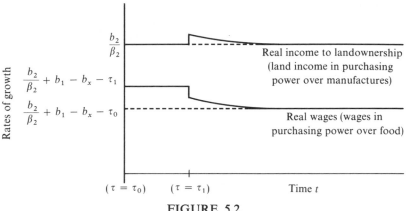

FIGURE 5.2

Growth rates of real labor and land income when the change in terms of trade rises. [SOURCE: Equations (5.15) and (2.15) in the long run, footnote 2 and Equation (5.12) in the short run.] τ_0 is the initial growth rate in terms of trade, while τ_1 is the higher level; the figure is drawn assuming

$$b_1 - b_x - \tau_0 < 0$$

the price elasticity of food demand is zero). Thus, on the one hand, if Equation (5.15) implies that real wages grow slower in an open economy, then land is being reallocated toward export production so that the export sector expands. On the other hand, if wages in the open economy are growing faster than the closed economy, eventually the export sector shrinks out of existence and the economy is closed. (Also, if the change in the terms of trade varies, the export sector may expand at certain times and contract at others.)

The results of this section may seem to depend upon the assumption that savings take place only in the secondary sector; this sector is the leading sector in that the capital accumulation in it leads to higher growth rates of secondary sector employment, higher migration to the city, and therefore higher rates of growth of agricultural labor productivity. However, savings may occur in the export sector; whether they do depends upon the economy. Thus, Levin (1960, pp. 181–182), in discussing the historical situation, notes:

> In the export industry there were higher income levels and saving could take place. In some economies, however, there was little saving by the luxury importers, and they spent their export-derived income in the maintenance of an extravangant imported standard of living. . . .

This was not the general case, however, and in many instances a considerable portion of export industry income went into savings and investments by foreign factors and luxury importers.

Seldom were the investment funds set aside from export industry earnings directed to the rest of the export economy, however.

In our model, if savings occur in the export sector and are reinvested in that sector so that our b_x rises, the results are similar to improved agricultural terms of trade: The rate of growth of real wages falls in both the short and long runs; the rate of growth of landowner income rises but only in the short run.

Growth of real wages (and then also of income to landownership) will be accelerated by improving terms of trade without governmental interference only if (1) the improving terms of trade substantially increase capital investment in the food sector (as manufacturing goods prices decrease) or (2) the improving terms of trade, resulting in an expansion of the export sector, lead to a substantially higher flow of savings from the export sector to either the food or, more likely, the manufacturing sector. Both situations are unlikely to occur without the government using its taxing powers.

Finally, one other implication of the real-wage-growth-rate equation here is that an equal increase in technological change in both the food and export sectors does *not* lead to an increase in the growth of real wages. However, this is only a long-run result. Using a procedure similar to footnote 1 on page 103, the short-run change in growth of real wages is the change in the rate of technological change (the same in both agricultural sectors) divided by $1 + [(1 - \beta_1)/(1 - \beta_2)]L_2/(L_1 + L_x)$ which, of course, is positive. The long-run result obtains because an equal change in b_1 and b_x implies that all relative price changes remain the same; therefore, after secondary sector labor-productivity growth returns to the rate of labor augmenting technical change b_2/β_2, growth of wages in terms of food returns to its long-run level while export growth is accelerating. Even the long-run result would not obtain if the increasing supply of imports were accounted for in real wages, and it does not obtain in our discussion in Chapter 6 where capital imports are crucial.

5.3 Exports Not Directly Substitutable in Production with Food

In Section 5.2 we assume that production for export and food are easily substitutable; in particular, there is a linear transformation curve between export and food production. In many circumstances, particularly when tree crops are exported, land is not completely interchangeable for producing one crop or the other; that is, the transformation curve is convex, as in Figure 5.1(b). In Section 5.1 we suggest that a convex production set be represented by allowing for decreasing returns to scale as land is shifted between crops. Does this generalization effect any results?[1]

First, note that if land area is not shifted between crops, then the returns to scale have no role and the results of Section 5.2 are unaffected. In particular, land distribution for crops remains constant whenever real wages happen to be growing at the same rate as in the closed economy, unconstrained by inability to import capital. When, in general, decreasing returns to scale are allowed in Section 5.2, production functions (5.2) and (5.3′) and the food price equation (5.11) must replace Equations (5.7), (5.8), and (5.12), respectively. Thus, the solution of the model is obtained by first using (5.11):

$$\frac{\dot{q}_1}{q_1} = \tau + b_x - b_1 + (1 - \beta_1 - \gamma_1)\left(\frac{\dot{A}_1}{A_1} - \frac{\dot{A}_x}{A_x}\right)$$

or, using (5.1),

$$\frac{\dot{q}_1}{q_1} = \tau + b_x - b_1 + (1 - \beta_1 - \gamma_1)\left(1 + \frac{A_1}{A_x}\right)\frac{\dot{A}_1}{A_1}$$

[1] Convexity also obtains when $\beta_1 + \gamma_1 = \beta_x + \gamma_x = 1$ but $\beta_1 \neq \beta_x$ (so that $\gamma_1 \neq \gamma_x$). In this case, the growth of real wages can be obtained as follows. As previously,

$$\frac{\dot{w}_1}{w_1} = \frac{b_2}{\beta_2} - \frac{\dot{q}_1}{q_1}$$

but, from Equations (5.6) and (5.9),

$$\frac{\dot{q}_1}{q_1} = \tau + b_x - b_1 + (\beta_x - \beta_1)\left(\frac{\dot{L}_x}{L_x} - \frac{\dot{A}_x}{A_x}\right)$$

Therefore, using (5.4) and (5.5),

$$\frac{\dot{w}_1}{w_1} = \frac{b_2}{\beta_2} + b_1 - b_x - \tau - (\beta_x - \beta_1)\left(\frac{\dot{L}_1}{L_1} - \frac{\dot{A}_1}{A_1}\right)$$

Thus, using (5.17) and (5.18) to substitute for $\dot{L}_1/L_1$ and $\dot{A}_1/A_1$ and then solving for $\dot{w}_1/w_1$, we have

$$\frac{\dot{w}_1}{w_1} = b_1 + \frac{1 - \beta_1}{1 - \beta_x}\left(\frac{b_2}{\beta_2} - b_x - \tau\right)$$

If $\beta_1 = \beta_x$, then the results of Section (5.2) obtain. Otherwise, the magnitude but not the direction of our previous results depends upon the relative labor intensities of the food and export sectors. In any case, the growth rate of real income to landowners is b_2/β_2.

[Note that if $\dot{A}_1/A_1 = 0$, we have Equation (5.12).] Therefore, using (2.2) and $\dot{Y}_2/Y_2 - \dot{L}_2/L_2 = b_2/\beta_2$,

(5.24) $\quad \dfrac{\dot{w}_1}{w_1} = \dfrac{b_2}{\beta_2} + b_1 - b_x - \tau - (1 - \beta_1 - \gamma_1)\left(1 + \dfrac{A_1}{A_x}\right)\dfrac{\dot{A}_1}{A_1}$

However, from (5.10),

$$\frac{\dot{Y}_1}{Y_1} = \epsilon + \alpha_1 \frac{\dot{w}_1}{w_1}$$

which, because $\dot{L}_1/L_1 = \dot{Y}_1/Y_1 - \dot{w}_1/w_1$, implies

$$\frac{\dot{L}_1}{L_1} = \epsilon - (1 - \alpha_1) \frac{\dot{w}_1}{w_1}$$

Therefore, from production function (5.2),

$$\frac{\dot{w}_1}{w_1} = b_1 - (1 - \beta_1)\frac{\dot{L}_1}{L_1} + \gamma_1 \frac{\dot{A}_1}{A_1}$$

$$= b_1 - (1 - \beta_1)\left[\epsilon - (1 - \alpha_1)\frac{\dot{w}_1}{w_1}\right] + \gamma_1 \frac{\dot{A}_1}{A_1}$$

or

$$\frac{\dot{A}_1}{A_1} = \frac{1}{\gamma_1}\left\{[1 - (1 - \beta_1)(1 - \alpha_1)]\frac{\dot{w}_1}{w_1} - [b_1 - (1 - \beta_1)\epsilon]\right\}$$

Substituting this equation into (5.24) gives

$$\frac{\dot{w}_1}{w_1} = \frac{b_2}{\beta_2} + b_1 - b_x - \tau - (1 - \beta_1 - \gamma_1)\left(1 + \frac{A_1}{A_x}\right)\frac{1}{\gamma_1}$$

$$\times \left\{[1 - (1 - \beta_1)(1 - \alpha_1)]\frac{\dot{w}_1}{w_1} - [b_1 - (1 - \beta_1)\epsilon]\right\}$$

Finally, remembering that $1 + A_1/A_x = 1/A_x$, then solving for $\dot{w}_1/w_1$ yields

(5.25)

$$\frac{\dot{w}_1}{w_1} = \frac{(1 - \beta_1 - \gamma_1)[b_1 - (1 - \beta_1)\epsilon] + \gamma_1 A_x(b_2/\beta_2 + b_1 - b_x - \tau)}{(1 - \beta_1 - \gamma_1)[1 - (1 - \beta_1)(1 - \alpha_1)] + \gamma_1 A_x}$$

In other words, growth of real wages for an economy exporting a crop not directly substitutable in production for the food crop and importing consumer goods is a weighted average of the growth rate for a closed economy unconstrained by inability to import capital and an open economy with the export crop substitutable in production for the food crop and also unconstrained by a need to import capital. The weights for averaging are $1 - \beta_1 - \gamma_1$ for the growth rate of real wages in the closed economy and $\gamma_1 A_x/[1 - (1 - \beta_1)(1 - \alpha_1)]$ for the open economy. If there are constant returns to scale, the first weight is zero; if there is no land area in the export crop, the second weight is zero. In any case, income to landowners in terms of manufactured goods grows at the rate b_2/β_2.

In summary, the effect of incomplete substitutability is to move the growth rate of real wages in Section 5.2 toward the rate for the closed economy while growth of income to landowners remains at b_2/β_2.

5.4 Downward-sloping Foreign Demand Curve

Throughout this chapter it has been assumed that the exporting country does not influence the price of its exports by the quantity it exports. However, some countries export a large share of the world's market of the export crop and thus do influence world prices. This possibility is now considered.

IMPORTS OF FOOD AND MANUFACTURERS

In the first instance, suppose that a developing country exports an agricultural crop under monopolistic conditions in its export market and imports food and manufactured goods both at fixed price. Further, suppose that the food imports could be or are produced at home. To be concrete, suppose that the country both produces and imports rice as its staple crop and that it exports tea. We now show that such an economy can be included in this chapter as a special case.

To begin, again assume that the food and export production functions have constant returns to labor and land and that the factor output elasticities are the same. This specification directly implies that food is not imported if the country faces a fixed export price: Because the production possibility curve is a straight line between the food and export goods, extra transportation costs are incurred if export land is not reallocated for producing food domestically to replace food imports. Therefore, the country must have a monopolistic influence on its export price.

The production conditions here are the same as in Section 5.1 and can be analyzed in a similar way. Competitive conditions in the domestic market for land use cause the change in the relative price of the export crop to be determined by the relative rates of technical change in the food sector versus the export sector. But because the international price of the food crop is fixed, the possibility of importing food ensures that the domestic price is also fixed (that is, in terms of manufactured goods). Therefore, the rate of growth of production of the export crop is determined by that level of export growth that leads to a change in the domestic price of the export crop of $b_1 - b_x$; that is,

$$\frac{\dot{q}_x}{q_x} = b_1 - b_x$$

This equation leads to an important conclusion. As long as we are willing to assume that the production functions in the food and export sectors can be treated as the same (except for technical change) and have constant returns to scale, then the rate of technical change in the export sector has no impact on economic growth: An increase in the rate of technical change b_x has the effect of causing the price of the export crop to fall by the same amount. Therefore, the value of the marginal product of labor and land is exactly the same as before the improvement in export technology, and the resultant decrease in food output is exactly compensated for by an increase in food imports obtained at a constant price.

This result has several implications: First, as long as the importation of food products is not restricted, there is little to be gained from disaggregating the export and food agricultural sectors; even equality of the rates of technical change in the sectors can be assumed. Second, the government should not pursue a policy of improving technology in the export sector because that technology has no impact. Third, if the conditions described here are thought to be realistic for an economy, then the results in Sections 5.2 and 5.3 obtain with the proviso that $b_1 = b_x$.

There are at least four reasons for believing that the economic structure described here is inapplicable, even apart from the nature of the assumed production conditions: First, imported agricultural goods may be specialized products which cannot be produced at home. Second, the country may face a fixed export price. Third, tariffs on agricultural imports or on exports may drive the domestic food price so high that food for domestic consumption is produced entirely at home. (This case is discussed in Chapter 6.) Fourth, the government may place a quota on food imports to increase capital imports. In all cases, the food import price does not determine the domestic food price.

IMPORTS OF MANUFACTURES ONLY

As a second possibility, suppose that the exporting country influences its export price but now imports only manufactured goods. However, as discussed previously, these imports are consumer goods (or, more generally, also inessential capital imports). The most important implication, then, is that the domestic food price is no longer exogenous; in fact, the domestic price is determined by the export price [see Equation (5.12)], which, in turn, is determined by the quantity exported. Therefore, we must first derive the relationship between export price and export quantity.

Suppose that world demand for the crop that a country exports is growing at a rate ω when world price is constant. For example, if in importing countries population is growing at 2 percent, the income elasticity of demand for the crop is 0.5, and per-capita real income is growing at 2 percent, then ω is 2 percent *plus* one-half of 2 percent, or 3 percent ($\omega = 0.03$). Suppose, further, that export supply from other countries is growing at the same rate ω when world price is constant (the assumption is not crucial, just convenient). Then, if exports Y_x from this country are also growing at ω, world price, in fact, remains constant.

If, on the other hand, the country is not increasing its exports at the rate ω, world price is influenced. Suppose that the (negative) reciprocal of the foreign demand elasticity for the country's export crop is labeled ρ.[1] Then, the change in world price $\dot{p}_x/p_x$ depends upon the change in

---

[1] The value of ρ can be obtained as follows. Let import demand for the crop by all importers D grow at the rate ω when world price is constant. Let the price elasticity of demand be $-\eta$. Then, world demand can be written $e^{\omega t}p^{-\eta}$ where p is the world price. World supply is this country's exports Y_x plus exports from the rest of the world R. Let the growth of exports from other suppliers be ω' when world price is constant and let their price elasticity of supply be v. Then,

$$e^{\omega t}p^{-\eta} = Y_x + ce^{\omega't}p^v$$

exports adjusted for increase in world demand $\dot{Y}_x/Y_x - \omega$.   In other words, $\dot{p}_x/p_x = -\rho(\dot{Y}_x/Y_x - \omega)$, or, replacing p_x by q_x (its equivalent when there are no export duties), we have

(5.26)
$$\frac{\dot{q}_x}{q_x} = \rho\omega - \rho\frac{\dot{Y}_x}{Y_x} \qquad 0 < \rho < 1$$

where ρ is less than one to ensure positive marginal revenue for exporting.   It would be expected that ρ is small in a long-run model because other exporters will respond in the long run to export levels of this country.   The remainder of the model is exactly the same as in Table 5.2; only Equation (5.26) is added to provide an endogenous explanation for the export price (and, thus, domestic food price).

---

where c is some constant.   Now,

$$\rho = -\frac{\partial p}{\partial Y_x}\frac{Y_x}{p} = -\frac{Y_x}{p}\left(\frac{\partial Y_x}{\partial p}\right)^{-1}$$

But,

$$\frac{\partial Y_x}{\partial p} = \frac{\partial[e^{\omega t}p^{-\eta} - ce^{\omega't}p^{v}]}{\partial p}$$

$$= -\eta\frac{e^{\omega t}p^{-\eta}}{p} - v\frac{ce^{\omega't}p^{v}}{p}$$

Therefore,

$$\rho = -\frac{Y_x}{p}\left(-\eta\frac{D}{p} - v\frac{R}{p}\right)^{-1}$$

or

$$\rho = \frac{Y_x}{D}\frac{1}{\eta + v(1 - Y_x/D)}$$

For example, if a country has one-third of the world market so that $Y_x/D = \frac{1}{3}$, if the (negative) price elasticity of importer's demand η is one-half, and if the price elasticity of supply from other exporters is one-half, then ρ is $\frac{2}{5}$ (0.40).
   Incidentally, a constant world price obtains when

$$\dot{Y}_x = \omega e^{\omega t}p^{-\eta} - \omega'ce^{\omega't}p^{v}$$
$$= \omega D - \omega'R$$

that is, when

$$\frac{\dot{Y}_x}{Y_x} = \omega + (\omega - \omega')\frac{R}{Y_x}$$

In the text, ω' is taken to equal ω.

The solution itself for growth in real wages is simple in conception: Substitute (5.18) of Table 5.2 into (5.21) and substitute that result into (5.26). Then, substitute into (5.15) with $\tau = \dot{q}_x/q_x$ to obtain

$$\frac{\dot{w}_1}{w_1} = \frac{b_2}{\beta_2} + b_1 - b_x - \rho\omega + \rho\left[b_x + \frac{\beta_1}{1 - \beta_1}\left(b_1 - \frac{\dot{w}_1}{w_1}\right)\right]$$

$$- \rho\frac{L_1}{L_x}\frac{[1 - (1 - \beta_1)(1 - \alpha_1)](\dot{w}_1/w_1) - [b_1 - (1 - \beta_1)\epsilon]}{1 - \beta_1}$$

or

$$\frac{\dot{w}_1}{w_1}\left[1 + \rho\frac{L_1}{L_x}\frac{1 - (1 - \beta_1)(1 - \alpha_1)}{1 - \beta_1} + \rho\frac{\beta_1}{1 - \beta_1}\right]$$

$$= \frac{b_2}{\beta_2} + b_1 - b_x - \rho\omega + \rho b_x + \rho\frac{\beta_1}{1 - \beta_1}b_1 + \rho\frac{L_1}{L_x}\frac{b_1 - (1 - \beta_1)\epsilon}{1 - \beta_1}$$

so that

(5.27)

$$\frac{\dot{w}_1}{w_1} = \frac{\begin{array}{c}[b_1 - (1 - \beta_1)\epsilon] + (L_x/L_1)(1 - \beta_1)[(b_2/\beta_2 + b_1 - b_x)/\rho \\ + b_1/(1 - \beta_1) + b_x - b_1 - \omega]\end{array}}{[1 - (1 - \beta_1)(1 - \alpha_1)] + (L_x/L_1)(1 - \beta_1)[1/\rho + \beta_1/(1 - \beta_1)]}$$

The other variables are given in Table 5.1, with the exception that (5.26) replaces τ in the import equation (5.22).

Two special cases of (5.27) are apparent: First, if the export sector is very small so that A_x/A_1 is close to zero, then the growth rate of real wages is approximately equal to the growth rate in the closed economy of Chapter 2 when the price elasticity of food demand is zero:

$$\frac{b_1 - (1 - \beta_1)\epsilon}{1 - (1 - \beta_1)(1 - \alpha_1)}$$

Second, if the country has very little influence on its export price so that ρ is close to zero, then the growth rate is approximately the growth rate of Section 5.2 (except that a trend growth in terms of trade is lacking because we have assumed that other suppliers have exports growing at the rate of world demand ω),

$$\frac{b_2}{\beta_2} + b_1 - b_x$$

The growth rate of (5.27) in the general case is not apparent without specific parameter values. However, one implication of Equation

(5.26) is that the export price will remain constant only if the volume of exports is growing at the rate ω, the increase in world demand for the export product. If, in fact, such is the case, then the implications of this section are formally equivalent to those of Section 5.2 with $\tau = 0$; in particular, the growth rate of exports given by Equation (5.21) must equal ω. Note, also, that increases in the growth rate of world demand ω decrease the growth rate of real wages because, as for the case of exogenous improving terms of trade, more laborers remain in agriculture. However, income to landowners grows more rapidly.

Chapter Six

CAPITAL IMPORTS AND TRADE POLICY

In the last chapter we focus upon those economies for which the presence of an export sector does not lead to any increased savings or leads to increased savings in the export sector only (see, for example, pp. 104 and 105). Thus, the export sector does not stimulate growth in the food or the secondary sector and so is an enclave (even if owned by domestic producers). Governments of most modern developing countries, however, do not permit the export sector to exist in isolation from the domestic economy. Rather, they undertake, in some way, policies to stimulate capital investment from the income of the export sector.

In the first of two sections of this chapter we extend the model of the previous chapter by considering the case in which imports are only capital machinery. An underlying presumption is that the economy has not yet been able to develop a domestic "heavy" industry so that the supply of capital equipment must come from abroad. Furthermore, it is presumed either that the demand for this capital equipment is sufficiently high so that all foreign exchange is used for importing capital, or that the government places a zero quota (or prohibitively high tariff) on other imports. Also, until the last paragraph of Section 6.1, it is presumed that all capital investment takes place in the secondary sector; capital investment by the export sector, as seen in Chapter 5, behaves like improving terms of trade, while capital investment in machinery by the subsistence food sector is still small in modern developing countries.

In Section 6.2 we remove the assumption that all imports are capital goods by allowing for the possibility that some imports are food which can be used to substitute for domestic food production (reduced, say, by growing export production). In such a circumstance, we examine the optimal import tariff or export tax policy for the purposes of maximizing capital imports. It is shown that, in virtually all cases, an optimal policy suggests that any food imports producable at home be eliminated by a high enough import tariff or export tax on food.

Note that linkages of the agricultural export sector to the rest of the economy are ignored in this chapter, as in Chapter 5. Thus, where relevant, an important extension of the analysis in these two chapters would be to consider such linkages, particularly to any export processing sector.

6.1 Imports of Capital Goods

Most developing countries do not import predominantly consumer goods; rather, they import capital goods (machinery) or raw materials. If these latter imports could, in fact, be produced at home without greatly increasing costs, then, as an economic problem, it does not really matter whether the imports are capital goods, raw materials, or consumer goods—the elasticity of substitution between home-produced and foreign-produced goods would be high. Chapter 5 could then be interpreted as the case where there is an infinite elasticity of substitution between home- and foreign-produced capital, with the level of investment determined by demand (savings in the secondary sector). In the terminology of the "two-gap" literature Chapter 5 thus represents the case in which the savings gap is binding.

However, in developing countries it is very common for the only low-cost supply of capital machinery to be foreign produced; capital imports are required for a supply of capital goods to meet demand. In fact, in many cases it is appropriate to treat the elasticity of substitution between home- and foreign-produced capital as zero. For example, Jaleel Ahmad (1970, p. 354) has remarked:

> In the *short run*, it would seem that the nature of production functions
> in capital-goods-making is such that a smooth transformation of

domestic resources into required capital goods is beyond the reach of non-industrial, non-diversified economies. In other words, the elasticity of substitution between imported capital goods and the available domestic resources is close to zero. In the *long run*, however, there is no presumption that this rigidity will persist. Indeed, the capacity of an economy to turn importables into exportables is one measure of its degree of industrialisation.

In this section, we take this latter supply-constrained view of investment. In particular, it is assumed that the domestic economy builds capital in structures, but that capital in equipment must come from imports. Furthermore, it is assumed that the bottleneck is in the imports, not the domestic construction industry (overbuilding of structures forces some of them to lie idle), so that total secondary sector investment is directly related to imports:[1]

$$(6.1) \qquad\qquad I_2 = k_2 M_2 \qquad k_2 \gtreqless 1$$

This equation replaces the investment equation (2.3) used in Chapter 5 (so that in the language of the two-gap literature the "foreign-exchange" gap is now binding); otherwise, the model remains the same as in Section 5.2, including the assumption that exports and food are substitutable in production.[2] Note that owners of capital consume some of their income if investment is less than the return to capital. (However, such expenditure is ignored here).

The solution of the model for this section is similar to the solution in Chapter 5, Section 5.2, and in Chapter 2 in that we obtain the long-run properties. Thus, note that $\dot{K}_2/K_2 = k_2(M_2/K_2) - \delta$, which rises when $\dot{M}_2/M_2 > \dot{K}_2/K_2$ and falls when $\dot{M}_2/M_2 < \dot{K}_2/K_2$. Therefore, *presuming stability*, in the long run $\dot{K}_2/K_2 \rightarrow \dot{M}_2/M_2$ and both approach a constant. However, unlike the two previous cases, $\dot{K}_2/K_2$ does not necessarily approach $\dot{Y}_2/Y_2$, so that the rate of growth of secondary

---

[1] If, as in the footnote on page 32, capital in structures is aggregated with labor in the secondary sector production function, then k_2 is unity.

[2] A model that considers a somewhat similar problem has been published recently by Bardhan and Lewis (1970). They analyze a one-sector economy producing under a constant returns-to-scale Cobb–Douglas production function with inputs of labor, domestic capital, and either imported capital or raw materials. The economy, facing a downward-sloping foreign demand curve, exports some of its output in return for capital or raw-material imports and reinvests another part of its output in domestic capital. Given the one-sector nature of the model, it is most applicable for a country exporting manufactured goods.

sector labor productivity is not necessarily b_2/β_2. In the solution of the model, therefore, we use the solution in Section 5.2, but replace b_2/β_2 by $\dot{Y}_2/Y_2 - \dot{L}_2/L_2$ in the equation for the growth of real wages [Equation (5.15)]. Thus, once we obtain the new value for $\dot{w}_1/w_1$, the solution for all other variables in terms of $\dot{w}_1/w_1$ is provided in Table 5.2, except that for Equation (2.15) $\dot{K}_2/K_2 = \dot{I}_2/I_2 = \dot{M}_2/M_2$ and $\dot{Y}_2/Y_2 = b_2 + (1 - \beta_2)(\dot{K}_2/K_2) + \beta_2(\dot{L}_2/L_2)$. The solution for $\dot{w}_1/w_1$ is given in Appendix D and is

(6.2)

$$\frac{\dot{w}_1}{w_1} = \frac{\left(\dfrac{L}{L_2} + \dfrac{L_1}{L_x}\right)[b_1 - (1 - \beta_1)\epsilon] + \dfrac{1 - \beta_1}{1 - \beta_2}\beta_2(b_2/\beta_2 + b_1 - b_x - \tau)}{\dfrac{L}{L_2} + \dfrac{L_1}{L_x}[1 - (1 - \beta_1)(1 - \alpha_1)] + \dfrac{1 - \beta_1}{1 - \beta_2}\beta_2}$$

which, in turn, is only somewhat less than

(6.3)

$$\frac{\dot{w}_1}{w_1} = \frac{\left(\dfrac{L}{L_2} + \dfrac{L_1}{L_x}\right)[b_1 - (1 - \beta_1)\epsilon] + \dfrac{1 - \beta_1}{1 - \beta_2}\beta_2(b_2/\beta_2 + b_1 - b_x - \tau)}{\left(\dfrac{L}{L_2} + \dfrac{L_1}{L_x}\right)[1 - (1 - \beta_1)(1 - \alpha_1)] + \dfrac{1 - \beta_1}{1 - \beta_2}\beta_2}$$

On the one hand, the long-run growth rate of real wages of an open economy that is constrained by its need to import capital is given by a weighted average of the growth rates for a closed economy that is unconstrained by need to import capital

$$\frac{b_1 - (1 - \beta_1)\epsilon}{1 - (1 - \beta_1)(1 - \alpha_1)}$$

and for an open economy also unconstrained by need to import capital

$$\frac{b_2}{\beta_2} + b_1 - b_x - \tau$$

in which the weights are, respectively, $L/L_2 + L_1/L_x$ and

$$\frac{[(1 - \beta_1)/(1 - \beta_2)]\beta_2}{1 - (1 - \beta_1)(1 - \alpha_1)}$$

If, as in Chapter 8, we take β_1 as $\frac{1}{4}$ and α_1 as $\frac{3}{4}$, and if $\beta_2 = 0.6$, then the latter weight is unity. In other words, because unity is small relative to $L/L_2 + L_1/L_x$, the growth rate of real wages is approximately the same as for the closed economy. [This, in turn, implies that agricultural acreage is relatively constantly distributed between the food and export crops; see Equation (5.18).]

On the other hand, the growth rate of income to landowners in terms of manufacturers is Equation (6.2) plus $\tau + b_x - b_1$ if the ratio of landowners to landless rural workers remains constant. Thus, landowners unequivocally benefit from improved terms of trade for capital importing, even in the long run. They may use their earnings for domestically produced manufacturers.

Some implications can be obtained. An often-mentioned argument by developing countries that face declining terms of trade in their international market, while at the same time requiring imports of machinery, is that their terms of trade must be improved so that they can purchase more capital machinery. We have now seen that for low-income laborers there will be *no appreciable effect* in the long run on real-wage-rate growth and perhaps there will be a slight retardation; the improved terms of trade lead to more capital imports for the secondary sector but also to higher food prices.[1] Landowners, however, benefit unequivocally.

Another implication of Equation (6.2) or (6.3) is that it is more likely here that improving terms of trade can indirectly accelerate the rate of technical change in agriculture sufficiently for a positive relationship to exist between terms-of-trade growth and real-wage-rate growth. For example, suppose the change in b_1 and b_x is the same in both agricultural sectors, while improving terms of trade decrease prices at the rate τ to farmers for fertilizers, farm machinery, and irrigation equipment bought from the manufacturing sector. Then, in Chapter 8, we shall see that the rate of decline in these input prices raises b_1 (and b_x) by an amount given by Equation (8.17)—somewhat greater than $\beta'\tau$ where β' is the sum of the elasticities of output with respect to these inputs. Thus, using (6.2) or (6.3) here, growth of real wages is a *positive* function of terms of trade growth if

$$\left(\frac{L}{L_2} + \frac{L_1}{L_x}\right)\beta'\tau > \frac{1 - \beta_1}{1 - \beta_2}\beta_2\tau$$

---

[1] Note that, as in Section 5.2, using a short-run analysis instead of the long-run would not affect the conclusion that improving terms of trade does not accelerate the growth of real wages: A larger growth in secondary sector labor productivity occurs only in the short run if secondary sector employment growth declines. But, if secondary sector employment growth declines so much that the real-wage-rate growth rises, then, according to Equation (5.23), secondary sector employment growth also rises—a contradiction.

that is, if

$$\beta' > \frac{1 - \beta_1}{1 - \beta_2} \frac{\beta_2}{L/L_2 + L_1/L_x}$$

If, empirically, $\beta_1 = 0.25$, $\beta_2 = 0.60$, and $L/L_2 = L_1/L_x = 4$, then β' must be greater than about 0.14.

6.2   Trade Policy for Increasing Domestic Investment

A difficulty with the often-mentioned policy of substituting some required capital imports with domestically produced capital goods in order to increase total domestic investment is that a low domestic capital supply may be due to the high expense of domestic production. Thus, the lack of domestic supply is the result of a domestic structural problem, and importation of capital (particularly, capital equipment) is the less expensive alternative source.   In this case the government may find it more desirable to increase the rate of technological change in agriculture so that the export of primary goods is accelerated.   In fact, such a policy could permit the per-capita growth rate of real consumer incomes to rise to, or even above, the rate of labor augmenting technical change in the secondary sector provided that the condition expressed by Equation (2.18) becomes nonpositive (i.e., provided agricultural technological change is such that agricultural prices would not rise if the economy were a closed economy).

Often, however, governmental controls in the international market seem to be a quicker way of achieving a higher rate of investment. Thus, governments may impose quotas on noninvestment import goods, or they may use changes in tariff rates to make capital importing or primary exporting more attractive or agricultural importing less attractive.   One interpretation of Section 6.1 is the case of a government-imposed zero import quota on noninvestment goods.

In this section, the use of tariff policy to increase investment is considered for the case in which total secondary sector investment is constrained by capital imports.   Throughout the section, the private economy exports an agricultural product under monopolistic conditions and both produces and imports the same food, while also importing capital goods.   As in Section 6.1, algebraic simplicity requires that the assumed technological conditions for producing both the domestic food crop and the export crop have the same production functions and constant returns to scale [cf., Equations (5.7) and (5.8)].   Implicitly, we are adopting the view that these production functions are not sufficiently different to warrant complicating the model any further. In countries where our technological assumptions are not totally unwarranted, our results should be suggestive of appropriate policy.

In the first part of this section, we examine the policy of imposing an export tax on the export crop to increase capital imports when government revenues are spent either on capital imports or on food imports. In the second part, we examine the imposition of a tariff on food imports—again to increase capital imports. In both cases, the international prices of the imported goods are assumed as fixed; therefore, because production conditions in the food and export sectors are the same, the country must have a monopolistic influence on its export price [otherwise food would not be imported (see Section 5.4)]. Thus, by undertaking a policy to discourage exports, the country can raise its export price and, at the same time, encourage the production of substitutes for food imports.

One central conclusion emerges from all the analyses in this section. Use of trade policy generally suggests that the tariff rate for food imports or the tax rate on exports should be high enough to eliminate food imports producible at home as long as the policy's primary objective is the raising of the level of capital imports. If food imports are, in fact, eliminated, then the fixed relationship between the domestic food price and manufacturing goods price, as determined by import prices, is broken. The economy can then be analyzed as if there is a zero quota on food imports and investment is determined by capital imports (see Section 6.1). If the government wishes to have command over more tax revenues, then an export tax is the preferable policy for eliminating food imports because tax revenues are not concomitantly eliminated, as with a tariff on food imports. However, the export tax rate should not be higher than that required to eliminate food imports; otherwise, foreign exchange earnings available for capital importing decline as exports decline.

A final comment should be made. This entire section considers only the case in which the volume of agricultural exports influences export price and agricultural goods are initially imported. However, suppose the country faces a horizontal demand curve for its exports and no agricultural goods are imported. In this case, then, any tax on exports lowers foreign exchange earnings and therefore capital imports because some export production is diverted to food production until the domestic export price is reduced by the amount of the tax. However, the government can increase foreign exchange earnings by subsidizing exports: Suppose that the subsidy rate is labeled ϕ; then the domestic price of the export crop to domestic producers is now $(1 + \phi)p_x$. Thus, land use is reallocated to export production until the price of food rises to $(1 + \phi)p_x$. Therefore, in practice, capital imports in this case are only limited by the ability of the government to raise tax revenues to pay the subsidy, by the constraints on raising domestic agricultural prices, and by the possibility of a demand developing for agricultural imports.

TAX ON EXPORTS

Suppose, in the first instance, that the country has a monopoly position in its export market and that it is importing food and capital goods, both under a fixed price (q_1 and unity, respectively). Suppose also that the government places a tax rate t_x on exports but leaves imports untaxed. If food is still imported after the tax, then the domestic relative price of food does not change. Furthermore, the domestic price of the export good q_x also does not change because it is produced domestically with the same technology as food. Thus, only the international price of the export crop p_x rises in proportion to the tax rate:

$$(6.4) \qquad p_x = (1 + t_x)q_x = (1 + t_x)q_1$$

The rise in the international price of the export crop causes demand on the international market to fall. Export volume falls, and some production for export Y_x is diverted to food production Y_1. Because there is no change in domestic relative prices, no labor moves between the primary and secondary sectors so that the increased food production is exactly equal to the decline in production for export.

The balance-of-trade equation can be easily formulated. Because the export price is p_x, export earnings are $p_x Y_x$, where Y_x is the level of total exports. The export earnings are distributed among private food imports M_1, which have a fixed price of q_1, private capital imports M_2, which have a unit price, and government tax revenues $t_x q_1 Y_x$. Thus,

$$(6.5) \qquad p_x Y_x = q_1 M_1 + M_2 + t_x q_1 Y_x$$

The objective of the export tax policy is to increase domestic investment by increasing capital imports. As in Section 6.1, we assume that capital imports are entirely capital equipment and that these imports can be matched by some domestic production of capital goods (e.g., capital in structures). Total investment is then k_2 times capital imports. Therefore, if we initially assume that all government export tax revenues are spent on capital imports,

$$(6.6) \qquad I_2 = k_2(M_2 + t_x q_1 Y_x) \qquad k_2 \geqq 1$$

In order to investigate the role of a governmental export tax policy, it is instructive to find that tax rate t_x^* which maximizes domestic investment. Therefore, first take the partial derivative of investment I_2 with respect to the tax rate t_x:

$$\frac{\partial I_2}{\partial t_x} = \frac{\partial k_2(M_2 + t_x q_1 Y_x)}{\partial t_x}$$

$$= \frac{\partial k_2(p_x Y_x - q_1 M_1)}{\partial t_x}$$

using (6.5). Or, using (6.4),

$$\frac{\partial I_2}{\partial t_x} = k_2 \frac{\partial[q_1(Y_x - M_1) + t_x q_1 Y_x]}{\partial t_x}$$

Now, we have already argued that food imports decline by the same amount as exports because land formerly used for export production is diverted to food production. Therefore,

$$\frac{\partial q_1(Y_x - M_1)}{\partial t_x} = q_1 \frac{\partial(Y_x - M_1)}{\partial t_x} = 0$$

so that domestic investment is maximized when $\partial t_x q_1 Y_x / \partial t_x = 0$. In other words, a maximum obtains when

$$(6.7) \qquad Y_x + t_x \frac{\partial Y_x}{\partial t_x} = Y_x + t_x q_1 \frac{\partial Y_x}{\partial p_x} = 0$$

Therefore,

$$t_x = -\frac{(p_x/q_1) Y_x}{p_x \, \partial Y_x / \partial p_x}$$

$$= -\frac{1 + t_x}{(\partial Y_x / \partial p_x)(p_x / Y_x)}$$

or

$$(6.8) \qquad t_x^* = \left(-\frac{\partial Y_x}{\partial p_x} \frac{p_x}{Y_x} - 1\right)^{-1}$$

But $-(\partial Y_x/\partial p_x)(p_x/Y_x)$ is the absolute value of the price elasticity of the foreign demand curve, calculated at the export price p_x^*. Therefore, this expression for the optimum tariff is nothing other than the standard expression in international trade theory for the optimum tariff.

Equation (6.8) provides that export tax rate which maximizes capital imports *given* that food is still imported at that tax rate; this is, in fact, unlikely. For example, in Section 5.4 the (negative) price elasticity of foreign demand is taken as a constant and labeled $1/\rho$, where ρ is the (negative) reciprocal of the foreign demand elasticity and is assumed less than 1 to assure positive marginal revenue from the country's exports. In this case,

$$(6.9) \qquad t_x^* = \left(\frac{1}{\rho} - 1\right)^{-1} \qquad 0 < \rho < 1$$

Therefore,

$$1 + \left(\frac{1}{\rho} - 1\right)^{-1} = \frac{p_x^*}{p_x} = \left(\frac{Y_x^*}{Y_x}\right)^{-\rho}$$

where Y_x^* is export volume after the tax rate t_x^* is imposed. Then,

$$(6.10) \qquad \frac{Y_x^*}{Y_x} = \left(1 + \frac{1}{1/\rho - 1}\right)^{-1/\rho} = (1 - \rho)^{1/\rho}$$

This expression is monotonically decreasing in $\rho > 0$. As $\rho \to 0$, $Y_x^*/Y_x \to e^{-1} = 0.37$; and as $\rho \to 1$, $Y_x^*/Y_x \to 0.0$. At $\rho = 0.50$, $Y_x^*/Y_x = 0.25$. Thus, exports are no greater than 37 percent of their original value in the constant elasticity case. Furthermore, we already know that food imports decrease by the same amount as exports when an export tax is imposed (unless food imports are eliminated). Thus, as long as the ratio of the initial level of food imports to initial exports is no greater than 1 less the value of Equation (6.10)—at least 0.63— then food imports are eliminated.

In summary, food imports generally are eliminated by an optimum tax on exports. If imports are, in fact, eliminated, the tax rate should be set at the level to cause just the elimination, not the level given by (6.8); otherwise, exchange receipts for capital importing are reduced.

Some extensions of this analysis are comparatively easy. Suppose the government taxes exports but uses the tax revenue to purchase primary goods abroad, not capital goods, in order to provide a supply of certain scarce food commodities. However, the government still wants to maximize private capital imports M_2. In this case, consider two possibilities: first, that the private economy places no value on the government imports and, second, that the private economy reduces its own food imports by the amount the government purchases.

When the private economy places no value on government food imports, then

$$I_2 = k_2 M_2$$
$$= k_2(p_x Y_x - q_1 M_1 - t_x q_1 Y_x)$$
$$= k_2[q_1(Y_x - M_1)]$$

In this case, as long as $M_1 > 0$, $\partial I_2/\partial t_x = 0$ because Y_x and M_1 fall together and the government uses the advantage of the increased export price to buy food imports. Thus, total capital imports remain constant. When the private economy reduces its own food imports by the amount that the government purchases food imports, then

$$I_2 = k_2 M_2$$
$$= k_2[p_x Y_x - q_1(M_1 - t_x Y_x) - q_1 t_x Y_x]$$
$$= k_2[p_x Y_x - q_1 M_1]$$

But this leads to the same problem analyzed above for the case when the government proceeds are used for capital imports.

Finally, our results for an export tax are formally equivalent to an equal tariff rate on both import goods. For, in such a case, the relative domestic food price would still be q_1 (the food import price divided by the capital goods import price), but the export price would be relatively lower. Thus, as before, land and labor would move from export production to food production until the export price rises to the food import price.

TARIFF ON FOOD IMPORTS

Suppose, again, that the country has a monopoly position in its export market and that it is also importing agricultural goods under a fixed price. Suppose, now, that the government places a tariff rate t_1 on importing primary goods but leaves capital imports and exports untaxed. If the imported food is still imported after the tariff, then the domestic relative price of domestic food products rises by exactly the amount of the tariff. Thus, if q_1 is the new domestic price of food,

(6.11) $q_1 = (1 + t_1)q_1'$

where q_1' is the initial price.

This price rise has two direct effects: On the one hand, because food crops have a higher price, more workers are induced to stay in the primary sector than formerly; production there rises, and agricultural imports fall. On the other hand, production for export becomes less attractive because the export price initially remains at q_1'. Thus, export production falls until the country's influence on its export price drives the export price to q_1.[1]

Now, because the objective of governmental policy in developing the tariff structure is to increase investment, assume that the entire tariff revenue is spent on imported capital goods. Then total investment expenditures, as above, are equal to k_2 times total capital imports $M_2 + t_1 q_1' M_1$ (private plus government capital imports), where M_1 is the level of total primary imports. Therefore, total investment is

$$(6.12) \qquad I_2 = k_2 M_2 + k_2 t_1 q_1' M_1$$

The balance-of-trade equation can then be formulated. Because the export price is q_1, export earnings are $q_1 Y_x$, where Y_x is total exports. The export earnings are distributed among private primary imports M_1, which have a fixed price of q_1' on the international market, private capital imports M_2, which still have a unit price, and government expenditures on capital imports $t_1 q_1' M_1$ (the level of tariff revenues). Thus,

$$q_1 Y_x = q_1' M_1 + M_2 + t_1 q_1' M_1$$

or

$$(6.13) \qquad q_1 Y_x = q_1 M_1 + M_2$$

Again it is instructive to find that tariff rate which maximizes investment, given that the food imports are not eliminated. First, take the partial derivative of investment I_2 with respect to the tariff rate t_1:

$$\frac{\partial I_2}{\partial t_1} = \frac{\partial [k_2 M_2 + k_2 t_1 q_1' M_1]}{\partial t_1}$$

$$= \frac{\partial [k_2 (q_1 Y_x - q_1 M_1) + k_2 t_1 q_1' M_1]}{\partial t_1}$$

$$= \frac{\partial k_2 q_1 Y_x}{\partial t_1} - \frac{\partial k_2 q_1' M_1}{\partial t_1} - \frac{\partial k_2 t_1 q_1' M_1}{\partial t_1} + \frac{\partial k_2 t_1 q_1' M_1}{\partial t_1}$$

$$= k_2 q_1' \frac{\partial (1 + t_1) Y_x}{\partial t_1} - k_2 q_1' \frac{\partial M_1}{\partial t_1}$$

[1] If the country does not affect its export price very strongly, then the drop in exports continues until primary goods are no longer imported and the domestic primary goods price lies between q_1' and $(1 + t_1) q_1'$. If primary imports are reduced to zero by the tariff, then, as above, the consequences can be analyzed as if the government imposes a zero quota on primary imports.

which, set equal to zero, gives

$$\frac{\partial(1 + t_1)Y_x}{\partial t_1} - \frac{\partial M_1}{\partial t_1} = 0$$

as the condition for a maximum. But $\partial M_1/\partial t_1 = \partial C_1/\partial t_1 - \partial Y_1/\partial t_1$, and so the condition becomes

$$\frac{\partial(1 + t_1)Y_x}{\partial t_1} - \frac{\partial C_1}{\partial t_1} + \frac{\partial Y_1}{\partial t_1} = 0$$

This equation can be also written as

(6.14) $$\frac{\partial t_1 Y_x}{\partial t_1} - \frac{\partial C_1}{\partial t_1} + \frac{\partial(Y_1 + Y_x)}{\partial t_1} = 0$$

On the one hand, the term $\partial(Y_1 + Y_x)/\partial t_1$ is positive: Increases in the import price of food cause increases in primary sector prices relative to secondary sector prices. Labor moves toward the primary sector and primary sector output increases. (In fact, because Y_x moves downward, Y_1 must increase more than Y_x falls.) On the other hand, the term $\partial C_1/\partial t_1$ is negative: The movement of labor to the primary sector reduces that output/labor ratio so that the marginal product of labor falls in terms of food. The resulting decline in real wages causes food consumption to fall.

In summary, the term $\partial t_1 Y_x/\partial t_1$ in Equation (6.14) must be negative. But,

(6.15) $$\frac{\partial t_1 Y_x}{\partial t_1} = Y_x + t_1 \frac{\partial Y_x}{\partial t_1}$$

which is directly related to Equation (6.7). Thus, by the same reasoning as for Equation (6.8), (6.15) here is negative only if the optimum tariff is *greater* than that given by Equation (6.8). In other words, the tariff rate on food imports which maximizes capital imports is greater than the tax rate on exports calculated previously. Therefore, the export price is higher and export volume is lower. Thus, because Y_1 increases more than Y_x falls and because C_1 falls, then $M_1 (= C_1 - Y_1)$ must fall more than Y_x. In short, the tariff on food eliminates food imports more quickly than the export tax calculated above.

If the government had spent the tariff revenues on food imports and not on capital goods, then

$$I_2 = k_2 M_2 = k_2 q_1(Y_x - M_1)$$

Therefore,

$$\frac{\partial I_2}{\partial q_1} = k_2 q_1 \frac{\partial (Y_x - M_1)}{\partial q_1} + k_2 (Y_x - M_1)$$

Now, $\partial M_1/\partial q_1 < \partial Y_x/\partial q_1 < 0$, as argued above, and so $\partial (Y_x - M_1)/\partial q_1$ is positive; furthermore, $Y_x - M_1$ is positive. Therefore, $\partial I_2/\partial q_1$ is always positive, and so the optimum tariff unquestionably eliminates food imports.

Chapter Seven

UNCERTAINTY IN FOREIGN EXCHANGE EARNINGS

In previous chapters we have not considered uncertainty in sectoral output levels or in prices because they are fundamentally concerned with characterizing the long-run determinants of economic growth: Random fluctuations in output and price above and below expected values are short-run effects. However, one of the important problems that hampers economic development for many countries is the considerable uncertainty in foreign exchange receipts from exporting an agricultural crop. As examples of the degree of this uncertainty, between 1949 and 1964 the standard deviation of rice export volume from Burma was 16 percent around its exponential trend; the standard deviation of rice export receipts was 13 percent. For Brazilian coffee, the figures were 14 and 15 percent; for Dominican sugar, 12 and 20 percent; for Honduran bananas, 14 and 15 percent; and for Ghanaian cocoa, 18 and 17 percent, respectively.[1] Thus, a considerable amount of academic discussion and many hours at international meetings center around stabilization of the export receipts of developing countries.

---

[1] The standard deviations are obtained from a regression of the logarithm of the export volume or export receipts on a constant and a time trend. The figures are taken from the International Monetary Fund's *International Financial Statistics, Supplement to 1966/67 Issues.*

The specific costs of the uncertainty in export receipts are very difficult to quantify but are more easily listed. First, fluctuations in export receipts directly cause fluctuations in incomes in the export sector. If these income fluctuations are transmitted to the farmer, then poor years can imply starvation on small farms and declines in wages and employment on large farms. Furthermore, the resulting expenditure fluctuations by the export sector cause fluctuations in incomes of other sectors so that the total effects are larger than the original fluctuations in receipts.

Second, a substantial portion of government revenues are obtained from the trade sector. Therefore, fluctuations in export receipts lead to fluctuations in revenues so that either government expenditures fluctuate (which can have quite harmful effects on investment projects, in particular) or the government budget must fluctuate between surpluses and deficits, a fiscal policy most governments are not capable of handling.

Third, fluctuations in export receipts lead to fluctuations in imports unless there are borrowing facilities abroad or substantial exchange reserves. Thus, planning for raw-material and capital imports becomes much more difficult and can increase the costs of investment projects considerably. Finally, the difficulties for both private and public investments in bad years may tend to make the economy generally risk-adverse. As a consequence, the level of investment as well as production for export may be reduced so that the growth rate is reduced.[1]

To avoid these costs, governments of developing countries pursue policies such as income-maintenance schemes for exporters, requesting foreign assistance in poor export years, holding emergency reserves of foreign exchange, and diversifying exports.

This chapter undertakes a characterization of the sources of uncertainty in export earnings. In the first two sections, the level of uncertainty in earnings is explicitly related to the level of uncertainty in

---

[1] This listing of costs of uncertainty benefits from Brainard and Cooper (1968). A first attempt to study analytically the welfare implications of the uncertainty has been undertaken by Berry and Hymer (1969). Alasdair I. MacBean (1966) has published a volume that purports to show, with a cross-country regression analysis, that countries with greater fluctuations in export earnings do not have lower growth rates or lower investment levels (see, especially, his chapter 4). However, the relevant question is whether a *given* country suffers when the variability of its export receipts increases, a question that cannot be answered with cross-country data without assuming the same structural characteristics in each of the countries considered.

agricultural output and export price.   In Section 7.1, we discuss the countries that mainly export the important domestically consumed crop (labeled a *subsistence* crop), for example, Asian countries that export rice; in Section 7.2, we discuss those countries that export a cash crop, for example, African, Asian, and Latin American countries that export coffee, cocoa, bananas, sugar, cotton, groundnuts, and rubber.[1] The conclusions of these two sections show that the most important factors determining the uncertainty of export earnings of an agricultural crop, given the variance of the random shocks in production and the world price, are: (1) for a subsistence export crop, the domestic income elasticity of demand for primary products, the percentage of domestic production intended for export, and the foreign price elasticity of demand for the country's export goods; (2) for a cash export crop, only the foreign price elasticity.

In Section 7.3 we analyze the effects on uncertainty of an economy diversified from a one- to a two-crop exporter.   In particular, export diversification more likely leads to reduced uncertainty when the secondary crop does not have highly variable receipts, has production disturbances that are not highly correlated with those of the principal crop, and/or has price disturbances on the international market that are substantially negatively correlated with those of the principal crop.

Finally, in Section 7.4 we investigate the governmental inventory policy of holding stocks of any export product (not just an agricultural product) to maximize foreign exchange earnings under uncertainty.   It is assumed that this year's output and international price are known but next year's are not, while only governmental stockpiling is considered because only the country as a whole (not individual producers) may face a downward-sloping demand curve for the export product.   The conclusion is that inventory holdings are usually too costly to be worthwhile unless this year's price is particularly low.

7.1   Uncertainty in Export Receipts of a Subsistence Crop

We shall now study the effects on foreign exchange earnings of unpredictable variation in agricultural output and world price for

---

[1] Countries that export primary metals or petroleum are not explicitly considered since production of these commodities is not particularly subject to *random* shocks.   However, primary metal or petroleum exports can be considered as a special case in our discussion of a cash crop, below, in which the variance of the random shocks to production is low.   In any case, the longer-term cyclical fluctuations in output from tree crops are not considered.

economies having a large production in a subsistence crop which is also exported. In these economies, farmers consume a large portion of the crop output at home but market a surplus to urban areas in exchange for manufactured goods. The surplus, in turn, is both consumed in the urban areas and exported for foreign exchange. Examples of countries exhibiting this behavior are Burma, Thailand, and Cambodia— all of which export rice. Burma and Thailand alone account for about one-half of world rice exports.

The predominant characteristic of the uncertainty in agricultural output is that plans based upon some predicted level of agricultural output are made by individual farmers at the beginning of the crop year, given acreage, capital stock (even if only traditional capital), and expected output price and rural wages; but that exact level of output is generally not obtained owing to the unpredictability of weather and pests (output may be higher or lower than expectations). To describe such an economy, we posit that the decision on expected, or planned, output at the beginning of the crop year cannot be altered; that is, decisions are made at planting time for the number of family members that are to remain on the farm to produce on a given land acreage, using a given stock of capital implements. (It is assumed that none of the output is stored beyond the given crop year so that there is no inventory accumulation undertaken.) Then, if the units of measurement of expected agricultural output Y_1^e are chosen so that $Y_1^e = 1$, and if total rural and urban food consumption when plans are fulfilled is summarized by a ratio v of consumption to output, we have $C_1^e = v Y_1^e = v$. Of course, the parameter v may vary from year to year (e.g., as population changes).

The effect of shocks on agricultural production is that expectations are not fulfilled; the random shocks due to weather and pests cause actual output to depart from expected output. Assuming the random variable e^u lognormally distributed, where u is normally distributed with mean zero and variance σ_u^2, actual output Y_1 can be written as [1]

(7.1) $$Y_1 = Y_1^e e^u = e^u \qquad u \sim N(0, \sigma_u^2)$$

Actual consumption is also affected by the variation in agricultural output; consumption will be determined by actual real income, not

---

[1] Actually, the mathematical expectation of $Y_1 = e^u$ is $e^{\sigma_u^2/2}$, not unity. However, this is close to 1 (for example, if $\sigma_u = 0.10$—68 percent of the time agricultural output is within about 10 percent of its mean—then $\sigma_u^2/2 = 0.005$ and $e^{\sigma_u^2/2} = 1.005$).

their expected levels (however, see the footnote on this page).   In Chapter 2, we derive the primary consumption function for the economy as

$$\frac{C_1}{L} = c_1 \left(\frac{Y_1}{L_1}\right)^{\alpha_1} q_1^{-\eta_1} \qquad 0 \leqq \alpha_1, \eta_1 \leqq 1$$

where L is total population, L_1 is agricultural population, α_1 is the income elasticity of demand, and η_1 is the (negative) price elasticity of demand.   But, because L is given and L_1 is fixed at the beginning of the year, these do not cause changes in consumption during the year and only Y_1 and q_1 affect C_1.   If we choose units of measurement so that q_1 is expected to be unity and if we remember that $C_1 = \nu$ when $Y_1 = 1$, we have

$$C_1 = \nu Y_1^{\alpha_1} q_1^{-\eta_1}$$

As in Chapter 2, this equation assumes that urban wages in terms of food rise and fall with rural wages (and thus rural consumer income) owing to food price movements.   If not completely accurate, the equation is still approximately correct because the majority of the population is in rural areas.   Furthermore, if necessary, the income elasticity can be interpreted as a short-run elasticity which is less than the long-run elasticity.[1]

If the international market is reasonably closely tied to the domestic economy in the sense that domestic producers are able to sell where the price is highest, then the domestic price q_1 will be brought into equality with the international price p_1.   In this case, the consumption function becomes

(7.2) $$C_1 = \nu Y_1^{\alpha_1} p_1^{-\eta_1}$$

However, some countries such as Burma fix the domestic price of their export crop so that consumption is influenced simply by income:

$$C_1 = \nu Y_1^{\alpha_1}$$

But notice that this equation is simply Equation (7.2) with $\eta_1 = 0$.

Finally, exports X_1 are the difference between production and domestic consumption.   Therefore, using (7.1) and (7.2) and dropping the unit subscripts for the remainder of this chapter gives

(7.3) $$X = Y - C = e^u - \nu e^{\alpha u} p^{-\eta}$$

---

[1] Another reason for interpreting α_1 as a short-run income elasticity is that consumption may be partly determined by "permanent" income.

This equation allows us to examine the variation in export volume. In order to do so, begin by assuming either that the domestic price elasticity of demand for the subsistence crop is zero or that domestic price is fixed (as in Burma). In both cases, η is zero. Then exports are given by

$$(7.4) \qquad\qquad X = e^u - ve^{\alpha u}$$

This expression can be understood most easily by examining two special cases.

Suppose, on the one hand, that the domestic income elasticity of demand for the subsistence crop equals zero so that Equation (7.4) becomes $e^u - v$. Essentially, therefore, domestic consumption levels are maintained in poor years and do not rise in good years; all of the randomness in output affects the residual, exports. If $v = 0.80$, for example, so that in a normal year consumption is 80 percent of output with exports 20 percent, then a standard deviation for u of 0.10 would imply that 90 percent of the time exports lie between 24 and 189 percent of its expected level. Thus, in this case, there is large variation in the level of exports.

On the other hand, if the income elasticity equals unity, Equation (7.4) becomes $(1 - v)e^u$. Then, a rise or fall in production leads to an equal percentage rise or fall in income and thus in consumption and exports; the coefficient of variation in quantity of exports is the same as the variance of the disturbance term in the production function. For cases in which the income elasticity lies between 0 and 1, the variation of exports is greater than the production variance but less than the variation when the income elasticity equals zero. For example, if the income elasticity of demand for rice is 0.5, then a standard deviation of 0.10 for u with $v = 0.80$ would imply that exports lie between 56 and 155 per cent of its expected level with 90 percent probability.

We now turn back to Equation (7.3) in which η is not zero. For this case, a possible upward rise in the export (and domestic) price in poor agricultural years owing to low exports would decrease the amount of the subsistence crop consumed so that the variation in exports is not so large as otherwise.[1] However, if the price elasticity is close to zero, or if the country only slightly influences its export price, the uncertainty in the quantity exported is not reduced by much. Because this influence,

---

[1] This conclusion ignores independent price fluctuations for the export crop on the world market. In the next subsection we allow for such influences.

in any case, is probably small relative to other causes of fluctuating exports, we assume $\eta = 0$ throughout the remainder of this chapter.

FOREIGN EXCHANGE EARNINGS

We have obtained the effects of uncertainty in output of a subsistence crop on the quantity of exports. Now the uncertainty in the foreign exchange earnings of this crop is examined. The exchange earned from exporting a product is the international price p times the quantity exported X. However, fluctuations in the demand by importers and in supply by other exporters affect the world price. Furthermore, the quantity exported influences the world price if a country has a large share of world exports in the crop. In summary, suppose that the fluctuations are lognormally distributed about a "normal" world price of unity and suppose that the export price is inversely related with constant elasticity ρ to the quantity exported (as in Chapter 5). Then

$$(7.5) \qquad p = \left[\frac{X}{1-v}\right]^{-\rho} e^v \qquad \begin{array}{l} 0 \leqq \rho < 1 \\[6pt] v \sim N(0, \sigma_v^2) \end{array}$$

The variable v represents the random influences of demand and other suppliers on the world market and is assumed to be normally distributed with zero mean and variance σ_v^2. The parameter ρ is 0 for the case of a small exporter and must be less than 1 in order that the country face positive marginal revenue.[1]

Using Equation (7.4), the foreign exchange earnings from exporting a subsistence crop are therefore given by

$$(7.6) \qquad pX = (1 - v)^\rho X^{1-\rho} e^v$$

$$= (1 - v)^\rho (e^u - v e^{\alpha u})^{1-\rho} e^v$$

When $u = 0$, earnings equal $(1 - v)e^v$, so that if $v = 0$ also, then earnings equal $(1 - v)$. Note, furthermore, that in Equation (7.6) if the income elasticity of demand α is unity, then

$$pX = (1 - v)e^{(1-\rho)u + v}$$

---

[1] Footnote 1 on page 110 discusses how a value for ρ could be calculated. In any case, the country is assumed to export in the elastic portion of its demand curve ($\rho < 1$) so that we do not need to analyze separately the policy implication of negative marginal revenue from increased exports. The interested reader, however, should examine the case of $\rho \geqq 1$.

If the foreign price elasticity of demand for the country's exports is infinite (i.e., the country faces a horizontal demand curve), then $\rho = 0$ and the uncertainty in export receipts in Equation (7.6) is a product of uncertainty in export volume [see Equation (7.4)] and in export price. However, if the price elasticity approaches unity, then ρ approaches 1 and the uncertainty in export receipts is the same as that in export price only [export receipts are simply $(1 - v)e^v$]. In general, when $0 < \rho < 1$, the uncertainty is less than when the country faces a horizontal demand curve because price declines in good years and price rises in poor years help maintain the average level of receipts.

The degree of uncertainty in the export earnings of a subsistence crop depends principally upon five parameters: (1) the variance of agricultural output around its expectation σ_u^2, (2) the variance of the international price σ_v^2, (3) the ratio of expected domestic consumption to expected production v, (4) the domestic income elasticity of demand α, and (5) the foreign price elasticity of demand $-1/\rho$. (The parameter for the domestic price elasticity of demand η, considered previously, is of second-order importance.) Given the production variance and export price variance,[1] the greater the percentage of the normal crop that is consumed domestically (i.e., the greater the value of v) the greater the variation of quantity exports and export receipts. Second, the lower the income elasticity of demand for the subsistence crop, the lower the influence on domestic consumption of fluctuations in production and in real income, and therefore, the greater the fluctuations in export quantity. Thus, the variation of quantity exports equals the variance of production when the income elasticity is unity but is greater when the income elasticity is below unity. Finally, the smaller the monopolistic influence of the country on the world market (i.e., the smaller the value of ρ), the greater the variation in export receipts.

---

[1] For simplicity, we have implicitly assumed that the covariance between the disturbances u and v is zero, and, in fact, it is probably small. However, the variance of export receipts may be somewhat smaller than predicted by the assumption of zero covariance: Suppose that competing exporters of the subsistence crop face similar weather conditions (e.g., rice exporters in Southeast Asia). Then, if the disturbance term u is negative in one country, it will also tend to be negative in other countries. Thus, the lower level of world exports should cause a higher world price so that the disturbance term v is positive. In summary, u and v should be negatively correlated. However, because u includes many additional influences other than weather and because v includes influences of many suppliers as well as demanders, the correlation is small.

A government has several methods of reducing the variation of export receipts of a subsistence crop through domestic policy, although the economic costs and benefits of any policy must be carefully evaluated. It can encourage the use of sprayers and irrigation in agriculture to reduce the variance of production.   It can pursue an inventory policy for stabilization of the quantity exported, or it can ration domestic supply.   Finally, it can encourage export of cash crops, primary metals, or industrial goods that are less subject to fluctuations in receipts or that do not fluctuate simultaneously with the subsistence export crop. (The variation in receipts of a cash crop is examined next.)

7.2   Uncertainty in Export Receipts of a Cash Crop

Most countries in the underdeveloped regions of Africa, Asia, and Latin America export petroleum, primary metals, or cash crops, not subsistence crops.   Although petroleum and primary-metal production are not subject to a great deal of purely random shocks in production, most cash crops are.   Thus, countries in Africa, Asia, and Latin America which depend primarily on the exchange earnings from coffee, bananas, sugar, cocoa, groundnuts, rubber, and cotton find that their level of production depends very greatly upon influences of weather and pests which are outside their immediate control.   In this section we discuss fluctuations in the earnings of a cash export crop.   We assume here, as in Section 7.1, that no inventory policy is being undertaken; some crops cannot be stored (e.g., bananas), and some have high storage costs.

Countries that depend upon a cash crop for foreign exchange earnings can be considered as a special case of our analysis in Section 7.1.   Cash crops are generally consumed in only a small portion at home, and any home consumption often is nonexportable, lower-quality output.   As a convenience, assume that domestic consumption of the export crop is zero so that exports are equal to domestic production; in Section 7.1 this would imply $v = 0$.   Then, export volume is simply equal to production e^u and foreign exchange earnings are given by

$$(7.7) \qquad\qquad pX = e^{(1-\rho)u+v}$$

A comparison of this equation with (7.6) reveals that the uncertainty in export receipts of a cash crop is less than that for a subsistence crop [i.e., the "normalized" variance of (7.6) decreases as v decreases until (7.6) becomes (7.7) when $v = 0$].

From Equation (7.7), the variance of a cash crop, as for a subsistence crop, is lower the larger ρ is ceteris paribus; that is, a country which has a large share of the world market decreases its variance of export receipts.[1] Furthermore, a country that has a large share of the world market will not find the supply from other countries having as large an influence on the international price so that the variance of v should be smaller.

Possible domestic governmental policies that may be used to reduce the uncertainty in export receipts of a cash crop are: (1) encourage use of production techniques that minimize the effects of weather and pests on output; (2) develop an inventory policy that can smooth out fluctuations; and (3) diversify exports.

7.3   Diversified Exports

In Sections 7.1 and 7.2 we have shown that the uncertainty in the level of export receipts depends upon the combined effects of uncertainty in export volume and in export price.   These sections, however, refer only to a single crop exporter when, in fact, one of the most frequently mentioned recommendations for reducing uncertainty is a diversification of exports, perhaps encouraged by governmental interference.   In this section we consider an economy which is diversified in its export receipts between two cash crops[2]; we show that the uncertainty in receipts is a complicated interaction of production and price effects and that in many cases diversification may be an inadvisable policy for reducing uncertainty.

Suppose that in an average year (say, when u and v in Sections 7.1 and 7.2 both equal zero) a country exports a principal cash crop and a secondary cash crop and that the sum of the receipts is unity.   In such an average year, label ψ the proportion of receipts earned by the principal crop so that $1 - \psi$ is the proportion of receipts earned by the secondary crop.   Then, in general, by using Equation (7.7), the level of foreign exchange receipts E is given by

(7.8) $$E = \psi e^{(1-\rho)u+v} + (1 - \psi)e^{(1-\rho')u'+v'}$$

where the primes refer to the secondary crop.   (When $u = v = u' = v' = 0$, then $E = 1$.)   In order to ascertain the factors that influence

---

[1] Assuming $COV(u,v) = 0$, the variance of (7.7) is $e^{(1-\rho)2\sigma_u{}^2+\sigma_v{}^2}[e^{(1-\rho)2\sigma_u{}^2+\sigma_v{}^2}-1]$.
[2] By far the more typical case is diversification of cash, not subsistence, crops. Furthermore, the mathematics is much simpler for this case.

the uncertainty in export receipts from these two crops, the variance of Equation (7.8) must be calculated; that is,

(7.9) $\quad V(E) = \psi^2 V[e^{(1-\rho)u+v}] + (1 - \psi)^2 V[e^{(1-\rho')u'+v'}]$

$\qquad\qquad + 2\psi(1 - \psi)COV[e^{(1-\rho)u+v}, e^{(1-\rho')u'+v'}]$

where V refers to variance (given in footnote 1 on page 137) and COV refers to covariance.

The most interesting term of this expression is the covariance term; however, because we show that this term may be zero, first assume it to be zero. In this case,

(7.10) $\quad V(E) = \psi^2 V[e^{(1-\rho)u+v}] + (1 - \psi)^2 V[e^{(1-\rho')u'+v'}]$

Thus, when all export receipts are earned by the principal export crop so that $\psi = 1$, then the variance of total earnings of course is given by the variance of earnings from the one crop (as obtained in Section 7.2). As ψ decreases and more and more of the export sector is diversified to the secondary export, the variance of total export earnings decreases until a minimum is reached at

$$\psi = \frac{V[e^{(1-\rho')u'+v'}]}{V[e^{(1-\rho)u+v}] + V[e^{(1-\rho')u'+v'}]}$$

Then, for higher values of export receipts being allocated to secondary exports, the variance of total receipts increases toward $V[e^{(1-\rho')u'+v'}]$ at $\psi = 0$. In summary, the variance of total receipts is always no more than the variance of receipts from the higher-variance export crop and generally will be smaller than the variance for either crop.

The third term of Equation (7.9) is the covariance term. By assuming that all covariances between u's and v's are equal to zero (see footnote on page 135) but that $COV(u,u')$ and $COV(v,v')$ are not equal to zero, this covariance term can be shown to be[1]

(7.11)
$COV[e^{(1-\rho)u+v}, e^{(1-\rho')u'+v'}]$

$= e^{[(1-\rho)^2\sigma_u^2 + \sigma_v^2 + (1-\rho')\sigma_{u'}^2 + \sigma_{v'}^2]/2}[e^{(1-\rho)(1-\rho')COV(u,u') + COV(v,v')} - 1]$

---

[1] $COV[e^{(1-\rho)u+v}, e^{(1-\rho')u'+v'}]$

$\qquad = E\{e^{(1-\rho)u+v} - e^{[(1-\rho)^2\sigma_u^2 + \sigma_v^2]/2}\}\{e^{(1-\rho')u'+v'} - e^{[(1-\rho')^2\sigma_{u'}^2 + \sigma_{v'}^2]/2}\}$

$\qquad = E\{e^{(1-\rho)u+v+(1-\rho')u'+v'} - e^{[(1-\rho)^2\sigma_u^2 + \sigma_v^2 + (1-\rho')^2\sigma_{u'}^2 + \sigma_{v'}^2]/2}\}$

$\qquad = e^{[(1-\rho)^2\sigma_u^2 + \sigma_v^2 + (1-\rho')^2\sigma_{u'}^2 + \sigma_{v'}^2]/2}[e^{(1-\rho)(1-\rho')COV(u,u') + COV(v,v')} - 1]$

where use has been made of the assumed zero covariances between u's and v's.

The first term on the right-hand side of this equation generally is only slightly greater than unity because the standard deviations are typically no larger than 0.3 so that the variances are no larger than 0.09. Thus, the second term

(7.12) $$e^{(1-\rho)(1-\rho')COV(u,u')+COV(v,v')} - 1$$

has a larger impact.

$COV(u,u')$ is the covariance between the disturbance terms of the production functions for the principal and secondary export crops. Its value is probably positive or perhaps zero, not negative, because a factor such as weather which affects one crop in a country also typically affects the other crop in the same direction. $COV(v,v')$ is the covariance between the disturbance terms of the exogenous influences on the international prices of the export crops and may be positive or negative. If $COV(v,v')$ is sufficiently negative so that the sum of the terms in the exponent is zero, then the whole covariance term is zero and Equation (7.10) describes the variance of total receipts.

In a common case, the country faces virtually a horizontal demand curve for its export crop so that $\rho = \rho' = 0$. Furthermore, remembering that $COV(u,u') = r_u \sigma_u \sigma_{u'}$ where r_u is a correlation coefficient, a likely value for $COV(u,u')$ may be $(0.25)(0.2)(0.2) = 0.01$. Thus, in order for the covariance term of Equation (7.9) to be zero or negative, $COV(v,v')$ must be equal to or less than -0.01.

W. C. Brainard and R. N. Cooper (1968) have published a paper on uncertainty and diversification in which they utilize Tobin's portfolio analysis to consider the question of the reduction in export-receipt variance (or risk) through diversification versus the return on investment in the export crops. They do not introduce the production variance, as we have done, but they do highlight the fact that the cost of diversification may be a lower rate of return. Of particular interest in our context is that they provide a table of correlation coefficients, variances, and covariances for world prices of some export products of developing countries, thus providing values for our $COV(v,v')$. In fact, they consider products which they consider to be either substitutes in production, fabricating processes, or "other." We report in Table 7.1 the values for the first category.[1] (They also report a correlation and

---

[1] Actually, their correlations are linear while ours are linear in logarithms, but the difference should be small. Also, they use time-series data without removal of trend so that their measures do not reflect precisely our notion of variance at a point in time (which more clearly implies uncertainty).

TABLE 7.1

Variation and Covariation in Wholesale Commodity Prices in World Trade,
1951–1963

COMMODITY PAIR	CORRELATION COEFFICIENT r_v	NORMALIZED STANDARD DEVIATIONS		NORMALIZED COVARIANCE $COV(v,v')$
		σ_v	$\sigma_{v'}$	
Substitutes in production				
Bacon-rice	−0.01	0.04	0.23	−0.0001
Beef-butter	−0.15	0.16	0.11	−0.0025
Beef-rice	−0.80	0.16	0.23	−0.0290
Beef-wheat	−0.53	0.16	0.10	−0.0083
Beef-wool	−0.86	0.16	0.32	−0.0430
Cocoa-coffee	0.65	0.28	0.24	0.0440
Copra-peanuts	−0.47	0.15	0.09	−0.0067
Copra-rubber	0.24	0.15	0.28	0.0150
Corn-wheat	0.48	0.16	0.10	0.0077
Cotton-peanuts	0.44	0.21	0.09	0.0084
Lumber-woodpulp	−0.49	0.02	0.22	−0.0026
Peanuts-abaca	−0.58	0.09	0.25	−0.0130
Rice-jute	−0.16	0.23	0.26	−0.0095
Rice-rubber	0.12	0.23	0.28	0.0079
Rice-sugar	0.10	0.23	0.38	0.0087
Rice-tea	−0.74	0.23	0.13	−0.0230
Wheat-wool	0.54	0.10	0.32	0.0170

SOURCE: Brainard, William C., and Richard N. Cooper (1968). "Uncertainty and Diversification in International Trade." *Food Research Institute Studies in Agricultural Economics, Trade, and Development*, 8: 270.

covariance matrix for prices of 12 commodities to which the reader may refer.)

The most important observation that can be made from the table is that few products (four in the list) have sufficiently negative covariances to compensate for a probable positive covariance in production levels. Thus, for only a few commodities will the last term of Equation (7.9) be negative. In other words, in order to obtain the greatest possible benefit from diversification, the choice of a secondary export must be considered carefully; and it may be that those commodities that reduce uncertainty the most do not yield a high return on the international market.

In summary, in order to reduce uncertainty of export earnings for a developing country, diversification is most beneficial if carefully conceived. First, any choice of a secondary export crop must yield a return that is high enough to make diversification worthwhile. Second, the expected variance in export earnings from the secondary crop must be determined. Third, an estimate of the covariance in output levels of the principal and secondary crops must be obtained. Finally, an estimate of the price covariance on the international market needs to be calculated. Only then can a decision be made on whether to diversify and in what direction.

7.4 Inventory Policy for Maximizing Export Receipts Under Uncertainty

Suppose that prices on the world market for an agricultural crop, a metal, or petroleum are low owing to high supply or low demand. Then a country which exports the product may find it desirable to withhold some of its available output from the world market in anticipation of future price rises. If so, the country, through the government, would desire an inventory policy to determine the amount of potential exports that should actually be exported. To study such a policy, we formulate in this section a two-period problem for maximizing export receipts when the output of the current period is known while that of the next period is not. The time period to which we refer is one year because this is most typical, but shorter or longer time periods could be considered.

First, assume that the country *expects* to retain for one year only any stocks held at the end of the current year; that is, it has a one-year time horizon. Although in the following year the country may decide to continue to hold some stocks, this assumption considerably simplifies the analytics and has little or no effect on most policy implications. The only effect of the assumption might be that stockholdings are biased slightly downward; a one-year horizon implies that accumulation this year is expected to be completely sold next year, but it may be more profitable to expect the drawing down of stocks to zero over several years.

Now, the foreign exchange earnings from exports is price times quantity. If the quantity exported influences the price with constant elasticity $-\rho$, as denoted before, then exchange earnings in the initial year $E(0)$ from the exports of the product $X(0)$ are

$$E(0) = [X(0)]^{-\rho}X(0) = [X(0)]^{1-\rho} \qquad 0 \leqq \rho < 1$$

with the appropriate choice of units of measurement. For the next year exchange earnings may rise or fall owing to changes in export volume or changes in price (caused by changes in demand and fluctuations in output in other countries). If we label the expected percentage *change* in world price $100p^*$ when the volume of exports is growing at a trend rate g, then expected foreign exchange earnings next year $E^*(1)$ from expected exports $X^*(1)$ can be described by

$$E^*(1) = e^{p^*}\left[\frac{X^*(1)}{e^g}\right]^{-\rho}X^*(1) = e^{p^*+\rho g}[X^*(1)]^{1-\rho}$$

The inventory policy problem derives from the attempt to maximize the expected earnings from the export of the two years

$$(7.13) \quad \max\{E(0) + e^{-r}E^*(1)\} = \max\{[X(0)]^{1-\rho} + e^{p^*+\rho g-r}[X^*(1)]^{1-\rho}\}$$

where r is the rate of interest used to discount earnings of the next year.

The problem itself is to decide the change in stocks in the initial year $\dot{S}(0)$, given total stocks at the beginning of the year $S(0)$, output available for exporting during the current year $Y_x(0)$, and expected output available during the next year $Y_x^*(1)$. For crops not consumed at home, current output available for exporting equals total current production and expected available output equals expected production.

Now available output $Y_x(0)$, of course, is subject to random disturbances from its expected level. Likewise, available output during the next year is subject to random disturbances. However, in the former case, output is known; in the latter it is not, so that only its expected value can be utilized in the inventory problem. For convenience later, available current output is written

$$Y_x(0) = e^z$$

where z is a known drawing from an independently distributed random variable with zero mean and variance σ^2. The value of $Y_x(0)$ for an agricultural crop can be ascertained from Sections 7.1 and 7.2; if in those sections the variation of export volume equals the production variance (e.g., when the export is a cash crop so that $v = 0$ or when $\alpha = 1$ and $\eta = 0$ for a subsistence export crop), then z is also normal.

The value of $Y_x(0)$ for a metal or petroleum export is close to 1 (random shocks to production are small). However, because any random shocks to production next year are not known this year, the disturbance term then is expected to be zero; with a trend growth in exports of g, expected exportable output next year is

$$Y_x^*(1) = e^g$$

Equation (7.13) therefore becomes

$$\max \{E(0) + e^{-r}E^*(1)\} = \max \{[e^z - \dot{S}(0)]^{1-\rho} + e^{p^* + \rho g - r}[e^g - \dot{S}(1)]^{1-\rho}\}$$

where $\dot{S}^*(1)$ is expected inventory change next year (to be discussed) and the maximization is carried out with respect to $\dot{S}(0)$. Because we have said that only a one-year time horizon is assumed, then remaining stocks are expected to be sold by the end of next year. However, there are storage costs associated with holding stocks. If $100s$ is the percentage annual storage costs, then

$$\dot{S}^*(1) = -S(1) = -e^{-s}[S(0) + \dot{S}(0)]$$

Consequently, the inventory problem becomes

$$(7.14) \quad \max \{E(0) + e^{-r}E^*(1)\} = \max\{[e^z - \dot{S}(0)]^{1-\rho} + e^{p^* + \rho g - r} \\ \times [e^y + e^{-s}S(0) + e^{-s}\dot{S}(0)]^{1-\rho}\}$$

The maximization of (7.14) with respect to $\dot{S}(0)$ is constrained by $\dot{S}(0) \geq -S(0)$: Sales of stocks in the initial year are limited by the total level of stocks at the beginning of the year. $\dot{S}(0)$ will not be greater than e^z because $e^z - \dot{S}(0)$, which is raised to a power, cannot be negative.

Differentiating the right-hand side of (7.14) with respect to $\dot{S}(0)$ and solving for $\dot{S}(0)$, we obtain

$$
\dot{S}(0) =
\begin{cases}
-S(0) & \text{if } e^z + S(0) \\
 & \leq e^{(r+s-p^*)/\rho} \\
\\
\dfrac{e^{z-(r+s-p^*)/\rho} - 1 - S(0)e^{-s-g}}{e^{-s-g} + e^{-(r+s-p^*)/\rho}} & \text{otherwise}
\end{cases}
$$

(7.15a) for the first case, (7.15b) for the second case.

Equation (7.15a) asserts that any inventory stocks held in the initial year should be depleted when total supply—exportable output e^z plus initial stocks $S(0)$—is less than or equal to $e^{(r+s-p^*)/\rho}$. To examine this condition, note that the rate of discount r is generally taken to be between 5 and 10 percent and the rate of annual storage costs s, including spoilage of an agricultural crop, is usually at least 5 percent.

The parameter p^* is the expected change in world price of the product *excluding* the influence of abnormal exports of the country under consideration.   It reflects the expected change in price between the current year and the next year due to the relation between expected growth in world supply (which includes fluctuations in exports from other countries) and the growth in world demand for the product (generally income inelastic when the export product is food).   If world export levels are particularly high in the current year so that price is particularly low, a rise in price can be expected in the next year.   Note, though, as long as the expected rise in world price is less than the rate of discount plus storage costs (together, at least 10 percent), then $r + s - p^*$ is positive.

The parameter ρ is the (negative) reciprocal of the price elasticity of demand for this country's commodity on the world market.   In the footnote on page 110, we see that its value is

$$\rho = \frac{X}{D} \frac{1}{\eta + v(1 - X/D)}$$

where X is this country's exports, D is world import demand equal to world exports, η is the (negative) price elasticity of demand by all importers, and v is the price elasticity of supply by other exporters.   If our country has a small share of the world market, or if other countries have a high price elasticity of supply, then $\rho = 0$. ρ must be less than 1 for the country to export in the elastic portion of its demand curve.

CASE I: $\rho = 0$.   The most probable case for $\rho = 0$ is with products having a small share of the world market.   This may involve, not the principal exports of the country, but rather the secondary exports.   In any case, if $r + s - p^*$ is positive, then $(r + s - p^*)/\rho$ is very large and current output e^z is less than $e^{(r+s-p^*)/\rho}$.   Then, by Equation (7.15a) inventory stocks should be held at or brought to zero.   In other words, countries which have only a small influence on the world market never build inventories when interest charges plus storage costs exceed the expected change in world prices.   When the expected rise in world price p^* is greater than interest plus storage costs, then $(r + s - p^*)/\rho$ becomes very large negatively so that inventory accumulation becomes desirable.   In fact, the country stores all of its available output in anticipation of the higher price next year [see (7.15b)] and sells all the

TABLE 7.2

Optimal Inventory Accumulation of an Export Product When $\rho = 0.2$[a]

EXPORTABLE OUTPUT		EXPECTED PERCENTAGE CHANGE IN WORLD PRICE ($100p^*$)				
z	e^z	0	10	20	30	40
−0.70	0.497	0	0	0	0.097	0.228
−0.40	0.670	0	0	0.041	0.227	0.372
−0.20	0.819	0	0	0.137	0.338	0.496
−0.10	0.905	0	0	0.193	0.403	0.567
0.00	1.000	0	0	0.254	0.474	0.646
0.10	1.105	0	0.055	0.322	0.553	0.734
0.20	1.221	0	0.116	0.397	0.640	0.831
0.40	1.492	0	0.258	0.572	0.843	1.056
0.70	2.014	0.146	0.532	0.909	1.235	1.490

[a] Assumptions: $S(0) = 0$ and $r = s = g = 0.05$.

stocks next year unless another large increase in the world price is anticipated.[1]

CASE II: $0 < \rho < 1$. The principal exports of developing countries often influence world price (that is, $\rho > 0$) because these exports often have an important share of the world market. In this case, the two important determinants of the optimal inventory policy are the expected change in the world price p^* and current exportable output e^z. Now, because p^* refers to the expected change in world price assuming *normal* exports of the country under concern, p^* is only determined by fluctuations in demand by importers and fluctuations in exports by other exporters. Except under wartime conditions, demand does not fluctuate markedly; however, exports of other countries may fluctuate rather considerably. Therefore, p^* may fluctuate rather widely with wider fluctuations associated with countries that do not have a very large share of the world market (because fluctuations in output of other countries are then more important determinants of p^*).

Because the extent of inventory accumulation $\dot{S}(0)$ given by Equation (7.15) is not apparent, Tables 7.2 and 7.3 are included to give examples

[1] Actually, the country may still want to maintain some export receipts in the current year so that it would not store all its available output. However, expected foreign exchange receipts are not then being maximized.

TABLE 7.3

Optimal Inventory Accumulation of an Export Product When $\rho = 0.5$ [a]

EXPORTABLE OUTPUT		EXPECTED PERCENTAGE CHANGE IN WORLD PRICE ($100p^*$)			
z	e^z	-10	0	10	20
-0.70	0.497	0	0	0	0
-0.40	0.670	0	0	0	0
-0.20	0.819	0	0	0	0
-0.10	0.905	0	0	0	0.049
0.00	1.000	0	0	0	0.104
0.10	1.105	0	0	0.055	0.165
0.20	1.221	0	0	0.116	0.231
0.40	1.492	0	0.128	0.258	0.387
0.70	2.014	0.222	0.376	0.532	0.686

[a] Assumptions: $S(0) = 0$ and $r = s = g = 0.05$.

of the accumulation that maximizes expected export receipts given alternative values of z and p^*. In both tables initial stocks $S(0)$ are assumed to be zero and the discount rate r, the annual rate of storage costs s, and the rate of growth of exportable output g are all taken to be 5 percent. In Table 7.2, the country is presumed to have only a moderate share of world exports so that $\rho = 0.2$. In Table 7.3 a larger exporter is presumed with ρ taken as 0.5; in this case, a smaller range for p^* is considered. In both tables, if z is normally distributed, as may be the case with a cash crop that is only exported, then knowledge of the standard deviations of z allows statements of probability of occurrence of different levels of output.

Examination of the tables demonstrates an important conclusion. In most circumstances a country maximizes discounted export receipts by selling all its output each year—storage costs and foregone interest earnings dominate inventory policy. Generally, positive inventory accumulation is desirable only when the *expected* change in world price during the next year, assuming normal exports of this country, is at least equal to interest plus storage costs (no less than 10 percent). Such a change usually is not expected, except during wartime. In any case, comparison of Tables 7.2 and 7.3 reveals that greater inventory accumulation occurs with lower ρ if $p^* > r + s$; but higher interest charges or storage costs decrease any inventory accumulation.

Part Four

THE AGRICULTURAL SECTOR

Chapter Eight

A THEORETICAL APPROACH TO THE SUPPLY OF AGRICULTURAL OUTPUT

In previous chapters, particularly 2 and 5, it is shown that one of the most important determinants of the rate of income growth to labor and landownership in developing countries is the rate of technological change in agriculture, given that food consists of a large proportion of family expenditures at low-income levels. In those chapters, technological change b_1 refers to all increases in agricultural output other than due to the labor input, that is, increases in output due to such sources as increased land area under cultivation, increased irrigation and fertilization, more use of physical capital, as well as technical improvements in the means of production. This chapter has two primary purposes: first, to reduce the mystery behind the previous use of b_1 insofar as it includes increases in traditional inputs and, second, to provide a model for the most important source of technological change in developing agriculture—the adoption of new seed varieties.

To accomplish these purposes, Section 8.1 is devoted to deriving a theoretical framework for studying the sources of increased agriculture output when a given variety of seed is used in planting and when agricultural production decisions are made as if there were no uncertainty in output levels once inputs were known. The theory is basically an application to agriculture of the powerful duality approach to production theory of Daniel McFadden (1972). In Section 8.2 the framework is utilized to study the impact of increases in aggregate cropped area and variable inputs, of surplus labor and improved marketing facilities, and of land-tenure arrangements. In Section 8.3 we begin by relating the results of the Sections 8.1 and 8.2 to Chapter 2. Then, a model for explaining the farmer's decision to adopt a new seed is developed by considering how the farm's maximized profits vary with changes in technology resulting from a new-seed adoption.

8.1 The Supply Function in Agriculture

In this section we are primarily interested in the total supply of agricultural output in a developing country. Consistent with Chapter 1, the microeconomic producing unit could be taken as a utility-maximizing family farm. Dale Jorgenson and Lawrence Lau (1969) have, in fact, taken this approach by considering an agricultural household whose welfare is maximized subject to a production function, a budget constraint, and a constraint "relating labor and leisure time of family members to the total time endowment of the household" (p. 2). The utility function of the individual members is taken to depend upon leisure, own consumption, and purchased consumption. Their most important result for our purposes is that the production decision is made before the consumption decision when there is a well-developed market for agricultural labor. In this case, all variable factor inputs, including labor, are employed until the price equals the marginal value product of the input [Jorgenson and Lau (1969, pp. 31–32)]:

> Thus, we note that given a competitive market for the factor inputs, and perfect substitution between family labor and hired labor, the production behavior of the peasant households is completely determined given the price of the output and the factor prices. It is completely independent of the consumption choices of the household. On the other hand, consumption behavior does depend on total net income, which is represented by the budget constraint and hence is not independent of the production decisions. As a result, one has a block recursive model in which the production decisions are first made without reference to the consumption decisions. Subsequently, the consumption decisions are made, taking the production decisions as given.

However, they also point out that the block recursive structure of the model is destroyed when there is no agricultural labor market.

Because in this chapter we focus on agricultural production, in particular, the sources of increasing output other than labor (which previously have been lumped together as b_1), we assume the simpler case represented by Jorgenson and Lau: That is, there is assumed to be an important agricultural labor market so that the household-production decision is made independent of the household-consumption decision. Thus, the farm unit behaves equivalent to a profit-maximizing firm facing a fixed output price and fixed prices for variable inputs (including labor), while having a given number of fixed inputs. The supply function of the farm can then be derived. From the farm supply function, the aggregate supply function is obtained, in which account is taken of the effects of aggregate agricultural output on the wage rate for labor.

First, write the production function for farm output y as

$$(8.1) \qquad y = f(x_1, \ldots, x_m; z_1, \ldots, z_n)$$

where x_i $(i = 1, \ldots, m)$ is the ith variable factor of production and z_i $(i = 1, \ldots, n)$ is the ith fixed factor and where the production function f has the usual neoclassical properties. Now, suppose that output price is labeled q and that the per-unit factor cost for the ith variable factor of production is labeled c_i. Then, the profit π of the farm per unit of time is

$$(8.2) \qquad \pi = qf(x_1, \ldots, x_m; z_1, \ldots, z_n) - \sum_{i=1}^{m} c_i x_i$$

in which the definition of profit excludes the costs to fixed factors because, under profit maximization, they do not affect the optimal combination of the variable inputs. But, given profit maximization, the value of the marginal product of each factor must equal the factor price:

$$(8.3) \qquad q\frac{\partial f}{\partial x_i} = c_i \qquad i = 1, \ldots, m$$

Therefore Equations (8.3) can be solved simultaneously in the m variable factors of production to yield factor demand equations:

$$(8.4) \qquad x_i^* = h_i\left(\frac{c_1}{q}, \ldots, \frac{c_m}{q}; z_1, \ldots, z_n\right) \qquad i = 1, \ldots, m$$

where x_i^* is the optimal input of the ith variable factor and h_i is a function of the factor prices and the fixed inputs. Substitution of (8.4) into (8.2) yields the profit function G, first introduced by McFadden

(1972), which relates the farmer's *maximized* profit π^* to the prices of his variable factors of production and to his fixed factors:

(8.5) $$\pi^* = qG\left(\frac{c_1}{q}, \ldots, \frac{c_m}{q}; z_1, \ldots, z_n\right)$$

Also, the supply function g, which has more interest here, can be obtained by substituting (8.4) into the production function (8.1),

(8.6) $$y^* = g\left(\frac{c_1}{q}, \ldots, \frac{c_m}{q}; z_1, \ldots, z_n\right)$$

where y^* is the optimizing quantity supplied.[1]

Here we have no particular interest in the precise functional form for either the production function or the supply function; therefore, the most convenient case is assumed—that the production function is Cobb–Douglas in all inputs. In other words, the production function (8.1) is written

(8.7) $$y = e^{bt} \prod_{i=1}^{m} x_i^{\beta_i} \prod_{i=1}^{n} z_i^{\gamma_i} \qquad \sum_{i}^{n} \beta_i < 1$$

with appropriate units of measurement where b is the rate of neutral technical change.

The factor demand functions (8.4) for the case of the Cobb–Douglas production function (8.7) have been obtained in Lau and Yotopoulos (1971), generally, and in Zarembka (1972) for two variable and one fixed inputs. They are

(8.8) $$x_i^* = \beta_i \left(\frac{c_i}{q}\right)^{-1} A e^{[b/(1-v)]t} \prod_{i=1}^{m} \left(\frac{c_i}{q}\right)^{-\beta_i/(1-v)} \prod_{i=1}^{n} z_i^{\gamma_i/(1-v)}$$

$$i = 1, \ldots, m$$

---

[1] A set of dual transformation relations connects the profit function and the production function. Most importantly, the Shepard (1953)–Uzawa (1964)–McFadden (1972) lemma states that the profit-maximizing factor demands are given by

$$x_i^* = -\frac{\partial G}{\partial c_i/q} \qquad i = 1, \ldots, m$$

and the supply function is given by

$$y^* = \frac{\pi^*}{q} - \sum_{i=1}^{m} \frac{\partial G}{\partial c_i/q} \frac{c_i}{q}$$

Thus, instead of first specifying a particular functional form for the production function (8.1) and deriving (8.4) to (8.6), the profit function (8.6) can be specified and then (8.4) and (8.5) derived.

where $A = \prod_{i=1}^{m} \beta_i^{\beta_i/(1-\nu)}$ and $\nu = \sum \beta_i$ (the returns to scale to variable inputs). Substituting this equation into the production function (8.7) or using the duality approach as outlined above (see footnote 1 on page 152) and used by Lau and Yotopoulos, the supply function becomes

$$(8.9) \qquad y^* = A e^{[b/(1-\nu)]t} \prod_{i=1}^{m} \left(\frac{c_i}{q}\right)^{-\beta_i/(1-\nu)} \prod_{i=1}^{n} z_i^{\gamma_i/(1-\nu)}$$

In logarithmic form, this equation is

$$(8.10) \quad \ln y^* = \ln A + \frac{b}{1-\nu} t - \sum_{i=1}^{m} \frac{\beta_i}{1-\nu} \ln \frac{c_i}{q} + \sum_{i=1}^{n} \frac{\gamma_i}{1-\nu} \ln z_i$$

Thus, the rate of change in the farmer's supply is given by

$$(8.11) \quad \frac{\dot{y}^*}{y^*} = \frac{b}{1-\nu} - \sum_{i=1}^{m} \frac{\beta_i}{1-\nu} \frac{\dot{c}_i}{c_i} + \frac{\nu}{1-\nu} \frac{\dot{q}}{q} + \sum_{i=1}^{n} \frac{\gamma_i}{1-\nu} \frac{\dot{z}_i}{z_i}$$

This important equation relates the rate of change in the farmer's profit-maximizing supply of output to the variables that can be considered exogenous to his decisions, the rate of technical change, the rate of change in input prices and output price, and the rate of change in fixed inputs. Thus, the following changes take place in supply of the farm output:

(1) It increases by the rate of technical change divided by 1 minus the returns to scale to variable inputs $(1 - \nu)$; the upward shift in the production function increases the marginal product of all factor inputs and leads to increased utilization of variable inputs.

(2) It reduces by the rate of increase in a variable factor price times the elasticity of that factor's output in production β_i divided by $1 - \nu$; an increase in the factor price reduces the utilization of that input and therefore of other variable inputs (otherwise, their marginal productivities would decline below their prices).

(3) It increases by the rate of increase in output price times the returns to scale to variable inputs ν divided by $1 - \nu$; an increase in the output price is equivalent in its effect to an equal decrease in all variable input prices.

(4) It increases by the rate of increase in a fixed factor input times the elasticity of that factor's output in production γ_i

divided by $1 - \nu$; an increase in the fixed input shifts the production function upward by the amount of the input increase times its output elasticity and therefore leads to an increased utilization of variable inputs (as in the case of technical change).

The general theoretical approach to the supply function for the farm has now been stated. To apply this approach to the farm-production circumstances of developing agriculture, first simplify the mathematics by assuming that the returns to scale in all inputs (variable and fixed) are constant *at the farm level* (on the national level, new land area is usually of lower quality); such an assumption is by no means crucial but is convenient. Furthermore, note that in the applications below we only refer to one fixed input. Therefore, in Equation (8.11) $n = 1$ and $\gamma_1 = 1 - \nu$, so that the equation becomes

$$(8.12) \qquad \frac{\dot{y}^*}{y^*} = \frac{b}{\gamma_1} - \sum_{i=1}^{m} \frac{\beta_i}{\gamma_1} \left(\frac{\dot{c}_i}{c_i} - \frac{\dot{q}}{q} \right) + \frac{\dot{z}_1}{z_1}$$

In other words, any increase in the unique fixed factor leads to an equal increase in the variable factors and thus in output.

Although Equation (8.12) can be applied to the circumstances of the farmer, it cannot necessarily be applied to the agricultural sector as a whole because some of the variables exogenous to the farmer are not exogenous to the whole sector. For certain variable inputs it is plausible to assume that the supply curve of the input is horizontal with respect to relative price c_i/q; supplies of fertilizer and chemical sprays, physical farm capital equipment, and irrigating tube wells and pumps are often controlled by the government. However, the wage rate to labor in agriculture does generally depend upon labor demand. Thus, if labor is a variable input to the farm, then Equation (8.12) cannot be used to describe the sector as a whole.

To overcome this difficulty, recall from Chapter 2 that the change in demand for agricultural output per capita is a function of the change in real consumer income and the change in the price of food. If we assume the price elasticity zero—because the empirical evidence is that it is low—and again define real consumer income and therefore real wages (which move with real consumer income) as the purchasing power over food, then

$$\frac{\dot{Y}_1}{Y_1} - \epsilon = \alpha_1 \left(\frac{\dot{w}}{w} - \frac{\dot{q}_1}{q_1} \right)$$

or

$$(8.13) \qquad \frac{\dot{w}}{w} - \frac{\dot{q}_1}{q_1} = \frac{(\dot{Y}_1/Y_1) - \epsilon}{\alpha_1} \qquad 0 < \alpha_1 \leqq 1$$

where w is nominal wages and the other notation is the same as in Chapter 2. Therefore, treating agricultural output as homogeneous so that $\dot{q}_1/q_1 = \dot{q}/q$, Equation (8.12) becomes

$$(8.14) \qquad \frac{\dot{y}^*}{y^*} = \frac{b}{\gamma_1} - \frac{\beta_1}{\gamma_1} \frac{(\dot{Y}_1/Y_1) - \epsilon}{\alpha_1} - \sum_{i=2}^{m} \frac{\beta_i}{\gamma_1} \left(\frac{\dot{c}_i}{c_i} - \frac{\dot{q}_1}{q_1} \right) + \frac{\dot{z}_1}{z_1}$$

In most applications, the fixed factor at the farm level is land, so that $\dot{z}_1/z_1 = 0$. At the national level, however, the growth of agricultural output depends upon the growth in productivity per acre on the average farm $(\dot{y}^*/y^*)$ and growth in effective acreage $\dot{A}/A$ (increases in cropped land, valuated in the constant quality units, due to expanded area under cultivation and double-cropping). Therefore,

$$\frac{\dot{Y}_1}{Y_1} = \frac{\dot{y}^*}{y^*} + \frac{\dot{A}}{A}$$

or, substituting into the left-hand side of (8.14),

$$\frac{\dot{Y}_1}{Y_1} - \frac{\dot{A}}{A} = \frac{b}{\gamma_1} - \frac{\beta_1}{\gamma_1} \frac{(\dot{Y}_1/Y_1) - \epsilon}{\alpha_1} - \sum_{i=2}^{m} \frac{\beta_i}{\gamma_1} \left(\frac{\dot{c}_i}{c_i} - \frac{\dot{q}_1}{q_1} \right)$$

where $\dot{z}_1/z_1$ is zero. In other words,

$$\frac{\dot{Y}_1}{Y_1} = \frac{b}{\Delta} + \frac{\beta_1/\alpha_1}{\Delta} \epsilon - \sum_{i=2}^{m} \frac{\beta_i}{\Delta} \left(\frac{\dot{c}_i}{c_i} - \frac{\dot{q}_1}{q_1} \right) + \frac{\gamma_1}{\Delta} \frac{\dot{A}}{A}$$

where $\Delta \equiv \gamma_1 + \beta_1/\alpha_1$, or, in terms of growth of output per capita,

$$(8.15) \qquad \frac{\dot{Y}_1}{Y_1} - \epsilon = \frac{b}{\Delta} - \sum_{i=2}^{m} \frac{\beta_i}{\Delta} \left(\frac{\dot{c}_i}{c_i} - \frac{\dot{q}_1}{q_1} \right) + \frac{\gamma_1}{\Delta} \left(\frac{\dot{A}}{A} - \epsilon \right)$$

(Growth in real consumer income, incidentally, is this expression divided by the income elasticity of food demand α_1.)

With Equation (8.15) at the macroeconomic level and (8.12) at the microeconomic level, we are prepared to investigate the sources of growth in agricultural output for developing countries. For future reference, it is useful to suggest a likely value for $\Delta \equiv \gamma_1 + \beta_1/\alpha_1$. In Chapter 9, the elasticity of farm output with respect to land γ_1 in India appears to be about one-half; the labor elasticity β_1, although uncertain, appears to be about one-quarter. In Chapter 10, the income elasticity of food demand α_1 varies from about 0.85 at low levels of income to about 0.65 at higher levels of income. If $\alpha_1 = \frac{3}{4}$, then $\Delta = \frac{5}{6}$ (0.83). Of course, the reader may employ other numerical values.

8.2 Applications of the Agricultural Supply Function

AGGREGATE CROPPED AREA

One of the most important sources of increases in aggregate agricultural output is a growth in the total area under crops. In densely settled areas, increases in cropped area occur primarily through large-scale irrigation projects which bring new land under cultivation and through increased use of double-cropping, often aided by irrigation. In newly settled areas, the increase in land area may be limited by the amount of labor and/or capital available to build transportation facilities to new land and by the amount of labor available to clear the land.

The rate of growth of cropped area in the densely settled regions (in which an adjustment should be made for any lower quality of double-cropped land and newly irrigated land) is rarely above the rate of population growth. For example, in India the annual rates, uncorrected for quality, have been 3.15 percent for 1951–1952 to 1955–1956, 1.33 percent for 1956–1957 to 1960–1961, and 0.13 percent for 1961–1962 to 1964–1965; in the Philippines the rate has been about 1 percent for 1948 to 1960; and in Taiwan, it has been 0.15 percent for 1951–1955 to 1961–1965 [for these data, see the authors in Shand (1969, pp. 34, 66, and 223)]. Thus, in many circumstances, the rate of population growth exceeds the rate of growth in cropped area by 2 percent. Using Equation (8.15) with the land elasticity equal to 0.5 and $\Delta = \frac{5}{6}$, the rate of any increase in per-capita food output is lower by 0.6 times 2 percent, or 1.2 percent. In other words, in densely populated areas, increases in per-capita food output and thus in wages depend crucially upon technical change and lower relative prices of variable inputs.

For newly settled areas, which still occur in much of Africa, in some of Latin America, and in a few parts of Asia, the fixed factor to production must be considered labor and/or capital infrastructure, not land. If transportation facilities, as the principal capital infrastructure required, are built mainly by labor, the effective price of land is then the wage rate to labor. Thus, Equation (8.15) is still the relevant equation for growth in output except that β_1 refers to the elasticity of output with respect to land, say, $\frac{1}{2}$; γ_1 is the labor elasticity, say, $\frac{1}{4}$; Δ is reinterpreted; and the growth in the fixed factor $\dot{A}/A$ refers to labor. Thus, if the agricultural labor force is growing at close to the same rate as population ϵ, the sources of growth in output are decreases in the prices of variable factor inputs (other than land) and technical change. The rate of growth will be about 1 percent higher than for densely settled areas if the changes in input prices, the rate of technical change, and the production parameters are similar.

VARIABLE INPUTS OTHER THAN LABOR

The important variable inputs in developing countries (other than labor) are fertilizer, physical capital, working cattle, tube-well or pump irrigation, and large-scale irrigation for which the farmer must pay according to use. Sprays for weed control and chemicals for insect and animal control may also be important. For our purposes, however, they can better be thought of as sources of technical change because their contribution to total variable costs is small (even if these inputs represent a larger proportion of "monetized" costs).

In the case of each of these inputs, per-capita agricultural output increases faster according to the elasticity of output with respect to the factor, divided by our Δ, times the rate of reduction in the relative price of the input. For example, J. G. Crawford [see Shand (1969, p. 74)] indicates that fertilizer prices in India, relative to wholesale prices of cereals, declined in 1965 to 63 percent of their 1952–1953 value, an annual rate of decline of 3.8 percent. Thus, if the fertilizer output elasticity happens to be 0.10 and we take Δ as $\frac{5}{6}$, then the rate of increase in output is about $\frac{1}{2}$ percent higher than it would have been if fertilizer prices were constant.

Physical capital and tube-well or pump irrigation can be purchased either by several farmers jointly or by one farmer who has access to credit. In the former case, the relevant price is the supply price *times* the rate of return on savings plus the rate of depreciation; in the latter case, it is the supply price *times* the cost of borrowing (which may be much higher than the rate of return on savings) plus the rate of depreciation. Thus, the factor costs can be reduced through a lower real supply price, through providing easier access to credit with lower interest rates, or through higher-quality and better repair facilities to reduce depreciation. The factor cost for irrigation from large-scale projects is the cost charged by the government to the user. If encouragement in usage is needed, the government can bring the marginal cost toward zero by taxing the land holdings of the affected rural population rather than by charging for direct usage.

Finally, working animals as a variable input is an important power source in many agricultural contexts. When these animals are purchased off the farm, they can be treated like capital expenditures on equipment, with the supply source from within the agricultural sector, not from manufacturing. However, feeding costs and any labor costs for training the animals for work must also be included. In any case, often the optimal amount of working cattle is fixed relative to labor if the cattle are primarily useful for field work in conjunction with labor, rather than for produce.

SURPLUS LABOR IN A WAGE ECONOMY

Many development economists have argued that much agricultural labor in developing countries is surplus [see, particularly, Lewis (1954) and Fei and Ranis (1964)]. Our principal focus in Chapter 1 is on surplus labor in the nonwage economy (except parts of Section 1.2). Here we discuss some implications of surplus labor in a wage economy that are not mentioned in Chapter 1.

First, surplus labor is sometimes taken to mean that the real wage rate to labor is institutionally fixed at a higher level than the level that leads to full employment in agriculture, but that farmers are able to determine the number of hired laborers. In this case, the microeconomic Equation (8.12) is appropriate at the aggregate level with the proviso that the change in the real wage is zero and that the growth in the fixed factor is taken as growth in gross cropped area. Therefore, changes in aggregate output depend upon technical change, variable input price changes other than wages, and cropped area. Each of these effects is larger in magnitude than obtains in Equation (8.15) because, in this surplus-labor circumstance, the effects are equivalent to taking Δ in Equation (8.15) equal to γ_1, not $\gamma_1 + \beta_1/\alpha_1$.

A second definition of surplus labor that may apply is that farmers are institutionally required to hire more laborers than dictated by profit maximization. In Indonesia, for example, this institution is enforced by requiring farmers to supply an ancient tool, the *ani-ani*, to harvesters rather than the much more efficient sickle. Harvesters are then paid a traditional 20 percent of harvested output.[1] For the Indonesian case, growth in agricultural output can be analyzed using Equation (8.12) by treating labor as a fixed (20 percent) cost relative to the value of output and so reducing net output price q.

This institutional surplus labor can also be enforced, however, by social pressure that requires that farmers hire laborers at a wage higher than their marginal product but directly related to their marginal product.   Then the marginal product of labor is institutionally equated to a lower supply price than the real wage; the relevant marginal product equation in (8.3) must multiply wage costs by some constant κ ($\kappa < 1$), where κ is the ratio of the marginal product to the real wage.   However, Equation (8.15) would still be appropriate at the macroeconomic level as long as κ remained constant.

Marketing Facilities

One important source of an increased growth rate of agricultural output is improved marketing facilities for bringing food from the farm to its final points of consumption.   By improving roads, transportation, and storage, the differential between the price paid to the farmer and the price paid by the final consumer can be reduced substantially, permitting an increase in the farmer's price and a decrease in the consumer's price. Such improvements would be particularly important in countries where a large portion of farm output is sold and not directly consumed.

Suppose that the increase in the output price to the farmer due to improved marketing facilities is $\dot{q}_1/q_1$.   Then, using Equation (8.15), the increase in q_1 is equivalent to a reduction in the relative price of all variable inputs.   Thus, the increase in agricultural output due to improved marketing facilities is

$$\frac{\nu}{\Delta}\frac{\dot{q}_1}{q_1} = \frac{1-\gamma_1}{\Delta}\frac{\dot{q}_1}{q_1}$$

If γ_1 is $\frac{1}{2}$ and Δ is $\frac{5}{6}$, then the increase due to improved marketing is $0.6(\dot{q}_1/q_1)$.

---

[1] See D. H. Penny in Shand (1969, pp. 263–265).   An example of the enforcement procedure is that "when a farmer tried to replace the *ani-ani* with the sickle, his neighbours, many of them landless, burned his fields because they feared their livelihood was threatened" (p. 265).

LAND TENURE: SHARECROPPING

A substantial amount of crop acreage in some developing countries is owned by a landlord who lives on or off the farm and offers land to tenants who then must share a percentage of their output with him. Sometimes this percentage is as high as 50. For the tenants, this arrangement implies that they retain only a fixed percentage of the value of their gross output, which is equivalent to facing an output price q lower by the same percentage. [For an interesting study of the economic motivation behind sharecropping versus fixed-cash rents, see Rao (1971). Also, note that a government imposed tax on privately produced output is equivalent to sharecropping in its economic effects for tenants.]

A natural question that arises in such a circumstance is the effect on agricultural output of reducing the percentage sharecropped or of enforcing a change in land tenure so that the tenants become owners of their plots of land. An analysis of such a question can best be carried out at the microeconomic level, using Equation (8.12), because only a portion of the land in the country is farmed under the tenant system. Suppose that the average change in *net* output price due to a change in tenancy arrangement is $\dot{q}/q$. As shown in Equation (8.12), this increase in $\dot{q}/q$ has the same effect as a lower change in real prices for all variable inputs; the change in average farm output $\dot{y}^*/y^*$ is then

$$\sum \frac{\beta_i}{\gamma_1}\frac{\dot{q}}{q} = \frac{1 - \gamma_1}{\gamma_1}\frac{\dot{q}}{q}$$

Thus, if the output elasticity with respect to land γ_1 is $\frac{1}{2}$, the percentage growth in output due to a change in the tenancy system is the same magnitude as the average increase in the net output price facing tenants. Furthermore, if one-quarter of the total farm area is under the tenant system, then the growth of total agricultural output $\dot{Y}_1/Y_1$ due to this change is $\frac{1}{4}\dot{q}/q$. In Section 8.3 the equally interesting question of the effect of sharecropping on the rate of technical change is mentioned.

LAND TENURE: *Latifundios*

A particularly common form of land tenure, especially in Latin America, is that of the landlord who owns a large acreage and runs his estate through a manager who, in turn, employs workers by paying wages or providing a small plot of land. Table 8.1 provides data indicating the prevalence of this form of land tenure in five Latin American countries. It is obvious that the *latifundios* use land very extensively and do not farm much of their land.[1]

The profits from the estate that accrue to the *latifundio* landlord are often so large that the marginal utility to that landlord of higher income through improved farming falls short of the marginal cost of worrying about improvements. If this happens, the model developed in Section 8.1 does not apply; the landlords do not maximize profits and do not encourage the adoption of technical improvements on their estates. Therefore, farm output is related to prices only to the extent that the manager of the estate responds to prices; and because the manager's income is distantly related to profits, the response is very small. In these circumstances, the government must come to realize that inherited wealth in land is inimical to economic progress in agriculture and is fundamentally inequalitarian.

8.3 A Model of Technological Change in Agriculture: The Case of New-seed Adoption

One of the most important parameters in Chapter 2 explaining the rate of growth in real consumer income for a closed economy is the rate of technical change in agriculture b_1. With the results of Sections 8.1 and 8.2, it is useful to pause briefly and reinterpret this aggregate b_1 by decomposing it into the sources of growth at the microeconomic level. Then we turn to a model of technical change by means of new-seed adoption on the farm.

In Chapter 2, the rate of growth in per-capita agricultural output is the income elasticity of food demand times the rate of growth of real consumer income (assuming the price elasticity of demand zero). That is,

$$\frac{\dot{Y}_1}{Y_1} - \epsilon = \alpha_1 \frac{b_1 - (1 - \beta_1)\epsilon}{1 - (1 - \beta_1)(1 - \alpha_1)}$$

However, by considering microeconomic behavior in agriculture, Section 8.1 gives the growth of per-capita agricultural output as Equation (8.15), or

$$\frac{\dot{Y}_1}{Y_1} - \epsilon = \frac{b}{\Delta} - \sum_{i=2}^{m} \frac{\beta_i}{\Delta} \left(\frac{\dot{c}_i}{c_i} - \frac{\dot{q}_1}{q_1} \right) + \frac{\gamma_1}{\Delta} \left(\frac{\dot{A}}{A} - \epsilon \right)$$

[1] See Barraclough and Domike (1966) for an excellent analysis of this land-tenure arrangement.

TABLE 8.1
Agrarian Structure in Five Latin American Countries

COUNTRY AND FARM TYPE	FARMS, %	TOTAL FARMLAND, %	LABOR EMPLOYED, %	VALUE OF AGRICULTURAL PRODUCT, %	INDEX OF VALUE OF OUTPUT (minifundios = 100)		
					PER HECTARE OF TOTAL FARMLAND	PER HECTARE OF CULTIVATED AREA	PER AGRICULTURAL WORKER
Argentina (1960)							
Minifundios	43	3	30	12	100	100	100
Family	49	46	49	47	30	51	251
Medium sized	7	15	15	26	51	62	471
Latifundios	1	36	6	15	12	49	622
Brazil (1950)							
Minifundios	22	—	11	3	100	100	100
Family	39	6	26	18	59	80	291
Medium sized	34	34	42	43	24	53	422
Latifundios	5	60	21	36	11	42	688
Chile (1955)							
Minifundios	37	—	13	4	100	100	100
Family	40	8	28	16	14	47	165
Medium sized	16	13	21	23	12	39	309
Latifundios	7	79	38	57	5	30	437

Colombia (1960)							
Minifundios	64	5	58	21	100	100	100
Family	30	25	31	45	47	90	418
Medium sized	5	25	7	19	19	84	753
Latifundios	1	45	4	15	7	80	995
Guatemala (1950)							
Minifundios	88	15	68	30	100	100	100
Family	10	13	13	13	56	80	220
Medium sized	2	32	12	36	54	122	670
Latifundios	—	40	7	21	25	83	706

SOURCE: Barraclough, Solon L., and Arthur L. Domike (1966). "Agrarian Structure in Seven Latin American Countries." *Land Economics*, 42:391–424. The definitions of farm types are: *minifundios*—farms too small to provide full employment for one family (two man-years); family—farms that provide work for two to four people; medium sized—farms that provide work for four to twelve workers; *latifundios*—estates providing employment for more than twelve workers.

163

where $\Delta = \gamma_1 + \beta_1/\alpha_1$ and $\gamma_1 = 1 - \beta_1 - \sum_{i=2}^{m} \beta_i$.

First, note that if labor and land are the only inputs, then the latter expression is just

$$\frac{b + (1 - \beta_1)(\dot{A}/A) - (1 - \beta_1)\epsilon}{1 - \beta_1 + \beta_1/\alpha_1}$$

which is identical to the former, except that

(8.16) $$b_1 = b + (1 - \beta_1)(\dot{A}/A)$$

In other words, in this case of only two factor inputs, the aggregate rate of technical change b_1 of Chapter 2 is the rate of technical change at the farm level *plus* the elasticity of output with respect to land times the rate of growth in aggregate effective land area (land area measured in the same quality units).

In the general case, technical change b_1 can be related to the microeconomic factors by equating the two expressions at the beginning of this section for per-capita agricultural output growth, after dividing by α_1:

$$\frac{b_1 - (1 - \beta_1)\epsilon}{1 - (1 - \beta_1)(1 - \alpha_1)} = \frac{b}{\alpha_1\gamma_1 + \beta_1} - \sum_{i=2}^{m} \frac{\beta_i}{\alpha_1\gamma_1 + \beta_1}\left(\frac{\dot{c}_i}{c_i} - \frac{\dot{q}_1}{q_1}\right)$$
$$+ \frac{\gamma_1}{\alpha_1\gamma_1 + \beta_1}\left(\frac{\dot{A}}{A} - \epsilon\right)$$

or, remembering that $\gamma_1 = 1 - \beta_1 - \sum_{i=2}^{m} \beta_i$ and solving for b_1,

(8.17) $$b_1 = \frac{1 - (1 - \beta_1)(1 - \alpha_1)}{1 - (1 - \beta_1)(1 - \alpha_1) - \alpha_1 \sum_{i=2}^{m} \beta_i}$$
$$\times \left[b - \sum_{i=2}^{m} \beta_i\left(\frac{\dot{c}_i}{c_i} - \frac{\dot{q}_1}{q_1}\right) + \gamma_1\frac{\dot{A}}{A} + \frac{\beta_1\epsilon \sum_{i=2}^{m} \beta_i}{1 - (1 - \beta_1)(1 - \alpha_1)}\right]$$

The term $[1 - (1 - \beta_1)(1 - \alpha_1)]/[1 - (1 - \beta_1)(1 - \alpha_1) - \alpha_1 \sum_{i=2}^{m} \beta_i]$ is somewhat greater than 1; for example, if $\beta_1 = \sum_{i=2}^{m} \beta_i = \frac{1}{4}$ and $\alpha_1 = \frac{3}{4}$, then it equals 1.3. In any case, this equation gives another way of examining the results of Chapter 2. That is, the important sources of aggregate agricultural technical change are (1) technical change at the farm level, (2) decreases in the relative prices of variable inputs such as fertilizers, farm machinery, and farm irrigation equipment, and (3) growth in aggregate land area under crops. The population growth rate also has a small positive impact insofar as a larger labor force increases utilization of other variable inputs.   Section 8.2 has discussed increases due to decreases in input prices and growth in aggregate land area.   We now turn to technical change at the farm level b, which often has the greatest impact on growth in agricultural output.

One of the most promising recent sources of technical change in developing agriculture is the adoption of new high-yielding seed varieties for staple crops such as wheat and rice.   Some of these seed varieties can yield two or three times as much per acre, require a shorter growing time, and permit double- or even triple-cropping in a year in some locations.   For these seeds, the problem for economists is to ascertain the economic forces that lead to acceptance by farmers and then to suggest appropriate government policy.

Unfortunately, the technical characteristics of new seeds, particularly the most high-yielding ones, are often that their yields are higher than traditional yields only when accompanied by higher utilizations of other variable inputs.   For example, J. G. Crawford, writing on India [in Shand (1969, p. 94)], has noted:

> The dwarf and hybrid varieties require two to three times the fertiliser dosage recommended for best results from traditional varieties.   India's traditional improved varieties yield almost as well as the dwarfs and hybrids when both are subjected to low levels of fertiliser application.   In addition they require less attention and less water, produce relatively more fodder, and fetch a better market price.   Thus the incentive to use high-yielding seed is directly related to the ease of obtaining fertiliser and to the security given to the higher-level investment by assured water supply.

In fact, increased utilization of fertilizers and human labor for these seeds is so important that K. N. Raj, in studying transformation of agriculture in Mexico, Taiwan, and two states of India, found that increases in aggregate land area under crops—not improved seed varieties—has made the more important contribution to past growth of agricultural output in these countries [Raj (1969, p. 34)]:

> A feature common to Mexico, Taiwan, the Punjab and Madras is that they had not only considerable irrigation facilities as a result of past investments but there was extension of irrigated area during the period in which high rates of growth were recorded.   Such extension led to an increase in the gross area under crops during the same period

and was responsible to a significant degree for the increases in output. When irrigation was extended to areas with good soil but where earlier productivity of land had been relatively low due to inadequate supplies of water, such extension led not only to increases in crop area but also to higher productivity all round.

No doubt, new and higher yielding plant varieties evolved by scientific research also made their contribution, more particularly in Mexico and Taiwan, but many of these new varieties only yielded more when complemented by substantial inputs of chemical fertilizers and other plant nutrients, which in turn required assured supplies of water at specified intervals.   Without such supplies there was danger not only of the complementary inputs being infructuous but, in some cases, of the yield being lower than from the use of the older varieties without these inputs.

In summary, a graphical representation of yield per acre would show that yield is *lower* for newer seed varieties when low levels of concomitant inputs are applied and is only above the old varieties when these inputs have reached a high enough level (see Figure 8.1).   Thus, the farmer attempting to maximize profits may find that the increased expenses required for a new variety (including, perhaps, interest costs for financing the purchase of new seeds) may not be sufficiently compensated for by higher revenue.   Therefore, in this section we shall set up a model to explain the farmer's decision as to whether or not to

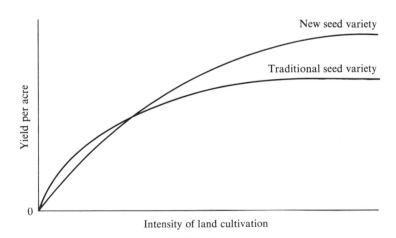

FIGURE 8.1

Hypothetical yields per acre from new and traditional seed varieties adopt a new seed variety.   First, it is assumed that the farmer has all of the technical data required for his decision; then uncertainties about the performance of the new seed and about the environment are discussed.

The core of designing a model for new-seed adoption is in describing the nature of the *change* in the technical conditions of production on the farm after a new seed variety is planted.   Thus, there seem to be three important changes that a model must include:

(1)   The maximum attainable yield under the new seed variety must be higher than under the traditional variety; this is not necessarily the optimum crop yield, which depends upon costs of inputs.

(2)   The yields at low levels of input utilization must be lower for the new variety.

(3)   The elasticity of substitution between inputs may, but not necessarily will, decline upon the adoption of the new seed; that is, it seems to be the case that the new seed varieties require simultaneously more utilization of each input (measuring land as effective area).

In Section 8.1, the Cobb–Douglas production function is used because the remarks made there do not focus on functional form.   It is apparent here that that function is no longer adequate.

To develop our theory, we consider two variable inputs in agriculture —labor and fertilizer—and one fixed input—land.   Irrigation is discussed later in connection with uncertainty; here we assume that either the farm has adequate rainfall for a more intensive utilization of fertilizer or it has irrigation.   Other inputs are ignored.   Suppose that we write the production function for farm output as a three-factor CES production function:

(8.18) $$y = [(\beta L)^\rho + (\alpha F)^\rho + (\gamma A)^\rho]^{1/\rho} \qquad \rho < 0$$

or

(8.19) $$\frac{y}{A} = \left[\left(\frac{\beta L}{A}\right)^\rho + \left(\frac{\alpha F}{A}\right)^\rho + \gamma^\rho\right]^{1/\rho} \qquad \rho < 0$$

where y is output, L is labor, F is fertilizer input, and A is acreage and where the elasticity of substitution between each input σ is $1/(1 - \rho)$ and is less than 1.   Constant returns to scale in all inputs are assumed.

It can then be shown that variations in parameters permit this function to characterize the three properties listed above. Thus:

(1) An improved seed variety shifts γ upward; holding land fixed and allowing labor and fertilizer usage to grow without limit, output approaches γA (yield approaches γ).

(2) A new seed shifts β and α downward. It can be derived that the marginal products of labor and fertilizer approach β and α, respectively, as variable input levels decline; thus, declines in β and α characterize lower yields at low variable input levels.

(3) A new seed may shift ρ downward; a shift of ρ downward decreases the elasticity of substitution between the inputs.

Given that farmers profit-maximize with a wage rate for labor w and a price for fertilizer c_f, under what conditions will they adopt the new seed? The answer is obtained by deriving the profit function for the farm, which gives maximized profit with respect to technical conditions of production and factor prices, and then ascertaining how maximized profit varies with changes in the parameters γ, β, α, and ρ (or σ), given the same factor prices.

The solution of the profit function is provided in Appendix E. Mathematically, it entails writing down the profit equation

$$\pi = p[(\beta L)^\rho + (\alpha F)^\rho + (\gamma A)^\rho]^{1/\rho} - wL - c_f F$$

taking the partial derivatives with respect to L and F and setting them equal to zero, and solving back into this equation to obtain the profit function:

(8.20) $\quad \pi^* = p\gamma\beta^2\left[1 - \left(\dfrac{w/p}{\beta}\right)^{1-\sigma}\dfrac{w'}{w}\right]^{1/(1-\sigma)}\left(\dfrac{w'}{w}\right)^{-2\sigma/(1-\sigma)} A$

$$0 < \sigma < 1$$

or

(8.21) $\quad \dfrac{\pi^*}{A} = p\gamma\beta^2\left[1 - \left(\dfrac{w/p}{\beta}\right)^{1-\sigma}\dfrac{w'}{w}\right]^{1/(1-\sigma)}\left(\dfrac{w'}{w}\right)^{-2\sigma/(1-\sigma)}$

$$0 < \sigma < 1$$

where π^* is maximized profit, p is output price, and

(8.22) $$\frac{w'}{w} = 1 + \left(\frac{c_f\beta}{w\alpha}\right)^{1-\sigma}$$

To ascertain whether a farmer will adopt an improved seed, Equations (8.20) and (8.21) must be examined for the change in profits that would occur.   In the first instance, suppose that the elasticity of substitution between inputs for the new and traditional seeds are the same, and suppose that β and α decline equally.   Then, w' and σ do not vary. Therefore, the term in (8.20) or (8.21)

$$(8.23) \qquad \left[1 - \left(\frac{w/p}{\beta}\right)^{1-\sigma}\frac{w'}{w}\right]^{1/(1-\sigma)}$$

decreases as well as β^2.   Thus, for a new improved seed to be adopted, γ must increase more than does (8.23) times β^2 decrease.   In other words, the improvement in yields at high input levels (γ) must be larger than the square of the decline in yields at very low input levels.   Additionally, if α declines more than β, w'/w increases so that the conditions for adoption are more stringent.   If α declines less than β, the conditions are less stringent.   Finally, if the elasticity of substitution between the inputs declines, w'/w increases and profits decline further.

In summary, new seeds are only adopted by profit-maximizing farmers if the increased yields at high input utilization are much larger than the decline in yields at very low input utilization; otherwise, the increased costs of using more inputs dominate over increased revenues at higher yields.   Therefore, the new seeds most likely to be adopted are those that have the highest yields at high input utilizations and/or that do not suffer much in yields if the same quantity of variable inputs as used for traditional seeds is used for improved seeds.   However, there are a number of additional factors that influence a farmer's decision as to adopt a new seed.

First, the quality characteristics of the crop output from an improved seed may be inferior to those of the traditional seed.   For example, some of the new "miracle" rice seeds produce rice that is more brittle and harder to mill and that tastes poorer.   In these cases, the price that the farmer receives from his output under an improved seed is lower, and, therefore, his profits are lower.

Second, the farmer is often only vaguely aware of yield response to input application under the new seed.   If the farmer has had bad experiences with adopting other seeds—perhaps, pushed by the government—his estimate of γ, in particular, under the new seed will be lower than its true value.   Because different farmers make different estimates of γ, diffusion of the new-seed adoption will be slower the lower the potential improvement in yields.   However, as long as the new seed is profitable, it will be adopted as farmers improve their estimate of γ by watching the experience of adopters.

Third, the new seed may, and often does, yield crops that are more disease-prone and more attractive to birds and rodents. Then, even if γ measures expected maximum yields taking account of diseases and animals, the greater damage the farmer suffers in bad years may not be compensated for by the good years. This factor is particularly important in developing countries, especially in near-subsistence agriculture where an assured annual minimum yield is essential to avoid crippling debts, attached labor, selling of land, or even starvation.

Fourth, the improved seeds generally require the application of more water due to greater fertilizer usage. If adequate irrigation is available, this factor should not present a problem. But if the farmer must rely upon rainfall, then, in fact, the effective fertilizer input is a random variable depending upon weather conditions. In other words, our α is a random variable, and expected profits are below the value obtaining from assuming a constant α. Furthermore, the more the elasticity of substitution declines from using the new seed, the more serious the decline in expected profits.

Finally, if the farmer is not independent in the sense that he lives under a sharecropping-tenancy arrangement, then the price he receives for any output is effectively lower. Thus, although it still may be profitable to adopt a new seed, the elements of uncertainty mentioned above may dominate his decision because he does not get all of the increase in profits; presumably he is at a lower level of average income and therefore more risk-adverse.

One extension of the model of this section might be mentioned. It has been assumed that a labor market exists in the sense that farms can hire (or sell) labor at a wage rate w. However, if the farm is worked only by family members, then a new seed requiring more labor input implies that family members must give up some leisure. Thus, the implicit wage rises according to hours worked. The model could thus be extended by having the wage rate w a function of profits per family worker. Or, alternatively, an indifference curve between hours of work per family member and profits per member (defined excluding family labor costs) could be formulated and then utility maximized.

Chapter Nine

PRODUCTION CONDITIONS IN INDIAN AGRICULTURE

An empirical application of the theoretical framework in Chapter 8 requires an estimate of the agricultural production function. Although data for developing agriculture are sparse, enough do exist to indicate at least the important factor inputs and to give some indication of the nature of the production function.

The most commonly used source for production and cost conditions in traditional agriculture is the *Studies in the Economics of Farm Management* undertaken by the Ministry of Food and Agriculture of the Government of India (1958–1960 and 1964–1968). These studies represent collection and interpretation of microeconomic data for the most important crops of India and are drawn from eight Indian states for selected crop years of 1945–1955 through 1959–1960. During the period of these studies, the most important foodgrain crop for India was rice, which was produced on 28 percent of the land under foodgrains (which was, in turn, 76.5 percent of the total sown area). Rice was followed by jowar (sorghum) with 16 percent of foodgrain land, by wheat with 10 percent, by bajri (millet) also with 10 percent, and by gram with 8 percent [for these figures, see Government of India (1958, pp. 11–12)].

In the following sections, factor inputs for each of these crops are examined using the cost accounting data from the *Studies*. When

171

available, production-function estimates based upon farm-unit, not more aggregate, observations are then reported.   In general, data are only utilized when the crop area constitutes at least 20 percent of the total crop area in the district studied.   At the end of the chapter, an attempt is made to draw the results together, with special reference to the theoretical chapters.

Before turning to the data, several remarks on production-function estimation are in order.   First, cross-section estimation of production functions requires variation in relative factor proportions.   If land is the only fixed input for a profit-maximizing farm facing constant returns to scale to all inputs, variable and the fixed, variations in factor proportions result from variations in variable factor prices.   For a utility-maximizing family farm, also with constant returns to scale (where utility depends upon leisure-income choice), variations in factor proportions depend upon variations in purchased input prices and variations in labor/land ratios (or in the utility functions).   However, all of the estimates reported here are based on small geographical areas, so that little variation in factor prices may be expected.

Fortunately for our purposes, the evidence on factor-price variations indicates that variations are significant even for small regions.   The most careful discussion of such variations is for wages by village in the districts studied in Bombay (see the *Study* for *Bombay, 1955–1956*, pp. 19–20, 23). Table 9.1 summarizes the results for field laborers, showing rather substantial variation.   Of particular interest is the rather detailed explanation of the causes of the variation across villages (as well as seasonal variations; *Study* for *Bombay, 1955–1956*, p. 23):

(1)   When a village is near a city the wage rate is not only high but also fairly constant throughout the year.   For example, in Nagardeola in Ahmednagar the wage rate for a man (field labourer) was Re. 1 and was constant during the whole year.

(2)   Construction work like that of a new canal (Ghod Project) increased the wage rates in the surrounding villages.   Madhevadgaon in Ahmednagar district was one of such villages in our sample.   The wage rate for men in the village had increased to Rs. 1.5 which was perhaps the highest in the selected villages of the district.

(3)   The fluctuation in the wage rates depended on the situation of the village.   Seasonal fluctuations were more in the interior villages than those touching the main road.   This could be inferred from the cases of Gundegaon, Chedgaon, Bhalwani and Goregaon in Ahmednagar.

TABLE 9.1
Daily Wages for Field Laborers in the Bombay Districts Studied,
1955–1956

	OVERALL AVERAGE, RS.	RANGE OF VILLAGE AVERAGE, RS.	WAGE PAID, RS.	
			LOWEST	HIGHEST
Ahmednagar				
Men	0.95	0.71–1.27	0.50	1.50
Women	0.49	0.36–0.63	0.31	0.75
Children	0.47	0.22–0.90	0.19	1.00
Nasik				
Men	0.88	0.75–1.08	0.75	1.25
Women	0.52	0.33–1.08	0.31	1.25
Children	0.39	0.22–0.52	0.12	0.75

SOURCE: India, Government of (1958–1960). *Studies in the Economics of Farm Management, Bombay, 1955–1956.* New Delhi, p. 20.

(4)   The wage rate depended also on the cropping pattern of the tract. Wakadi in our sample which is situated in the Sugarcane tract of Ahmednagar district had a higher wage rate compared to other villages in the district.

(5)   The subsidiary occupation of "Bidi" making in Dubere seems to be the cause of higher wage rate of field labourers because it gives an opportunity for alternate employment. As the employment in "Bidi" making could be had throughout the year it resulted also in making the wage rate fairly constant throughout the year.

(6)   The opportunities of employment in "Hamali" (porterage) at the Manmad railway station has affected the wage rates of the village Vanjarwadi in Nasik. The wage rate for men there was Re. 1 throughout the year.

Data available for Madras and Uttar Pradesh indicate similar variation in wages. Data on bullock-hire rates in Bombay also show considerable variation. In summary, variation in observed factor proportions could result from variation in factor prices.[1]

[1] If, instead, much of the variation in observed factor proportions results from errors of measurement in quantity or quality of inputs, then the estimates are virtually meaningless. We should note, in any case, that, except where indicated, the input and output measures for the production-function estimates are in physical units, with human and bullock labor measured on an hourly basis.

A second remark on the production-function estimates is that they are all for the Cobb–Douglas function. The reasons are that the Cobb–Douglas function is one of the simplest functions to estimate and that departures from the implied unit elasticity of factor substitution are not important, we believe, relative to correct specification of factor inputs. In any case, the estimates provided here are obtained from other sources where estimates of more general production functions are unreported.

Third, all of the estimates use simple least squares on primarily cross-section data. Theoretically, to justify least squares we can rely on the results of Zellner, Kmenta, and Drèze (1966) that the coefficient estimates are unbiased if the level of utilization of factor inputs is determined before the disturbance term of the production function is known. On the one hand, such a possibility would hold, for example, if land planted and labor employed on the land are determined before the exogenous influences of weather and pests are known. On the other hand, the possibility would not hold if known differences in managerial talent are excluded from the list of inputs. Therefore, least-squares estimates are reported in the belief that the utilization of inputs is largely independent of the production-function disturbance term, so that any simultaneous equation bias is small.[1]

9.1   Rice

The states of Assam and Kerala had the largest percentage of food-grain area under rice of any state in India—both with 94 percent [see Government of India (1958, p. 12)]—but no *Studies* have been undertaken for them because they are small states. For area under rice, these states were followed by Orissa (83 percent), West Bengal (81 percent), Bihar (54 percent), Madras (43 percent), Andhra Pradesh (29 percent), Madhya Pradesh (27 percent), and Uttar Pradesh (20 percent). Rice production in Orissa and Andhra Pradesh has been studied for the crop years 1957–1958 through 1959–1960, while rice production in West Bengal, Madras, and Uttar Pradesh has been studied for the crop years 1954–1955 through 1956–1957.[2] However, only the studies for

---

[1] The disturbance term after writing the production function in the logarithms of the variables is also assumed to be normally and independently distributed with zero mean and constant variance. Standard errors of elasticity estimates are reported when available; standard errors of returns-to-scale estimates are unavailable.

[2] Rice was not studied in Madhya Pradesh, and no *Study* has appeared for Bihar.

TABLE 9.2
Direct and Imputed Factor Costs of Unirrigated Aman Paddy Rice Production

	24-Parganas, West Bengal			Sambalpur, Orissa[a]		
	1954–1955	1955–1956	1956–1957	1957–1958	1958–1959	1959–1960
Operating Costs, %						
Human labor	55.8	49.6	39.4	39.4	34.9	36.6
Bullock labor	10.4	8.8	9.4	15.5	25.3	19.9
Seed	7.8	5.0	4.7	16.9	14.1	14.5
Manure and fertilizer	1.1	0.4	0.2	2.4	4.7	3.7
Overhead Costs, %						
Rental value of land	12.1	10.7	14.9	d	16.3	18.4
Depreciation of implements[b]	1.0	2.4	1.7	3.5	1.5	1.6
Interest on fixed capital[c]	11.7	17.8	24.8	d	1.4	2.3
Land revenue and other charges	0	5.2	5.0	1.3	1.8	3.1
Average Cost in Rupees per Acre	146.94	129.13	163.83	101.17	108.55	102.58
Average Yield in Maunds per Acre	15.18	14.69	16.70	12.00	14.01	11.81

SOURCE: India, Government of (1958–1960). *Studies in the Economics of Farm Management, West Bengal, 1954–1955. New Delhi*, pp. 62–64, A–48; *1955–1956*, pp. 77, 178; *1956–1957*, pp. 84–85. Also India, Government of (1964–1968). *Orissa, 1957–1958*, pp. 85, 87; *1958–1959*, pp. 50–51; *1959–1960*, pp. 90, 92–93.

a Average irrigated area per farm for the farms in the sample was 17.6 percent in 1957–1958, 2.8 percent in 1958–1959, and 9.9 percent in 1959–1960. Rice was produced on more than 90 percent of the area sown.

b And nonresidential farm buildings in Orissa.

c Unlike the usual definition of fixed capital which includes livestock, implements, and nonresidential farm buildings, for West Bengal, fixed capital includes all farm assets except land (in particular, residential buildings).

d Rental value of land and interest on fixed capital together equal 21.0 percent.

Orissa, Andhra Pradesh, and West Bengal are discussed here; Madras and Uttar Pradesh are not discussed because the two particular districts studied there had only small percentages of total crop area under rice.

Table 9.2 provides the average direct and imputed factor costs as a percentage of total costs for unirrigated *aman* paddy rice production in the districts of 24-Parganas, West Bengal, and Sambalpur, Orissa. 24-Parganas is chosen in West Bengal instead of the other district studied (Hooghly) because the former is used in a production-function study reported below. Only the one district was studied in Orissa.

The first obvious result from the table is that labor is by far the most important input for unirrigated rice production, accounting for from 35 to 50 percent of total production costs. Bullock labor is the second most important operating input, particularly in Orissa, and is followed by seed and manure and fertilizer. The only important fixed input is land—interest on fixed capital is a high percentage of costs in West Bengal only because interest on nonproductive assets (such as residential buildings) is inappropriately included.[1] In summary, the three most important inputs are human labor, bullock labor, and land.

Rice production in these districts occurred in areas with very little irrigation. In Table 9.3, factor costs for both unirrigated and irrigated rice production in West Godavari, Andhra Pradesh, are reported. (Unirrigated production is included for comparison, although it accounts for less than 5 percent of total cropped area.) A notable result in Table 9.3 is that the imputed cost of land for both the unirrigated and irrigated crops is about one-half of total costs, much higher than in West Bengal and Orissa. Wellisz et al. (1970, p. 664) argue that this result is due to improper calculation of rent in the *Studies*, that "...since there is still some uncultivated land in Andhra, the worst land under cultivation carries no rent, and all rent can be decomposed into Ricardian differentials in natural endowment and quasi rent on improvements." Thus, since our district of West Godavari is a particularly productive one, rent is overstated.

Table 9.3 also shows that irrigation leads to a much higher output yield per acre (somewhat less than twice as high) and costs increase proportionally. Evidently, irrigation increases the intensity of land

---

[1] The inclusion of interest on nonproductive assets in the West Bengal study also helps explain why average cost per acre is calculated to be higher there than in Orissa. Incidentally, through all of the *Studies*, a 3 percent interest rate is utilized to calculate interest on fixed capital. This rate seems to be too low in almost any country and particularly in an underdeveloped one.

TABLE 9.3
Direct and Imputed Factor Costs of Paddy Rice Production in West Godavari, Andhra Pradesh

	Unirrigated			First Season Irrigated		
	1957–1958	1958–1959	1959–1960	1957–1958	1958–1959	1959–1960
Operating Costs, %						
Human labor	25.8	26.3	18.6	21.7	22.7	18.0
Bullock labor	8.6	7.2	9.8	10.8	11.5	14.5
Seed	2.3	2.3	2.6	4.8	6.1	6.2
Manure and fertilizer	9.5	7.1	9.6	3.6	4.3	2.5
Overhead Costs, %						
Rental value of land	51.5	52.9	56.2	52.9	49.6	52.3
Depreciation of implements	0.7	1.3	0.8	1.2	1.4	1.3
Interest on fixed capital	0.1	0.8	0.2	0.3	0.5	0.6
Irrigation charges				0.1	0.9	0.7
Land revenue and other charges	1.4	2.0	2.2	4.7	3.0	3.8
Average Cost in Rupees per Acre	170.84	161.40	200.05	331.25	301.54	326.71
Average Yield in Maunds per Acre	12.70	14.09	12.22	23.46[a]	26.18[b]	21.12

SOURCE: India, Government of (1964–1968). *Studies in the Economics of Farm Management, Andhra Pradesh, 1957–1958.* New Delhi, pp. 109, 111, 124–125; *1958–1959*, pp. 82, 85, 102, 104; *1959–1960*, pp. 198, 204, 245, 247.
[a] 27.45 by crop-cutting tests.
[b] 28.64 by crop-cutting tests.

TABLE 9.4

Cobb–Douglas Production-function Estimates for Rice

	24-Parganas, West Bengal[a] (Unirrigated) 1956–1957		Sambalpur, Orissa[b] (Unirrigated)			West Godavari, Andhra Pradesh[c] (Irrigated) 1957–1958
	Hired Labor	No Hired Labor	1957–1958	1958–1959	1959–1960	
Human labor	0.395	−0.073	0.477	0.114	0.760	0.227
	(0.151)	(0.142)				(0.115)
Bullock labor	0.009	0.030	0.159	0.250	0.180	
	(0.118)	(0.154)				
Land	0.512	0.911	0.321	0.559	0.030	0.490
	(0.157)	(0.171)				(0.098)
Value of implements	0.093	0.098	0.045[d]			0.000[e]
	(0.035)	(0.065)				(0.048)
Production expenses[f]						0.272
						(0.074)
Sum of elasticities	1.009	0.966	1.002	0.923	0.970	0.989
R^2	0.846	0.818	0.891	0.847	0.905	0.926
Number of observations	64	34	100	100	100	67

SOURCE: For West Bengal: Desai, M., and D. Mazumdar (1970). "A Test of the Hypothesis of Disguised Unemployment." *Economica*, 37:53. For Orissa: India, Government of (1964–1968). *Studies in the Economics of Farm Management, Orissa, 1957–1958.* New Delhi, p. 105; *1958–1959*, p. 63; *1959–1960*, p. 112. For Andhra Pradesh: Chennareddy, V. (1967), "Production Efficiency in South Indian Agriculture." *Journal of Farm Economics*, 49:818.

a For West Bengal, the land input is measured as size of cultivating unit, not gross cropped area.

b All point estimates reported are statistically significant at 5 percent, but the standard errors are not reported in the *Studies.* Also, note that for Orissa for 1958–1959, human and bullock labor refers to preharvesting input only. Finally, in Orissa a small proportion of the land cultivated in rice is irrigated (see footnote a, Table 9.2).

c Value of all crops in "rice zone."

d Manure only [measured as quantity ot manure in maunds *plus* unity (*sic*)].

e Including, also, value of draught cattle, storage sheds, and share of the draught cattle in the cattle sheds.

f Seed, manure and fertilizers, hired bullock labor, cost of maintenance of draught cattle apportioned to crop production, and minor repairs.

179

cultivation and, thus, each cost.   Indeed, Wellisz et al. (1970, p. 671) calculate only a 3 to 4 percent return from investment in major irrigation projects in Andhra Pradesh.   In any case, human labor is again an important input, with bullock labor of less importance.

M. Desai and D. Mazumdar (1970, p. 53) have reported production-function estimates for the district of 24-Parganas, West Bengal, using unpublished data for the crop year 1956–1957 obtained for the *Studies*. Their most useful estimate for our purposes is of a Cobb–Douglas production function with inputs of human labor, bullock labor, land, and value of major and minor implements.   Their measure of output is the total value of farm output; however, rice accounts for 90 percent of cultivated area.

Table 9.4 reports the West Bengal estimates for two types of farms, those utilizing some hired labor and those utilizing no hired labor. An interesting result, as Desai and Mazumdar emphasize, is that the human labor input has a positive marginal product only for those farms hiring labor.   Thus, they conclude that some, but not all, farms in India have surplus labor in the sense that labor's marginal product is close to zero.   Other results from the West Bengal estimates are that land is a statistically significant input while bullock labor is not, and that the value of farm implements seems to be marginally significant. Finally, the estimates indicate that there are constant returns to scale at the farm level.

The next three columns of Table 9.4 provide estimates of a Cobb–Douglas production function for rice in Orissa, reported in the *Studies*. All these point estimates are statistically significant (although separate, unreported estimates for 1958–1959 and 1959–1960, including manure input, yielded an insignificant coefficient for this input).   Note that there is a wide variation in the estimates of the land and human-labor coefficients, while the bullock-labor coefficient seems to be rather well defined around 0.2.   Also, there is an indication of constant or slightly decreasing returns to scale.

Finally, one production-function estimate is available for rice in West Godavari, Andhra Pradesh.   It is reported in Chennareddy (1967, p. 818) for the *rice zone* in 1957–1958 where virtually all of the rice is irrigated and rice is grown on 72 percent of cultivated area.   The estimate is repeated in the last column of Table 9.4.   Statistically significant inputs are land, labor, and "production expenses", while the coefficient estimate for fixed capital is 0.000(!).   Approximately constant returns to scale prevail.

9.2   Jowar (Sorghum)

Jowar was produced on 40 percent of the land under foodgrains in Bombay, making it the largest jowar-producing state in India.   The state of Mysore allocated 37 percent of its land under foodgrains to jowar, while Andhra Pradesh allocated 28 percent.   No other state allocated more than 15 percent.   The *Studies* do not survey Mysore, while the Andhra Pradesh *Studies* do not survey jowar.   Therefore, we examine only the results for Bombay.   Table 9.5 provides the direct and imputed factor costs for both unirrigated and irrigated jowar production in Ahmednagar, Bombay.[1]

Table 9.5 first indicates that human labor is the most important input, followed closely by bullock labor and land, which are of about equal importance; other inputs are relatively unimportant.   Second, the table indicates that average cost per acre is about three times higher for irrigated farms than for those that are unirrigated, but yield is about five times greater.   Thus, irrigation is very profitable.   Finally, as we found for rice production in Andhra Pradesh, irrigation greatly increases the intensity of use of each input.

Production-function estimates for jowar production in Admednagar, Bombay, have been reported previously only for 1956–1957, but estimates for 1954–1955 can be obtained from the individual farm observations reported in that year's *Study*.   The 1954–1955 estimates for both unirrigated and irrigated jowar are unacceptable: The labor elasticities are greater than 1, the bullock and land elasticities are negative, and the constant term is smaller for irrigated farms.   (Regressions were also run, without any improvement, using the value of jowar output as the dependent variable and including a dummy variable for each village.)   Furthermore, although the 1956–1957 estimates, by and large, give appropriate point estimates—the human-labor-coefficient estimates are about 0.55, with bullock labor and land lower and "crop service charges" close to zero—the standard errors of the estimates are so high, presumably owing to multicollinearity, that none of the point estimates differ significantly from zero at any reasonable confidence level.   Thus, we might note here only that the returns-to-scale estimates for 1956–1957 unirrigated and irrigated jowar in

---

[1] In 1954–1955, 19 percent of area under jowar in the Ahmednagar sample was irrigated; in 1955–1956, 23 percent; and in 1956–1957, 17 percent.   Incidentally, the other district of Bombay that was studied, Nasik, allocated only a small proportion of total cultivated area to jowar and so is not reported here.

TABLE 9.5

Direct and Imputed Factor Costs of Jowar Production in Ahmednagar, Bombay

	UNIRRIGATED			IRRIGATED		
	1954–1955	1955–1956	1956–1957	1954–1955	1955–1956	1956–1957
Operating Costs, %						
Human labor	36.8	33.0	38.6	39.1	34.7	35.2
Bullock labor	25.2	30.0	21.5	23.5	23.9	19.8
Seed	4.2	3.0	5.3	2.6	1.2	2.5
Manure and fertilizer	0	1.0	0.8	1.2	4.3	5.9
Overhead Costs, %						
Rental value of land	29.2	26.4	25.6	24.0	20.1	17.7
Depreciation of implements	1.4	2.5	3.3	6.0	3.6	4.5
Interest on fixed capital	1.3	1.6	1.6	1.7	7.5	9.4
Irrigation charges					3.2	3.3
Land revenue and other charges	1.9	2.5	3.2	1.9	1.5	1.7
Average Cost in Rupees per Acre	24.41	31.07	24.6	79.80	97.70	85.0
Average Yield in Maunds per Acre	2.00	1.09[a]	2.0	10.08	6.09[b]	7.0

SOURCE: India, Government of (1958–1960). *Studies in the Economics of Farm Management, Bombay, 1954–1955.* New Delhi, pp. 87, 90, 239, 244; *1955–1956,* pp. 163–165, 170, 172; *1956–1957,* pp. 155, 159, 164, 168.
[a] 2.25 by crop-cutting tests.
[b] 10.34 by crop-cutting tests.

Ahmednagar are 1.024 and 1.070, respectively [Government of India, (1958–1960), *Bombay 1956–1957*, pp. 257–259].

9.3 Wheat

In Punjab, 28 percent of the foodgrain area was devoted to wheat, with 22 percent of such area devoted to wheat in Uttar Pradesh.   The *Studies* for Punjab for the crop years 1954–1955 through 1956–1957 are reported for districts for which area under wheat as a single crop was less than 20 percent of total cultivated area.   Although these *Studies*, consequently, are not used here, the Government of Punjab (1964, 1966) has undertaken its own *Studies* for the crop years 1961–1962 through 1963–1964, which we do use.   Data from the *Studies* for Uttar Pradesh are also available and are reported here.

Table 9.6 provides the factor costs in Punjab.   As previously, the three major inputs are human labor, bullock labor, and land, for both irrigated and unirrigated wheat production.   Like jowar, but unlike rice, bullock labor accounts for over 20 percent of production expenses.   Much more surprising, though, irrigation increases yield by only 20 percent.   Judging from rather small cost increases, evidently irrigation in Punjab does not lead to more intensive production techniques as it does for rice and jowar in the studies reported above.

The results for Uttar Pradesh differ from those for Punjab.   First, in Table 9.7, note that even though irrigation does not greatly increase intensity of cultivation, it does almost double the yields.[1]   Thus, irrigation is more profitable in Uttar Pradesh than in Punjab.   Second, the distribution of factor costs differs substantially.   Unlike wheat production in Punjab or the production of either rice or jowar studied above, bullock labor in wheat production in Uttar Pradesh is a much more important input than human labor.   The apparent explanation for this difference is that cattle upkeep in the two districts of Uttar Pradesh was very intensive but led to a higher operating cost.   The actual physical difference in hours of bullock input per acre in producing wheat in Punjab and Uttar Pradesh was small.[2]

---

[1] Yield for Uttar Pradesh is measured in *maunds* per acre, while it is measured in *quintals* per acre for Punjab.   Thus, the yields in the two tables cannot be compared directly.

[2] In Table 9.7, the rental value of land has not been calculated—only actual rent paid, which is a small proportion of rental value.

TABLE 9.6
Direct and Imputed Factor Costs of Wheat Production in Sangrur, Punjab

	UNIRRIGATED			IRRIGATED		
	1961–1962	1962–1963	1963–1964	1961–1962	1962–1963	1963–1964
Operating Costs, %						
Human labor	26.2	28.9	26.1	22.0	28.6	25.3
Bullock labor	23.6	27.3	23.9	20.3	24.4	23.0
Seed	10.5	8.0	8.9	7.1	7.0	6.3
Manure and fertilizer	0.3	0.1	0.3	0.1	1.5	2.6
Overhead Costs, %						
Rental value of land	30.6	29.2	31.2	38.7	29.8	31.7
Depreciation of implements	2.5	1.9	3.8	1.8	1.8	3.3
Interest on fixed capital[a]	3.6	2.5	3.6	4.7	2.1	2.9
Irrigation charges				3.1	3.2	3.1
Other	2.7	2.1	2.2	2.2	1.6	1.8
Average Cost in Rupees per Acre	149.26	192.99	206.70	206.44	236.88	269.75
Average Yield in Quintals per Acre	4.60	4.20	3.78	5.58	4.74	4.95

SOURCE: Punjab, Government of (1964, 1966). *Studies in the Economics of Farm Management in the Punjab, 1961–1962.* Chandigarh, pp. 122, 125, 135, 137–138; *1962–1963,* pp. 99, 102, 110, 112; *1963–1964,* pp. 94, 97, 104, 106.
[a] Based on a 5 percent interest rate, not the 3 percent of other tables.

184

TABLE 9.7

Direct and Imputed Factor Costs of Wheat Production in Meerut and Muzaffarnagar, Uttar Pradesh

	UNIRRIGATED			IRRIGATED		
	1954–1955	1955–1956	1956–1957	1954–1955	1955–1956	1956–1957
Operating Costs, %						
Human labor	20.0	21.0	21.6	22.1	20.9	20.4
Bullock labor	60.9	55.1	53.2	55.8	52.6	50.0
Seed	8.7	6.5	9.3	6.7	6.3	7.0
Manure and fertilizer	—	—	0.7	0.6	0.6	0.5
Overhead Costs, %						
Rent paid[a]	4.3	6.5	3.7	2.5	4.4	2.7
Depreciation of implements	4.3	7.3	8.6	4.3	7.0	8.1
Interest on fixed capital	1.8	3.6	2.9	0.6	3.8	5.4
Irrigation charges				7.4	4.4	5.9
Average Cost in Rupees per Acre	115.	138.	139.	163.	158.	186.
Average Yield in Maunds per Acre	6.9	5.0	7.3	13.3	9.8	11.0

SOURCE: India, Government of (1958–1960). *Studies in the Economics of Farm Management, Uttar Pradesh, 1954–1955.* New Delhi, pp. 75–77; *1955–1956*, pp. 80–81, 84; *1956–1957*, pp. 65, 69.

[a] Unlike other tables, land costs are only rent paid (a very small proportion of direct and imputed land costs).

TABLE 9.8

Cobb–Douglas Production-function Estimates for Irrigated Wheat

	PUNJAB			UTTAR PRADESH[a]		
	1961–1962	1962–1963	1963–1964[b]	1954–1955	1955–1956	1954
Human labor	0.323[c]	0.019	−0.081	−0.023	−0.261	0.020
					(0.151)	(0.008)
Bullock labor	0.301[c]	0.044		0.016	0.508	0.508
						(0.067)
Land	0.477[c]	0.300[c]	0.518[c]	0.937[c]	0.504	0.235
					(0.150)	(0.050)
Operating expenses[d]	0.128	0.889[c]	0.713[c]		0.536	0.143
					(0.124)	(0.034)
Value of implements					0.166	
					(0.086)	
Sum of elasticities	1.219	1.252	1.150	0.930	0.945	0.906
R^2	0.65	0.79	0.69	0.775	0.823	0.87
Number of observations	133	164	156	50	60	43 ?

SOURCE: Punjab, Government of (1964, 1966). *Studies in the Economics of Farm Management in the Punjab, 1961–1962.* Chandigarh, pp. 131–132; *1962–1963,* p. 106; *1963–1964,* p. 101. Also India, Government of (1958–1960). *Studies in the Economics of Farm Management, Uttar Pradesh, 1954–1955.* New Delhi, pp. 79–80; *1955–1956,* pp. 91–92. Also Hopper, W. D., (1965). "Allocative Efficiency in Traditional Indian Agriculture." *Journal of Farm Economics,* 47:615.

[a] For 1955–1956, value of output, not physical output, is used as the dependent variable, and human and bullock labor are combined by using their values. No estimate is reported for 1956–1957. For the 1954 estimate of Hopper, output is *expected* physical output (less seed used) before harvesting, human labor is hours used for "land preparation and sowing other than those directly used with bullocks," and bullock labor is hours of a bullock team, including attending human labor, used for land preparation and sowing. A quality adjustment for bullock labor is included. The data are obtained from a village in the district of Jaunpur. [See Hopper (1965, pp. 613–614)].

[b] According to the *Studies* for Punjab, bullock labor is excluded because, when included, the coefficient of human labor is negative and statistically significant.

[c] Significant at 5 percent where no standard errors of estimates are reported.

[d] For Punjab: seed, manure and fertilizer, and irrigation charges. For Uttar Pradesh: in 1955–1956, seed and manure and fertilizer charges; in 1954, irrigation water (not expenses) only.

187

In both the Punjab and Uttar Pradesh *Studies*, about twice as much acreage is used for irrigated wheat as for unirrigated wheat so that, in both the *Studies*, production-function estimates are reported for irrigated wheat only.   Table 9.8 summarizes these estimates in the first five columns.   In all cases, the land coefficients are significantly different from zero.   However, only for the 1961–1962 Punjab result are the human- and bullock-labor estimates significantly different from zero at 5 percent, while seed, manure and fertilizer, and irrigation charges generally are significantly different from zero.   Increasing returns to scale are indicated in Punjab, and constant or slightly decreasing returns are indicated in Uttar Pradesh.

One other estimate of a production function for irrigated wheat in Uttar Pradesh has been reported by W. David Hopper (1965, p. 615). It is repeated in the last column of Table 9.8 and indicates that the highest coefficient estimate is associated with bullock labor, followed by land, then irrigation water.   The human-labor-coefficient estimate is positive but quite small.   Decreasing returns to scale are reported.

9.4   Bajri (Millet) and Gram

Bajri was grown on 36 percent of the area under foodgrains in the state of Rajasthan and on 20 percent in Bombay.   Because no studies were undertaken for Rajasthan, we report the results for the districts of Ahmednagar and Nasik, Bombay, where bajri is grown unirrigated. Table 9.9 reports the factor costs.   As in the production of unirrigated rice and jowar, human labor is the most important input, followed by land, and then bullock labor.

One production-function estimate for unirrigated bajri is available for the Nasik district for 1956–1957 (see pp. 259–260 of the 1956–1957 Bombay *Study*).   However, with an R^2 of 0.06, the null hypothesis of all zero input coefficients can be accepted.   The poor regression result may be partly due to poor weather conditions for this crop in 1956–1957.

Gram was produced on 34 percent of the foodgrain-crop area in Punjab; no other state uses more than 15 percent of its crop area for gram.   However, the particular districts studied in Punjab for the crop years 1954–1955 through 1956–1957 produced most of their gram in combination with wheat rather than as a separate crop.   Therefore, we again use separate data provided by the Government of Punjab (1964, 1966).   The usual production data are given in Table 9.10.

TABLE 9.9

Direct and Imputed Factor Costs of Unirrigated Bajri Production
in Ahmednagar and Nasik, Bombay[a]

	AHMEDNAGAR		NASIK	
	1955–1956	1956–1957	1955–1956	1956–1957
Operating Costs, %				
Human labor	43.4	41.6	40.2	39.5
Bullock labor	17.8	19.0	21.2	20.9
Seed	2.6	4.3	3.7	4.9
Manure and fertilizer	5.6	7.9	2.8	4.1
Overhead Costs, %				
Rental value of land	22.2	17.2	25.5	22.0
Depreciation of implements	4.3	5.7	3.1	5.6
Interest on fixed capital	2.0	1.8	1.7	1.5
Land revenue and other charges	2.3	2.5	1.9	1.5
Average Cost in Rupees per Acre	30.04	27.9	36.35	39.2
Average Yield in Maunds per Acre	1.51[b]	1.1	2.25[c]	1.8

SOURCE: India, Government of (1958–1960). *Studies in the Economics of Farm Management, Bombay, 1955–1956.* New Delhi, pp. 241–242, 245–246; *1956–1957*, pp. 239, 244, 248, 252.

[a] Bajri was not surveyed in Bombay in 1954–1955.

[b] 1.97 by crop-cutting tests.

[c] 3.58 by crop-cutting tests.

The most important input is the rental value of land, which accounts for 40 to 45 percent of costs.   It is followed by human labor and then by bullock labor.   Again, other inputs are of much less importance. Irrigation, surprisingly, does not increase yields greatly but does increase intensity of land cultivation somewhat.   Evidently, irrigation was used on poorer land.

Production-function estimates were undertaken for only two years— 1961–1962 and 1963–1964—in the *Studies*.   Because unirrigated gram is much more important in terms of area of cultivation than irrigated gram, only the former estimates were calculated.   They are reported in Table 9.11.   The land-coefficient estimate is statistically significant,

TABLE 9.10
Direct and Imputed Factor Costs of Gram Production in Sangrur, Punjab

	UNIRRIGATED			IRRIGATED		
	1961–1962	1962–1963	1963–1964	1961–1962	1962–1963	1963–1964
Operating Costs, %						
Human labor	21.4	22.8	19.8	22.5	21.8	20.6
Bullock labor	15.3	15.4	16.6	15.3	14.8	16.2
Seed	6.0	7.8	7.8	5.2	6.2	5.8
Manure and fertilizer	—	—	0.1	0.5	—	—
Overhead Costs, %						
Rental value of land	44.8	43.0	45.5	40.6	43.0	43.7
Depreciation of implements	3.2	3.5	5.2	2.7	3.5	5.0
Interest on fixed capital[a]	5.5	4.1	2.6	6.4	3.4	3.4
Irrigation charges				3.4	4.7	3.2
Land revenue and other charges	3.8	3.4	2.4	3.4	2.6	2.1
Average Cost in Rupees per Acre	111.37	102.00	124.82	154.96	122.25	144.23
Average Yield in Quintals per Acre	2.91	2.56	2.55	3.08	2.53	2.69

SOURCE: Punjab, Government of (1964, 1966). *Studies in the Economics of Farm Management in the Punjab, 1961–1962*. Chandigarh, pp. 168, 170–171, 178, 180; *1962–1963*, pp. 134, 136, 142, 144–145; *1963–1964*, pp. 127, 130, 135, 138.
a Based on a 5 percent interest rate, not 3 percent.

TABLE 9.11

Cobb–Douglas Production-function Estimates for Unirrigated Gram in Punjab

	Human Labor	Bullock Labor	Land	Seed, Manure, and Fertilizer Charges	Sum of Elasticities	R^2	Number of Observations
1961–1962	0.206[a]	0.214[a]	0.430[a]	0.034	0.884	0.63	143
1963–1964	0.048	0.012	0.540[a]	0.539[a]	1.139	0.71	163

SOURCE: Punjab, Government of (1964, 1966). *Studies in the Economics of Farm Management in the Punjab, 1961–1962.* Chandigarh, pp. 184–185; *1963–1964*, pp. 141–142.

while the other three coefficient estimates are significant in only one of the two years. The returns to scale are decreasing in one year and increasing in the other.

9.5 Conclusions

The first empirical result that can be drawn from our survey of production conditions in Indian agriculture is that, in the case of each crop, the most important inputs in terms of factor costs for the farmer are land, human labor, and bullock labor. Although no other input accounts for more than about 10 percent of total costs, the relative importance of these three inputs varies with the crop. In general, human labor and land are the most important inputs for rice, while human labor is most important for jowar and bajri and land is most important for gram. However, the fact that human labor and bullock labor are equally important for producing wheat in Punjab but bullock labor is much more important in Uttar Pradesh indicates that location as well as crop determines relative factor costs.

For rice and jowar, we found that irrigation leads to a large increase in the crop yields for the districts studied, while irrigation showed smaller but noticeable increases in yields for wheat and bajri. Thus, we have direct evidence of the importance of irrigation for increasing agricultural output. However, such irrigation leads to higher costs owing to a more intensive utilization of the factor inputs on the land.

The conclusions that can be drawn from the production-function estimates are much more tenuous because the point estimates vary from crop to crop and from year to year. However, a few broad conclusions can be drawn: First, land is a statistically significant input in all estimates except for jowar, and an output elasticity with respect to land of 0.5 is consistent with most of these estimates. Second, human labor is generally a statistically significant input for rice but not for wheat; no useful results are available for jowar and bajri, and the gram results are ambiguous. Third, the bullock-input-coefficient estimates are not at all well defined. Finally, approximately constant returns to scale are indicated for rice and jowar, while increasing and decreasing returns are alternately estimated for both wheat and gram.

In this chapter we have investigated cost conditions and production functions in Indian agriculture primarily to give the empirically oriented economist a framework with which to examine developing agriculture; we have provided relevant characteristics of agriculture that must be examined.   In addition, we have attempted to build a foundation for further generalizations of the theoretical models given in previous chapters.   Nevertheless, the results reported in this chapter cannot be viewed as a complete empirical study of agricultural production. First, the crops grown and the nature of cost conditions differ widely among countries, so that an economist working on a particular country must know the technical conditions in that country. Second, our results are only as reliable as the underlying data. Although we have been careful to utilize data that are conceptually acceptable, we have little information on the degree of unaccounted quality variation in inputs across observations and of measurement errors.

In any case, two theoretical implications about traditional agriculture can be drawn.   First, a production function for traditional agriculture must include, explicitly or implicitly, at least land and labor; and it should include working animals when relevant.   In Chapters 2 and 5, working animals are assumed to be used in fixed proportion with labor to produce crops, and total cultivated land area is assumed to be either fixed or growing at an exogenously determined rate; further work could generalize either of these assumptions.   Second, the evidence seems to suggest that constant returns to scale is a safe assumption in agriculture: About one-half of the estimates here indicates constant returns, while the other half is split between increasing and decreasing returns.   Furthermore, Cline (1970, pp. 62–74) finds that returns to scale generally are constant in Brazilian agriculture.   Thus, there is no important evidence that either small or large farms are inherently more productive (so that land-tenure policy does not hinge on technical considerations of farm size).

These remarks establish a reasonable characterization of the static production function but ignore the important factor of technical change. In the context of our theoretical models in Chapters 2 and 5, technical change is exogenous but includes a potpourri of factors such as increases in land area, irrigation, fertilizers, and physical capital as well as improvements in seed and managerial ability.   In Chapter 8 these sources of increased agriculture productivity are discussed theoretically. In this chapter we found empirically that irrigation can lead to a much more intensive cultivation of land, along with a more than proportional increase in yields, but that the actual effects vary considerably among crops and regions.   However, much more empirical work, of course, needs to be undertaken.

Chapter Ten

AN ECONOMETRIC ANALYSIS OF THE FOOD-CONSUMPTION FUNCTION

In Chapter 2, the other crucial relationship besides the agricultural production function that determines the growth rate of consumer income in a closed economy is the consumption function for food. This function continues to play an important role in problems discussed in subsequent chapters. In this chapter, the theoretical characterization of the food-consumption function is first reexamined. Then, after some econometric considerations, estimates provided by other sources of the income elasticity of food demand are summarized. Finally, a new functional form for the consumption function is developed that introduces an additional parameter for characterizing the behavior of the income elasticity of demand for food as income level changes. Some estimates of this functional form are undertaken.

10.1 Theoretical and Econometric Specification of the Food-consumption Function

At the most general level, an individual's consumption of one commodity is determined simultaneously with consumption of other commodities, present and future. Because future consumption is often aggregated as one item—savings—the consumer is portrayed as

194

choosing among items of current consumption and savings. This choice is determined by his income (or wealth), by commodity prices, and by the interest rate. However, a convenient special case is to assume that commodity prices do not affect the level of savings and that the interest rate either is constant or also does not affect the level of savings. Commodity consumption is then determined only by income and prices. A number of demand systems have been developed based upon these last determining variables [for a summary, see Yoshihara (1969) or Parks (1969)].

In this chapter we are only interested in the consumption function for one commodity—food. At a deterministic level, the problem of consistency of one demand function with the demand functions for other commodities and total expenditures can be ignored by assuming, as we do in Chapter 2, that the demand functions for other commodities are consistent with total expenditures. However, inclusion of stochastic terms, as is necessary in econometric work, complicates such a formulation. In this section we develop a stochastic model of food demand that leads to the econometric approach relied upon in subsequent sections.

Most data on food demand are cross-sectional, so that the prices facing consumers are not expected to vary much across observations. Therefore, the influence of prices on food consumption cannot be accurately determined, and, in fact, relevant price data usually are not even collected. Thus, the key parameter that is estimated here is the income elasticity of demand. In this section we discuss first the influence of income on food consumption, and then introduce the possible influence of household size insofar as there are effects of household-age distribution and economies of scale.

Suppose that the current income y of a consumer can be thought of as consisting of two elements: a permanent component y_p, which represents the individual's long-run earning potential, and a transitory component y_T, which represents temporary influences on his income level (such as unexpected unemployment, inheritance, or the selling of a crop harvest); that is,

(10.1) $$y = y_p + y_T$$

Now it might be expected that the individual's food demand is determined by his long-run earning potential, not by what his current income just happens to be. Certainly the shorter the time period of the data, the more likely it is that this will be the case. (As an extreme

case, daily data would reflect enormous fluctuations in income—high
on paydays and perhaps zero at other times, while food consumption
would not show large fluctuations.   Also, most consumer household
data refer to a time period of a month or less—still a short period.)
Then, current food consumption c_1 may be formulated most accurately
as depending upon permanent income subject to a stochastic disturbance
term [see Friedman (1957)].   For example, in a linear formulation we
would have

(10.2) $c_1 = a_0 + a_1 y_p + u$

where u is a random variable independent of y_p.[1]
    Equation (10.2) cannot be estimated directly because permanent
income is not an observable concept but, rather, an abstraction.   A
number of techniques have been developed to relate permanent income to observable magnitudes, including grouping data, utilizing a
distributed lag of measured income, and introducing instrumental
variables.   As an example of the last technique, Liviatan (1961) has
developed a consistent estimator of the marginal propensity to consume
one commodity out of total expenditures by using measured income as
an instrumental variable.   In Liviatan's model, data are needed on
both current income and total expenditures, but unfortunately they are
often unavailable.   Also, income is usually subject to considerable
measurement errors.
    In this chapter we rely upon the use of grouped data to obtain con-
sistent estimates of our parameters because most data are reported in
grouped form.   To clarify in principle the value of grouped data, first
consider ungrouped data where permanent income is replaced by current
income in Equation (10.2):

(10.3) $c_1 = a_0' + a_1' y + v$

when, in fact, permanent income is the correct influence on food con
sumption.   Then we ask whether the least squares estimate $\hat{a}_1'$ is a
consistent estimate of a_1 in Equation (10.2).   Now,

$$\hat{a}_1' = \frac{COV(c_1, y)}{VAR(y)}$$

<hr>

[1] Friedman labels the deterministic portion of Equation (10.2) as permanent
consumption and u as transitory consumption.

where COV stands for covariance and VAR stands for variance. Therefore,

$$\hat{a}'_1 = \frac{COV(a_0 + a_1 y_p + u, y_p + y_T)}{VAR(y_p + y_T)}$$

or, writing the probability limit as *plim*,

(10.4) $$plim \ \hat{a}'_1 = a_1 \frac{VAR(y_p)}{VAR(y_p) + VAR(y_T)}$$

Thus, in general, $\hat{a}'_1$ is downward biased as an estimator of a_1, where the degree of bias depends upon the relative variance of transitory income to permanent income.

Suppose, however, as also discussed by Liviatan (1961, pp. 357–359), that the individual observations from a cross-section sample are grouped by some scheme such that the method of grouping is correlated with the level of income but *not* with the disturbance term v in Equation (10.3). Then, because of the averaging over several observations, the variance of transitory income moves in inverse proportion to the number of observations in each group. Thus, with the grouping undertaken using a correlate of income level, the variance of permanent income in the grouped sample can be quite large while the variance of transitory income can be quite small. In summary, the use of grouped data permits an essentially consistent estimate of the marginal propensity to consume out of permanent income.

In many cases, expenditure data used for estimating the consumption function include only expenditure by commodities and total expenditures, not income. Therefore, in the consumption function income is often replaced by total expenditures. Analytically, this can be justified by noting that the expenditure data, in principle, can also be grouped by a procedure uncorrelated with the disturbance term in the commodity-expenditure function. Then the grouped total expenditure data serve as a proxy for permanent income: The random fluctuations in total expenditures, in addition to the influence of permanent income on expenditures, are reduced to having a very small variance in the grouped data. If the total expenditure elasticity out of permanent income is unity, an estimate of the total expenditure elasticity for a commodity is an estimate of the income elasticity.

To summarize the resulting model of consumer expenditure on food, we hypothesize that this expenditure depends upon permanent income and a random variable that is independent of permanent income. We then use grouped data to obtain a measure of permanent income. Thus, an essentially consistent estimate of the income elasticity of food demand is obtained. When total expenditures are utilized instead of income, there is no ambiguity between the income and total expenditure elasticity of food demand if the income elasticity of total expenditures equals 1. For convenience, we always refer only to the income elasticity.

The principle difficulty with using published grouped data is that in surveys for developing countries they are usually grouped by total expenditures, often because income data are unmeasured. Thus, the grouping procedure is, in fact, correlated with the disturbance term in the commodity-consumption function (regardless of whether income or total expenditures is the independent variable). In other words, exogenous shocks to consumption of one commodity influence total expenditures (the grouping variable). Additionally, even if income data are available but income is the independent variable in the regression, then grouping either by income level or total expenditure level is still correlated with the disturbance term in the commodity consumption function. *Only if* total expenditure is the independent variable and the grouping is by income level can it be plausibly argued that the grouping method is correlated with the independent variable but not with the commodity disturbance term (because income level is not influenced by commodity consumption). In summary, a consistent estimate of the food-consumption function can be obtained only from household surveys grouped by income level. Indeed, very few surveys are appropriate.

In the preceding discussion, a linear relationship between food consumption and income has been assumed. This relationship permits a focus on the central point that grouped data are preferable for estimating the food-consumption function. However, a linear relationship has come into disrepute because the implied income elasticity of demand is $a_1 y / c_1 = y/(y + a_0/a_1)$, which increases toward unity as income rises given an initial elasticity below unity. Because it is believed empirically that the food elasticity is below unity and falls or stays constant as income rises, the linear form is unacceptable.

L. M. Goreux (1960, pp. 1–4), in a summary of a larger FAO[1] study, has surveyed seven other functional relationships between food

---

[1] Food and Agricultural Organization of the United Nations.

consumption and income.   His a priori preference is for the log–log-inverse function

$$(10.5) \qquad \ln c_1 = a_0 - \frac{a_1}{y} - a_2 \ln y \qquad \text{log–log-inverse}$$

which implies an income elasticity of $(a_1 - a_2 y)/y$.   Thus, at very low levels of income, food is a luxury good with a high-income elasticity; then it becomes a necessity with an income elasticity below unity; and, finally, it becomes an inferior good with an income elasticity less than zero.   We do not believe that food ever becomes an inferior good.

The most commonly used functional forms are the logarithmic form, which implies a constant elasticity a_1,

$$(10.6) \qquad \ln c_1 = a_0 + a_1 \ln y \qquad \text{logarithmic}$$

and the semilog form, which implies an elasticity of a_1/c_1,

$$(10.7) \qquad c_1 = a_0 + a_1 \ln y \qquad \text{semilog}$$

The latter, of course, requires that the income elasticity falls as the reciprocal of rising consumption.   Actually, Goreux places most emphasis on the empirical results from these two and the log-inverse function

$$(10.8) \qquad \ln c_1 = a_0 - \frac{a_1}{y} \qquad \text{log-inverse}$$

with its implied elasticity of a_1/y.   Goreux believes that Equation (10.5) is only useful when a very broad range of income levels is being utilized.   [Note that (10.6) and (10.8) are special cases of (10.5).]

In Section 10.2, elasticities derived from food-consumption functions obtained previously are reported.   Each of the studies utilizes some of the functional forms (10.5) through (10.8).   In Section 10.3, a new functional form is introduced, which permits the data to directly discriminate the behavior of the food income elasticity as income changes.

Two additional econometric problems involved in estimating a food-consumption function should be mentioned.   First, most cross-sectional expenditure data are reported in per-capita units for a household. Unfortunately for econometric purposes, the level of per-capita household food consumption may depend upon the sex and, particularly, the age of the household members as well as upon per-capita income. Furthermore, there may be economies of scale from the purchase, storage, and preparation of food for a larger household, so that household size may be important.   If, by chance, we are willing to assume that these three factors are independent of per-capita income (as we do for taste differences), then there is no bias from these factors in estimating income elasticities.   But, almost assuredly, sex, age, and household size are correlated with household per-capita income.

The influence of sex on food consumption can probably be ignored as a small effect.   Age is most conveniently summarized for the household by a conversion to equivalent adult units, as most succinctly discussed by F. G. Forsyth (1960).   However, most survey expenditure data in developing countries do not provide age distribution of households, so that conversion to equivalent adult units is impossible.   Nevertheless, it is likely that household size is inversely correlated with equivalent adult units per capita; that is, larger households tend to have more children and thus fewer adult units per person.   Therefore, for lack of any better measure, household size may be a useful variable to include in the regression framework for food consumption in order to capture, in part, the age effect, together with any possible economies-of-scale effect.   When included, we expect the coefficient of household size to be nonpositive as an influence on per-capita consumption.   In any case, both the age and economies-of-scale effects are labeled as economies of scale.

The second econometric problem is the use of *nominal* food consumption as the dependent variable and *nominal* expenditure as an independent variable.   One consequence is that if there is some variation in food prices across observations due to regional price variation, both nominal food consumption and nominal expenditure may rise in high-food-price areas.   Thus, the expenditure-coefficient estimate will have an upward bias relative to the demand model which is based upon real magnitudes.   Therefore, it is important that the household data utilized in estimation come from a geographical area that can reasonably be expected to have constant prices.   Alternatively, if income data are available and income is not correlated with prices in the cross section, then income data could be used in place of total expenditures *provided* that an appropriate grouping method is available.[1]

A second effect of using nominal food consumption as the dependent variable is that higher nominal consumption at higher-income levels may be due partly to the purchase of better quality food at higher prices.   Again, the estimate of the income elasticity for real consumption

[1] Also, if income data are more subject to errors in measurement, then use of income data leads to a downward bias in the estimated income elasticity.

has an upward bias. Quirino Paris (1970, pp. 17–22) provides an empirical summary that shows that this bias can be serious for individual food commodities. Whether the bias is serious for total food is not known. In any case, if data on real consumption are unavailable, there seems to be no immediate solution to this possible bias in using nominal consumption.

One final comment is necessary. Whenever grouped data are utilized, it is standard econometric procedure to weight each observation of the dependent and independent variables by the square root of the number of households composing the observation. Such a procedure has the effect of generating homoskedasticity of the disturbance term in the consumption function and thus yielding efficient regression estimates of the coefficients.

10.2 Survey of Previous Estimates of the Income Elasticity of Food Demand

In virtually all published studies of the income elasticity of food demand for developing countries, the estimates are biased on three counts. As seen in Section 10.1, the estimates are biased downward because the independent variable is total expenditures—or, infrequently, income—while the basic data are grouped according to the level of this same variable. Second, the estimates are biased upward because the dependent variable is food expenditures, so that no correction for improved quality at higher-income levels is introduced. Third, most studies permit no economies of scale in food consumption because household size is not included as a separate independent variable. Because household size is presumably negative correlated with household income per capita, and because, if there are economies of scale, larger households should have smaller food consumption per capita at the same level of per-capita income, the omission of household size should bias the income elasticity estimates upward.

In this section we review previous estimates of the income elasticity of food demand and, in two cases, the household-size effect, with the hope that these econometric biases are equally strong in the downward and upward directions. To do otherwise would be to discard these previous studies. In any case, in Section 10.3, we do make use of data that are properly grouped and include household size.

A final comment before turning to the results is needed. Many economists have argued that in urban areas the income elasticity for food is lower than in rural areas because of the greater urban marketing services, which lead to a larger number of competing goods, and because of the demonstration effect. However, an empirically obtained lower elasticity might be caused by only higher urban income or relatively higher urban food prices resulting from transportation or processing costs. To cast some light on this discussion, except for brief mention of an FAO study, only those estimates that consider the rural and urban sectors separately are surveyed.

For many years, the Food and Agriculture Organization of the United Nations has been developing agricultural commodity projections and thus information on income elasticities of demand. Their latest study, published in 1967, analyzes 80 developing and developed countries for about 100 household surveys [see Food and Agricultural Organization of the United Nations (1967)]. In general, the study reports quantity estimates of income demand for individual food commodities, but an estimate is also provided for "total cereals." For developing countries, their income elasticity estimate for quantity of total cereals varies from 0.2 to 0.4 in most cases, with a few estimates of 0.1 or 0.5 and 0.6. The functional forms used are the log–log-inverse or the semilog. For our purposes, the most serious limitation of these estimates is that they refer only to total cereals, not to total food.

By far the most extensive survey of consumer expenditures in developing countries is the continuous one undertaken by the Indian Statistical Institute and issued by the Cabinet Secretariat of the Government of India (from 1952 to present). To date, eighteen rounds have been published, with sufficient consumer-expenditure data to allow estimates of the income elasticity for both the rural and urban sectors [see Government of India, Cabinet Secretariat (1952 to present)].

The most comprehensive study of the income elasticity of food demand, based upon the Indian data, has been published by R. P. Sinha (1966), although earlier studies were undertaken by Ravi Varma (1959) and M. K. Chatterji (1962). We shall summarize Sinha's results first and then discuss those of Varma and Chatterji. As far as can be determined from these papers, the basic data are grouped by total expenditure level, and simple rather than weighted regressions are used. Also, we should note that the dependent variable in all the Indian studies is nominal consumption and the independent variable is total expenditures. Sinha bases all of his results upon the log–log-inverse function [Equation (10.5)], but he reports only estimates of income (i.e., expenditure) elasticities. Table 10.1 summarizes his estimates for

TABLE 10.1

Estimates of the Income Elasticity of Food Demand for India[a]

SURVEY ROUND	TOTAL FOOD		FOODGRAINS	
	RURAL	URBAN	RURAL	URBAN
2nd: April–June 1951	0.79 (0.06)		0.53 (0.15)	
3rd: Aug.–Nov. 1951	0.78 (0.06)	0.73 (0.05)	0.56 (0.09)	0.28 (0.07)
4th: April–Sept. 1952	0.73 (0.05)	0.72 (0.05)	0.53 (0.09)	0.27 (0.10)
5th: Dec. 1952–March 1953	0.70 (0.12)	0.68 (0.06)	0.36 (0.13)	0.29 (0.11)
6th: May–Sept. 1953	0.83 (0.03)	0.75 (0.10)	0.50 (0.06)	0.33 (0.17)
7th: Oct. 1953–March 1954	0.73 (0.07)	0.71 (0.07)	0.30 (0.13)	0.22 (0.17)
8th: July 1954–March 1955	0.62 (0.14)	0.69 (0.04)	0.31 (0.08)	0.23 (0.08)
9th: May–Nov. 1955	0.60 (0.07)	0.71 (0.04)	0.34 (0.11)	0.28 (0.08)
10th: Dec. 1955–May 1956	0.76 (0.09)	0.74 (0.05)	0.52 (0.10)	0.25 (0.07)
11th: May–Nov. 1956	0.66 (0.04)	0.67 (0.04)	0.36 (0.05)	0.17 (0.06)
12th: March–April 1957	0.66 (0.06)	0.67 (0.08)	0.39 (0.05)	0.21 (0.05)

SOURCE: Sinha, R. P. (1966). "An Analysis of Food Expenditure in India." *Journal of Farm Economics*, 48:117–118.

[a] Each estimate is based upon the log–log-inverse functional form where the elasticity is calculated at the mean level of income in a particular survey round.

various rounds of the consumer survey for both total food and food-grains in the rural and urban areas.[1]

From this table three results are striking: First and most important,

---

[1] Sinha also provides some estimates for different geographical regions of India, but for total food and foodgrains there is no striking regional variation.

the income elasticity for total food is about 0.7 and is approximately the same in rural and urban areas.   Second, the income elasticity for foodgrains is less than that for total food and corresponds roughly with the estimates for foodgrains (i.e., cereals) obtained by the FAO. Finally, the foodgrain income elasticity is higher in the rural areas. Sinha suggests and provides some evidence that this last difference results from a higher elasticity for home-produced commodities (rural sector only) than for cash purchases.   (The source of the difference is not rural versus urban average income level because the differential is small.)

The major addition of Varna's (1959) study to the results reported by Sinha is that the foodgrain elasticity is shown to be even lower in big cities than in urban areas as a whole.   This result is consistent with Sinha's discussion of home-produced food if more foodgrains are obtained from family farms in smaller urban areas than in big cities. The most interesting contribution of Chatterji's (1962) study is an analysis of the possible contribution of household size toward explaining total food and foodgrain consumption per capita.   On the one hand, out of twenty regressions undertaken for total food, five household-size coefficient estimates are negative and significantly different from zero at 5 percent; out of twenty regressions for foodgrains, three coefficient estimates are negative and significant and one is positive and significant.   For all other estimates, we can accept the null hypothesis of no influence.

On the other hand, if observations are grouped according to household size, then in the rural sector families with three or less members have a higher elasticity for total food than any larger family, while in the urban sector there is a rather uniform decline according to family size.   For foodgrains, families with less than three members have a considerably higher elasticity than those with three or more members, while there is no important variation in urban areas.   In summary, particularly for total food, household size does seem to have some impact on per-capita consumption, but that influence is not linear.   Thus, a regression framework including household size as a regressor does not uniformly demonstrate size as having an influence.   Perhaps household-size groups should be included as dummy variables when a regression is undertaken.

Turning away from the Indian data, we shall now report estimates of the income elasticity of food demand in the Philippines and Jamaica and then report a summary for other countries provided by Quirino

Paris.   Allen C. Kelley (1969) has published an article which relies upon a 1961 household survey in the Philippines to obtain an estimate of the income elasticity of food demand in both rural and urban areas. He uses the weighted-regression technique on data grouped apparently by total expenditure level, with nominal food consumption per *household* (not per capita) as the dependent variable and both total expenditures per *household* and household size as independent variables.   His estimates of the income elasticity, using the logarithmic form, are given in Table 10.2.   The estimate is 0.75 in rural areas and 0.67 in urban areas.   Thus, the urban estimate is close to the rural but somewhat lower.

In rural areas the household-size elasticity estimate is 0.19 with a standard error of 0.12; for urban areas it is 0.41 with a standard error of 0.10.   Thus, with food consumption and income in per-capita units, the implied coefficient estimates are −0.06 for rural areas and 0.08 for

TABLE 10.2

Estimates of the Income Elasticity of Food Demand for the
Philippines and Jamaica

| FUNCTIONAL FORM | PHILIPPINES | | JAMAICA | | |
	RURAL	URBAN	RURAL	MAIN TOWNS	METROPOLITAN
Logarithmic	0.75	0.67	0.859	0.556	0.553
	(0.05)	(0.03)	(0.069)	(0.045)	(0.033)
Semilog[a]			0.849	0.702	0.575
			(0.066)	(0.083)	(0.038)
Average weekly income (shillings)			10.2	27.3	46.7

SOURCE: For the Philippines: Kelley, Allen C. (1969).   "Demand Patterns Demographic Change and Economic Growth."   *Quarterly Journal of Economics*, 83:117.   For Jamaica: Harris, Donald J. (1964).   "Econometric Analysis of Household Consumption in Jamaica."   *Social and Economic Studies*, 13:477–478.

[a] The elasticities reported for the semilog functional form are calculated at the sample means for average household consumption divided by average number of persons per household.

urban areas (the standard errors for these estimates cannot be ascertained with the reported information). For rural areas there are some
economies of scale, while for urban areas the coefficient has the wrong
sign (it indicates diseconomies).

Donald J. Harris (1964) has undertaken an econometric analysis of
household consumption in Jamaica, using 1958 household-expenditure
data. His regressions for total food expenditures use the value of per-
capita food consumption as the dependent variable and a measure of
per-capita income as the independent variable. These are weighted
regressions that use both the logarithmic and semilogarithmic functional
forms for grouped data on rural areas, main towns, and metropolitan
areas. These results are also summarized in Table 10.2. As for the
Philippines, the income elasticity is higher in rural than in urban areas,
but for Jamaica the spread is much greater. However, for both the
Philippines and Jamaica the difference may be due to higher-income
levels in the urban areas. Harris (p. 479), in considering the possibility,
finds no contradictory evidence.

Finally, Quirino Paris (1970, pp. 47–52) has provided a survey of the
point estimates of the income elasticity of food demand for those
countries carrying out separate rural and urban surveys. In each case,
the logarithmic function has been used with food expenditures as the
dependent variable and total expenditures as the independent variable.
Table 10.3 reports his results except for India and the Philippines
(countries which we have already discussed). Except in Morocco and,
particularly, Malaysia, the income elasticities are lower in urban areas.

To test the possibility that the higher-income elasticity estimates in
rural sectors are due to lower income per-capita, Paris (p. 50) calculated
values of the elasticity at different levels of income for Egypt, Iran, and
India using the semilog and the log-inverse functional forms; he found
that the elasticities at the same level of income tend to be *higher* in
urban areas. He suggests, though, that the difference is due to higher
food quality in urban areas resulting in an upward bias for these
functional estimates, to larger rural families, or to higher variability of
rural income.

To summarize previous estimates of the income elasticity of food
demand, it appears that the elasticity (1) is about 0.7 in rural areas and
lower in the urban areas (but the difference may be due to different
income levels), (2) falls with rising income, and (3) is influenced somewhat by household size. The elasticity for foodgrains is lower than for
total food.

TABLE 10.3

Point Estimates of the Income Elasticity of Food Demand in Some
Developing Countries

COUNTRY AND YEAR	NUMBER OF HOUSEHOLDS		PERCENTAGE OF FOOD IN TOTAL EXPENDITURES		ELASTICITIES[a]	
	RURAL	URBAN	RURAL	URBAN	RURAL	URBAN
Iran, 1963–1964 (rural) and 1960 (urban)	823	3237	58.5	46.5	0.74[b]	0.67[c]
Egypt, 1958–1959	3037	3145	64.3	48.3	0.72[d]	0.63[e]
Sudan, 1960–1961	352	94	59.0	54.0	0.84	0.76
Morocco, 1959–1960	2370	1955	75.9	59.7	0.88	0.90
Mexico, 1960	2364	——	——	——	0.77	0.67
Malaysia, 1957–1958	——	——	60.0	55.8	0.52	0.64

SOURCE: Paris, Quirino (1970). "An Appraisal of 'Income' Elasticities for Total
Food Consumption in Developing Countries." Technical Papers, Development Centre of the Organization for Economic Cooperation and
Development.   Paris, p. 49.
[a] Each estimate is based upon the logarithmic functional form.
[b] 0.69 using semilog function, 0.61 using log-inverse; valuated at the weighted
means of consumption and total expenditures.
[c] 0.68 using semilog function, 0.62 using log-inverse.
[d] 0.74 using semilog function, 0.73 using log-inverse.
[e] 0.68 using semilog function, 0.58 using log-inverse.

10.3   A New Functional Form for Estimating the Income Elasticity of Food Demand

One of the key issues in estimating the income elasticity of food
demand is the appropriate functional form.   There seems to be clear
empirical support for the proposition that the income elasticity is
below 1 and declines as income rises.   Therefore, economists are often
dissatisfied with estimating a logarithmic functional form for food consumption that exhibits a constant income elasticity; rather, they prefer
to utilize such functional forms as the semilog, the log-inverse, or the
log–log-inverse.   Unfortunately, the semilog and log-inverse functional

forms yield a well-defined a priori response of changes in the income
elasticity to changes in the income level; in fact, in our judgment, the
response is too rapid [for an example of the response, see Paris (1970,
p. 50)]; the log–log-inverse form implies that food is an inferior good
at high income levels.

Fortunately, there exists another functional form, suggested by
Zarembka (1968) in another context, that introduces an additional
parameter for characterizing the response of the income elasticity to
changes in the level of income. Furthermore, this generalized functional form is rather easy to estimate. The new functional form that
we wish to introduce is a linear relation between a power transformation
λ of food consumption as the dependent variable and the same power
transformation on income as the independent variable:

$$(10.9) \qquad\qquad c_1^\lambda = a_0 + a_1 y^\lambda$$

This functional form has the following properties: (1) If $\lambda = 1$, then we
have a linear relationship between c and y; (2) if $\lambda \to 0$, then we have a
logarithmic relationship;[1] and (3) in general, the income elasticity of
food demand η_y is

$$(10.10) \qquad\qquad \eta_y = a_1\left(\frac{y}{c_1}\right)^\lambda$$

Thus, for example, we have the important property for food-demand
studies that if $\lambda < 0$, the income elasticity declines as income rises
because y/c_1 rises (as long as $0 < \eta_y < 1$). In summary, an additional
parameter is introduced into the food-consumption function which
allows the data to discriminate the behavior of the income elasticity
with changing income level.[2]

---

[1] As indicated in Zarembka (1968, p. 503, footnote 3), by noting that

$$\lim_{\lambda \to 0} \frac{c_1^\lambda - 1}{\lambda} = \ln c_1$$

and similarly for y.

[2] Actually, the functional form could be complicated by utilizing different power
transformations on consumption and income:

$$c_1^{\lambda_1} = a_0 + a_1 y^{\lambda_2}$$

with the logarithmic, semilog, and log-inverse forms [Equations (10.6 to 10.8)]
all special cases. In such a case, $\eta_y = a_1 y^{\lambda_2}/c_1^{\lambda_1}$. Although this functional
form can also be estimated by the technique suggested below, the complication
seems unnecessary; the special case $\lambda_1 = \lambda_2$ still introduces an additional
parameter to describe the variation in the income elasticity as income level rises.

In order to estimate this functional form, first rewrite the function as

(10.11)
$$\frac{c_1^\lambda - 1}{\lambda} = a_0 + a_1 \frac{y^\lambda - 1}{\lambda}$$

where a_0 has been appropriately redefined. This form is preferable to (10.9) only in that it is continuous at $\lambda = 0$ (see footnote 1 on page 208) and has a simpler Jacobian in the likelihood transformation below.[1] Now introduce a stochastic disturbance term u, which is assumed to be normally and independently distributed with zero mean, constant variance, and independent of y:

(10.12)
$$c_1^{(\lambda)} = a_0 + a_1 y^{(\lambda)} + u$$

where (λ) expresses the transformation given by (10.11).[2] Then, using the maximum likelihood approach, the likelihood function in terms of the original N observations is expressed by

$$\mathscr{L}(\theta | \text{data}) = 2\pi^{-N/2} \sigma^{-N} \exp\left\{ \frac{-\sum_{n=1}^{N}[c_1^{(\lambda)} - a_0 - a_1 y^{(\lambda)}]}{2\sigma^2} \right\} J$$

where θ is the vector $(a_0, a_1, \sigma^2, \lambda)$ and J is the Jacobian of the transformation on the dependent variable, or

$$J = \prod_{n=1}^{N} \left| \frac{dc_1^{(\lambda)}}{dc_1} \right| = \prod_{n=1}^{N} c_1^{\lambda - 1}$$

First, the logarithm of the likelihood is maximized with respect to a_0, a_1, and σ^2 given λ. The maximum likelihood estimate of σ^2 for the given λ, $\hat{\sigma}^2(\lambda)$, is then just the estimated variance of the disturbance of the regression of $c_1^{(\lambda)}$ on unity and $y^{(\lambda)}$. Replacing σ^2 by $\hat{\sigma}^2(\lambda)$ in the

[1] Schlesselman (1971) points out that (10.11) is a valid rewriting of (10.9), in the sense that estimates of λ are invariant to changes in units of measuring c_1, only if a constant term a_0 is included in the equation.

[2] Actually, another way of viewing the operator λ is that it is that operator which leads to a normally distributed and homoskedastic disturbance term [see Box and Cox (1964, pp. 211–212)].

Also, as noted in Zarembka (1968, p. 504, footnote 6), the stochastic term u is only approximately normal because the dependent variable cannot take on the full range of values between $-\infty$ and ∞ unless $\lambda = 0$. However, note that even if we utilize the linear functional form, with $\lambda = 1$ here or as in Equation (10.2) or (10.3), then u is still only approximately normal: Food consumption cannot take on negative values. In each of these cases, only a portion of the left-hand tail of u with very low probability is discarded.

maximized log likelihood function, the maximum log likelihood for a given λ, $L_{max}(\lambda)$, is (except for a constant)

$$(10.13) \qquad L_{max}(\lambda) = -\frac{N}{2} \ln \hat{\sigma}^2(\lambda) + (\lambda - 1) \sum_{n=1}^{N} \ln c_1$$

Note that with an appropriate change in units of measurement for c_1, $\sum \ln c_1$ may be set equal to zero.   Then,

$$(10.14) \qquad\qquad\qquad L_{max}(\lambda) = -\frac{N}{2} \ln \hat{\sigma}^2(\lambda)$$

the value of which can be calculated from the output of any regression program.

The value of Equation (10.14) for different values of λ can now be plotted to arrive at the maximized log likelihood over the whole parameter space and the maximizing $\hat{\lambda}$.   Using the likelihood-ratio method, an approximate 95 percent confidence region for λ can be obtained from

$$L_{max}(\hat{\lambda}) - L_{max}(\lambda) < \tfrac{1}{2}\chi_1^2(0.05) = 1.92$$

At the point of maximum likelihood, estimates of a_0, a_1, and σ^2 can also be obtained.

To illustrate the usefulness of our functional form in food-demand studies of developing countries, Equation (10.12) has been estimated with data from the Philippines taken from the 1961 and 1965 household surveys [see Republic of the Philippines (1964, 1968)].   These data provide a total of 72 observations—24 each from metropolitan Manila, other urban areas, and rural areas—for 12 income classes in the two years.   Because the data are grouped by income level and include total expenditures as well as food expenditures, we can obtain an estimate of Equation (10.12) that has the desirable econometric property of consistency (see page 198).   Furthermore, average household-size data are also available so that any economies-of-scale effects of household size can be introduced.   Thus, the only potentially important econometric problem with estimating the food-consumption function that is not corrected for here is the possible increase of food quality at higher-income levels.

The precise equation that we estimate is

$$(10.15) \qquad c_1^{(\lambda)} = a_0 + d_U + d_M + d_Y + a_1 y^{(\lambda)} + a_2 h^{(\lambda)} + u$$

where

c_1 = food consumption per household divided by average household size (giving food consumption per capita)

d_U = dummy variable for urban (including metropolitan Manila) areas

d_M = dummy variable for metropolitan Manila only

d_Y = dummy variable for year (1961 is zero)

y = total expenditures per household divided by average household size (giving total expenditures per capita)

h = average household size

u = disturbance term (as discussed above)

In other words, average household size is included with the same power transformation as consumption and total expenditures. Also, both urban and rural observations are included in the same estimating equation; but a dummy variable is included for urban areas to ascertain whether the consumption function shifts from rural to urban areas, and a dummy variable is included separately for metropolitan Manila to ascertain if the consumption function differs there from other urban areas. A shift in either case would be due to regional price variation of food or of other goods or taste differences. Additionally, a dummy variable is included to represent any shift between 1961 and 1965 due to price or taste changes.

Before running the regression after each λ power transformation, each dependent and independent variable before any transformation is multiplied by the square root of the number of sample households in the grouped aggregate.[1] Regressions are then undertaken for the alternative values of λ, and the values of $L_{\max}(\lambda)$ given by Equation (10.14) are calculated. These values are then plotted.

In Figure 10.1 the likelihood curve for λ in Equation (10.15) is given for both when food consumption refers to total food consumption and when it refers to cereals only. As can be seen, the maximum likelihood estimate of λ for total food is -0.53, with an approximate 95 percent confidence interval of $(-0.67, -0.39)$. For cereals only, the estimate of λ is -0.46, with a 95 percent confidence interval of $(-0.66, -0.24)$.

---

[1] Actually obtained by multiplying reported population in a grouped aggregate by the sampling ratio of households sampled to total households (for 1961, 1:850 in rural areas and 1:425 in urban areas; for 1965, 1:1717 in rural areas and 1:574 in urban areas).

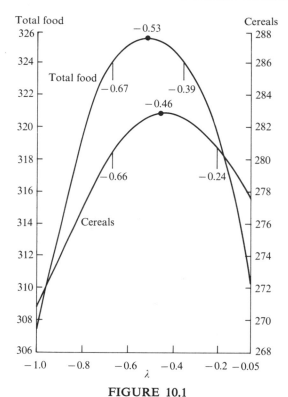

FIGURE 10.1

Values of $L_{max}(\lambda)$ using 1961 and 1965 Philippine household data

Thus, because $\lambda < 0$, the income elasticity of food demand does decline with rising income; the logarithmic functional form, with $\lambda = 0$ (and, of course, the linear form with $\lambda = 1$) is indeed inappropriate for food demand. We report the pattern of this decline below.

In Table 10.4 the estimates of the coefficients at the points of maximum likelihood are reported. First, for both total food and cereals only, there is a downward shift in the consumption function as we move from rural to urban Philippines; moreover, the shift is further increased as we move into metropolitan Manila. This shift may be due to higher food prices in urban areas, a lower taste for food in urban areas, or a higher propensity to consume home-produced goods [i.e., in rural areas (see p. 204)]. Second, in both results the consumption function shifts upward in 1965 relative to 1961. This result may be due to lower food

TABLE 10.4
Estimates of Equation (10.15) Using 1961 and 1965 Philippine Household Data

	$\hat{\lambda}$	CONSTANT	$\hat{d}_U$	$\hat{d}_M$	$\hat{d}_Y$	$\hat{d}_1$	$\hat{d}_2$
Total food	−0.53	−35.11	−0.019	−0.013	0.108	19.65	−0.478
		(0.54)	(0.008)	(0.012)	(0.010)	(0.36)	(0.099)
Cereals only	−0.46	−14.99	−0.095	−0.172	0.273	7.673	−0.563
		(0.70)	(0.015)	(0.022)	(0.018)	(0.427)	(0.157)

SOURCE: See the text discussion. The units of measurements for total food have been adjusted by dividing each observation by $e^{(5.5149)}$; for cereals only, by $e^{(4.4138)}$ so that the mean of the logarithm of c_1 is zero in both cases (see page 210).

213

TABLE 10.5

Values of the Income Elasticity of Food Demand for Varying Ratios
of Food Consumption to Total Expenditures

Total food					
$\dfrac{c_1}{y}$	0.70	0.60	0.50	0.40	0.30
η_y	0.875	0.806	0.732	0.650	0.558
Cereals only					
$\dfrac{c_1}{y}$		0.30	0.20	0.10	0.05
η_y		0.579	0.481	0.349	0.254

SOURCE: Equation (10.10) with coefficient values given in Table 10.4. The range
of c_1/y is the approximate range of the Philippine data.

prices in 1965 or a taste change toward food. Third, the coefficient of
household size is negative and statistically significant. Thus, there are
economies of scale from a larger household size.

The income elasticity of food demand given by Equation (10.10) is
reported in Table 10.5 for a varying ratio of food consumption to
total expenditures. Note that the change in the income elasticity with
rising income level (falling c_1/y) is definitely evident but not nearly as
rapid as suggested by the semilog or log-inverse functional forms [see
Paris (1970, p. 50)]. Note also that, as suggested by other studies, the
income elasticity of demand for cereals is decidedly below that for total
food.

10.4 Summary

The results from estimating the new functional form of food demand
are consistent with independent results of other researchers but give a
more accurate description of the response of the income elasticity of
food demand to changing income levels. We have thus seen that, at
very low levels of income, the income elasticity for total food is in the
order of 0.8 to 0.9 and falls rather slowly as income rises. However,
the income elasticity of demand for cereals (foodgrains) is considerably
lower than that for total food. We have also seen that there are
economies of scale in food consumption for larger household size.
Further, we have seen that urban households, particularly in larger

urban areas, consume less food than rural households but that this difference may only be due to higher urban food prices (an untested hypothesis).

The most important implication of these results is that the dependency of a developing economy upon its agricultural sector declines as its income level rises because the income elasticity of food demand is both below unity and falling.   Thus, given a theoretical framework such as in Chapter 2, the growth rate of real wages increases somewhat as income level rises ceteris paribus.   Furthermore, there is virtually conclusive evidence that the foodgrain income elasticity is below that for total food (but well above zero), so that the structure of food demand shifts away from foodgrains as income rises.   Finally, there is some suggestive evidence that a decline in average family size, which could result from lower birth rates, will somewhat increase food demand.

APPENDICES

Appendix A

THE ASYMPTOTIC CAPITAL/OUTPUT RATIO FOR THE SECONDARY SECTOR

In this appendix, the asymptotic capital/output ratio for a Cobb–Douglas production function is derived given a constant rate s of output being reinvested. Using the notation in Chapter 2 for secondary sector production but dropping subscripts, we have

$$Y = e^{bt} K^{1-\beta} L^{\beta}$$

$$I = sY$$

$$\dot{K} = I - \delta K$$

Therefore,

$$\frac{\dot{Y}}{Y} = b + (1 - \beta)\frac{\dot{K}}{K} + \beta\frac{\dot{L}}{L}$$

or

$$\frac{\dot{Y}}{Y} - \frac{\dot{K}}{K} = b - \beta\frac{\dot{K}}{K} + \beta\frac{\dot{L}}{L}$$

$$= b - \beta s\frac{Y}{K} + \beta\delta + \beta\frac{\dot{L}}{L}$$

after substituting for $\dot{K}$ and I. However,

$$\left(\frac{\dot{K}}{Y}\right) = \frac{K}{Y}\left(\frac{\dot{K}}{K} - \frac{\dot{Y}}{Y}\right)$$

so that

(A.1) $$\left(\frac{\dot{K}}{Y}\right) = -\left(b + \beta\delta + \beta\frac{\dot{L}}{L}\right)\frac{K}{Y} + \beta s$$

Now, taking the rate of change in employment to be determined by the change in labor supply and thus independent of the capital/output ratio (as is the case in Chapter 2 when the price elasticity of food demand is zero), Equation (A.1) is a simple first-order differential equation of the form

$$\dot{x} = cx + \delta$$

which has a solution

$$x = \frac{e^{ct+k} - \delta}{c}$$

where k is some constant. In other words,

(A.2) $$\frac{K}{Y} = \frac{\beta s}{b + \beta\delta + \beta(\dot{L}/L)} - \frac{e^k}{b + \beta\delta + \beta(\dot{L}/L)}\, e^{-[b + \beta\delta + \beta(\dot{L}/L)]t}$$

Therefore, the asymptotic capital/output ratio given $\dot{L}/L$ is obtained by letting $t \to \infty$, or

(A.3) $$\left(\frac{K}{Y}\right)_\infty = \frac{\beta s}{b + \beta\delta + \beta(\dot{L}/L)} = \frac{s}{b/\beta + \delta + \dot{L}/L}$$

Note that the asymptotic capital/output ratio is directly related to the savings rate s. As an example of the value of this asymptotic capital/output ratio, suppose that $s = 0.3$, $b/\beta = 0.02$, $\delta = 0.05$, and $\dot{L}/L = 0.05$. Then,

$$\left(\frac{K}{Y}\right)_\infty = 2.50$$

The second term on the right-hand side of Equation (A.2) can be calculated by using the initial condition that $K/Y = (K/Y)_0$ at time $t = 0$. Then Equation (A.2) becomes

(A.4) $$\frac{K}{Y} = \left(\frac{K}{Y}\right)_\infty + \left[\left(\frac{K}{Y}\right)_0 - \left(\frac{K}{Y}\right)_\infty\right]e^{-[b + \beta\delta + \beta(\dot{L}/L)]t}$$

This solution implies that the gap between any current capital/output ratio and the asymptotic capital/output ratio declines at the rate $b + \beta\delta + \beta(\dot{L}/L)$ annually. Using the parameter values given in the preceding paragraph, this rate equals 9 percent annually, while the gap is closed by 50 percent after eight years. In other words, the capital/output ratio does not approach its asymptote quickly.

Appendix B

EXACT SOLUTION OF THE MODEL OF CHAPTER 2

In this appendix, the exact solution of the model in Chapter 2 is provided for a point in time, given the distribution of the labor force between the primary and secondary sectors and given the current value of the capital/output in manufacturing. It is also demonstrated how to reinterpret the solution in the text to give exact results. First, substitute Equation (2.11) into (2.10) to obtain

$$[\beta_1(1 - \alpha_1 - \eta_1) + \alpha_1 + \eta_1] \left[\epsilon\left(1 + \frac{L_2}{L_1}\right) - \frac{\dot{L}_2}{L_2}\frac{L_2}{L_1} \right]$$

$$= \epsilon - (1 - \alpha_1 - \eta_1)b_1$$

$$- \eta_1 \left[b_2 + (1 - \beta_2)^2 \frac{Y_2}{K_2} - (1 - \beta_2)\delta - (1 - \beta_2)\frac{\dot{L}_2}{L_2} \right]$$

In other words,

$$-[\beta_1(1 - \alpha_1 - \eta_1) + \alpha_1 + \eta_1]\frac{\dot{L}_2}{L_2}\frac{L_2}{L_1} - \eta_1(1 - \beta_2)\frac{\dot{L}_2}{L_2}$$

$$= -[\beta_1(1 - \alpha_1 - \eta_1) + \alpha_1 + \eta_1]\epsilon\left(1 + \frac{L_2}{L_1}\right)$$

$$- \eta_1(1 - \beta_2)\epsilon + \eta_1(1 - \beta_2)\epsilon + \epsilon - (1 - \alpha_1 - \eta_1)b_1$$

$$- \eta_1 \left[b_2 + (1 - \beta_2)^2 \frac{Y_2}{K_2} - (1 - \beta_2)\delta \right]$$

Therefore, solving for $\dot{L}_2/L_2$,

$$\frac{\dot{L}_2}{L_2} = \epsilon + \frac{\begin{array}{l}[\beta_1(1 - \alpha_1 - \eta_1) + \alpha_1 + \eta_1]\epsilon - \eta_1(1 - \beta_2)\epsilon - \epsilon \\ + (1 - \alpha_1 - \eta_1)b_1 + \eta_1[b_2 + (1 - \beta_2)^2(Y_2/K_2) - (1 - \beta_2)\delta]\end{array}}{[\beta_1(1 - \alpha_1 - \eta_1) + \alpha_1 + \eta_1](L_2/L_1) + \eta_1(1 - \beta_2)}$$

or

(B.1)
$$\frac{\dot{L}_2}{L_2} = \epsilon + \frac{\begin{array}{l}[b_1 - (1 - \beta_1)\epsilon](1 - \alpha_1 - \eta_1) \\ + \eta_1\{b_2 - (1 - \beta_2)[\epsilon + \delta - (1 - \beta_2)(Y_2/K_2)]\}\end{array}}{[1 - (1 - \beta_1)(1 - \alpha_1 - \eta_1)](L_2/L_1) + \eta_1(1 - \beta_2)}$$

Comparing this exact solution of secondary sector labor-force growth with the solution in the text (2.14), it can be seen that, on grounds of simplicity, the solution in the text is preferable. However, if the capital/output ratio (2.12) assumed in the text differs considerably from empirically observed values, then some realism has been lost. We now show how departures from the capital/output ratio assumed in (2.12) affect the solution.

Suppose that we label the output/capital ratio given by (2.12) as

$$\frac{Y_2}{K_{2\infty}} = \frac{b_2/\beta_2 + \delta + \dot{L}_2/L_{2\infty}}{1 - \beta_2}$$

where $\dot{L}_2/L_{2\infty}$ is given by (2.14). Then, Y_2/K_2 in (B.1) can be written

$$\frac{Y_2}{K_2} = \frac{Y_2}{K_2} - \frac{Y_2}{K_{2\infty}} + \frac{b_2/\beta_2 + \delta + \dot{L}_2/L_2}{1 - \beta_2} - \frac{\dot{L}_2/L_2 - \dot{L}_2/L_{2\infty}}{1 - \beta_2}$$

Therefore, (B.1) can be written

(B.2)
$$\frac{\dot{L}_2}{L_2} = \epsilon + \frac{L_1}{L_2}\frac{\begin{array}{l}[b_1 - (1 - \beta_1)\epsilon](1 - \alpha_1 - \eta_1) \\ + \eta_1[b_2/\beta_2 + (1 - \beta_2)^2(Y_2/K_2 - Y_2/K_{2\infty}) \\ - (1 - \beta_2)(\dot{L}_2/L_2 - \dot{L}_2/L_{2\infty})]\end{array}}{1 - (1 - \beta_1)(1 - \alpha_1 - \eta_1)}$$

so that, using (2.14),

$$\frac{\dot{L}_2}{L_2} - \frac{\dot{L}_2}{L_{2\infty}} = \frac{\dot{L}_2}{L_2} - \epsilon - \frac{L_1}{L_2}\frac{\eta_1(b_2/\beta_2) + [b_1 - (1 - \beta_1)\epsilon](1 - \alpha_1 - \eta_1)}{1 - (1 - \beta_1)(1 - \alpha_1 - \eta_1)}$$

$$= \frac{L_1}{L_2}\frac{\begin{array}{l}\eta_1(1 - \beta_2)^2(Y_2/K_2 - Y_2/K_{2\infty}) \\ - \eta_1(1 - \beta_2)(\dot{L}_2/L_2 - \dot{L}_2/L_{2\infty})\end{array}}{1 - (1 - \beta_1)(1 - \alpha_1 - \eta_1)}$$

Solving for $\dot{L}_2/L_2 - \dot{L}_2/L_{2\infty}$,

$$\frac{\dot{L}_2}{L_2} - \frac{\dot{L}_2}{L_{2\infty}} = \frac{\eta_1(1 - \beta_2)^2(Y_2/K_2 - Y_2/K_{2\infty})}{(L_2/L_1)[1 - (1 - \beta_1)(1 - \alpha_1 - \eta_1)] + \eta_1(1 - \beta_2)}$$

and substituting for the same in (B.2), the term

$$\frac{b_2}{\beta_2} + (1 - \beta_2)^2\left(\frac{Y_2}{K_2} - \frac{Y_2}{K_{2\,\infty}}\right) - (1 - \beta_2)\left(\frac{\dot{L}_2}{L_2} - \frac{\dot{L}_2}{L_{2\,\infty}}\right)$$

becomes

(B.3) $\quad \dfrac{b_2}{\beta_2} + \dfrac{(1 - \beta_2)^2(Y_2/K_2 - Y_2/K_{2\infty})}{1 + (L_1/L_2)\eta_1(1 - \beta_2)/[1 - (1 - \beta_1)(1 - \alpha_1 - \eta_1)]}$

But, note that Equation (B.2) is now merely Equation (2.14) with b_2/β_2 replaced by (B.3). In other words, the exact solution for $\dot{L}_2/L_2$ can be obtained simply by reinterpreting b_2/β_2 in Equation (2.14).

For example, if secondary sector capital stock is low so that the current output/capital ratio is high (relative to the long-run value), then b_2/β_2 in Equation (2.14) must be reinterpreted to a larger value which includes the fact that the current output/capital ratio is high. However, of course, if $\eta_1 = 0$, then the value of $\dot{L}_2/L_2$ remains unchanged.

Given the exact solution for $\dot{L}_2/L_2$, $\dot{Y}_2/Y_2 - \dot{L}_2/L_2$ can be obtained from (2.11). Thus,

$$\frac{\dot{Y}_2}{Y_2} - \frac{\dot{L}_2}{L_2} = b_2 + (1 - \beta_2)^2\frac{Y_2}{K_2} - (1 - \beta_2)\delta - (1 - \beta_2)\frac{\dot{L}_2}{L_2}$$

$$= \frac{b_2}{\beta_2} + (1 - \beta_2)^2\left(\frac{Y_2}{K_2} - \frac{Y_2}{K_{2\,\infty}}\right) - (1 - \beta_2)\left(\frac{\dot{L}_2}{L_2} - \frac{\dot{L}_2}{L_{2\,\infty}}\right)$$

or (B.3). Therefore, $\dot{Y}_2/Y_2 = \dot{I}_2/I_2$ equals $\dot{L}_2/L_2$ *plus* (B.3)—the same reinterpretation of b_2/β_2 is required. As in the text, exact solutions for $\dot{L}_1/L_1$, $\dot{Y}_1/Y_1$, and $\dot{q}_1/q_1$ can easily be obtained and also merely lead to replacing b_2/β_2 by (B.3).

On the other hand,

(B.4) $\quad \dfrac{\dot{K}_2}{K_2} = (1 - \beta_2)\dfrac{Y_2}{K_2} - \delta$

$$= (1 - \beta_2)\left(\frac{Y_2}{K_2} - \frac{Y_2}{K_{2\,\infty}}\right) + \frac{b_2}{\beta_2} + \delta + \frac{\dot{L}_2}{L_{2\,\infty}} - \delta$$

or

(B.5) $\quad \dfrac{\dot{K}_2}{K_2} = \dfrac{b_2}{\beta_2} + (1 - \beta_2)\left(\dfrac{Y_2}{K_2} - \dfrac{Y_2}{K_{2\,\infty}}\right) + \dfrac{\dot{L}_2}{L_{2\,\infty}}$

Thus, for this one variable, b_2/β_2 must be reinterpreted to be $b_2/\beta_2 + (1 - \beta_2)(Y_2/K_2 - Y_2/K_{2\infty})$, not (B.3), and $\dot{L}_2/L_{2\infty}$ should still be used, not the exact $\dot{L}_2/L_2$. However, (B.4) can be used directly.

Appendix C

THE PONTRYAGIN PROBLEM
FOR CHAPTER 4

This appendix sets up the Pontryagin optimal control problem for the consumption and work-hour choices of Section 4.3 and indicates the special case implying the problem of Section 4.2 (when work hours are fixed). The problem of consumption and work-hour choice of Section 4.3 is to maximize

$$U(a) = \int_a^\infty \ell(t)e^{-mt}u[c(t),H(t)]\, dt$$

subject to the equality constraints

$$\dot{\ell}(t) = \ell(t)\{d(t) + f[c(t)]\}$$
$$\dot{S}(t) = y^*[t,H(t)] + rS(t) - c(t)$$

and the inequality constraint

$$S(t) \geqq 0$$

This problem may be rewritten, after dropping time subscripts,

$$\text{Max } U(a) = \int_a^\infty Du(c, H)\, dt$$

subject to

$$\dot{D} = -D[d + f(c) + m]$$
$$\dot{S} = y^*(t,H) + rS - c$$

and

$$S \geqq 0$$

The Hamiltonian G for this problem is

$$G = Du(c,H) + p_1 \dot{D} + p_2 \dot{S}$$
$$= Du(c,H) - p_1 D[d + f(c) + m] + p_2[y^*(t,H) + rS - c]$$

where p_1 and p_2 are the imputed prices of the constraints. The Lagrangian K is therefore

$$K = Du(c,H) - p_1 D[d + f(c) + m] + p_2[y^*(t,H) + rS - c]$$
$$+ \lambda_2[y^*(t,H) + rS - c]$$

where λ_2 is a Lagrangian multiplier for the inequality constraint such that

$$\lambda_2 \geqq 0 \qquad \lambda_2 S = 0 \qquad \text{and} \qquad \lambda_2 \dot{S} = 0$$

That is, the Lagrangian multiplier λ_2 is zero in the interior of the solution (when $S > 0$) and is greater than zero along the boundary (when $S = 0$).

For a maximum,

$$(C.1) \qquad \frac{\partial K}{\partial c} = \frac{D \, \partial u(c,H)}{\partial c} - p_1 D f'(c) - p_2 - \lambda_2 = 0$$

and

$$(C.2) \qquad \frac{\partial K}{\partial H} = \frac{D \, \partial u(c,H)}{\partial H} + \frac{p_2 \, \partial y^*(t,H)}{\partial H} + \frac{\lambda_2 \, \partial y^*(t,H)}{\partial H} = 0$$

with $\qquad \dot{p}_1 = -\dfrac{\partial K}{\partial D} \qquad$ and $\qquad \dot{p}_2 = -\dfrac{\partial K}{\partial S}$

or

$$(C.3) \qquad \dot{p}_1 = -u(c,H) + p_1[d + f(c) + m]$$

and

$$(C.4) \qquad \dot{p}_2 = -(p_2 + \lambda_2)r$$

and with

$$(C.5) \qquad \dot{D} = -D[d + f(c) + m]$$

and

$$(C.6) \qquad \dot{S} = y^*(t,H) + rS - c$$

This system of six differential equations in the six unknowns c, H, D, S, p_1, p_2 and the Lagrangian λ_2 can be restated by writing (C.1) as

$$\text{(C.7)} \qquad p_2 + \lambda_2 = \frac{D \, \partial u(c,H)}{\partial c} - p_1 D f'(c)$$

and then substituting into (C.2) to give

$$\text{(C.8)} \qquad \partial u(c,H)/\partial H + \frac{\partial u(c,H)}{\partial c} \frac{\partial y^*(t,H)}{\partial H} = p_1 f'(c) \frac{\partial y^*(t,H)}{\partial H}$$

where division by D is permitted because $D > 0$. The system then consists of Equations (C.3) through (C.8).

In the text, Equation (C.8) is Equation (4.10). If work hours are fixed, then the other five equations provide the system that must be solved in the optimal control problem of Section 4.2. However, the solution for c in the latter case leads to a third-order nonlinear differential equation when the inequality constraint is not binding (i.e., in the interior of the solution where $\lambda_2 = 0$).

One additional result for the consumption and work-hour-choice case is worth obtaining; that is, it is possible to provide expressions for the time rate of change both in the marginal disutility of work along the optimum interior path and in the marginal total disutility of work along the boundary. First, when $\lambda_2 = 0$ (in the interior), Equation (C.2) and (C.4) become, respectively,

$$\frac{D \, \partial u(c,H)}{\partial H} + \frac{p_2 \, \partial y^*(t,H)}{\partial H} = 0$$

and

$$\dot{p}_2 = -p_2 r$$

The first equation can be written

$$p_2 = -\frac{D \, \partial u(c,H)/\partial H}{\partial y^*(t,H)/\partial H}$$

because $\partial y^*(t,H)/\partial H > 0$, so that

$$\dot{p}_2 = -\frac{[\partial y^*(t,H)/\partial H][\dot{D} \, \partial u(c,H)/\partial H + D \, \partial^2 u(c,H)/(\partial t \, \partial H)]}{[\partial y^*(t,H)/\partial H]^2}$$

$$+ \frac{[D \, \partial u(c,H)/\partial H][\partial^2 y^*(t,H)/(\partial t \, \partial H)]}{[\partial y^*(t,H)/\partial H]^2}$$

Thus, substituting into the second equation and multiplying by $\partial y^*(t,H)/\partial H$ and dividing by $\partial u(c,H)/\partial H) < 0$, we have

$$-\dot{D} - D\,\frac{\partial^2 u(c,H)/(\partial t\,\partial H)}{\partial u(c,H)/\partial H} + D\,\frac{\partial^2 y^*(t,H)/(\partial t\,\partial H)}{\partial y^*(t,H)/\partial H} = rD$$

Substituting Equation (C.5) for $\dot{D}$ and dividing by $D > 0$ gives, after rearranging,

$$(C.9) \qquad -\frac{\partial^2 u(c,H)/(\partial t\,\partial H)}{\partial u(c,H)/\partial H} = r - d - f(c) - m - \frac{\partial^2 y^*(t,H)/(\partial t\,\partial H)}{\partial y^*(t,H)/\partial H}$$

The left-hand term is the rate of change in the disutility of work along the optimum interior path (without the negative sign, the term is the rate of change in the marginal utility of work where the marginal utility is negative). The right-hand term is the rate of return on savings *less* the subjective rate of discount *less* the rate of change in the marginal productivity of a work hour. If the rate of change of the marginal productivity of work is zero (e.g., for workers whose choice of work hours does not influence their wage and who expect no changes in wage), then the equation reduces to

$$(C.10) \qquad -\frac{\partial^2 u(c,H)/(\partial t\,\partial H)}{\partial u(c,H)/\partial H} = r - d - f(c) - m$$

Finally, assume that the utility function is separable so that the level of consumption does not affect the marginal disutility of work. Then, when the right-hand side is negative [e.g., at low-income levels, so that $f(c)$ is high], the marginal disutility of work is decreasing over time, implying that work hours are decreasing over time. In other words, at low-income levels, the worker *plans* (subject to revision) to work hard now, to increase the probability of survival, and to relax more later. However, the discussion in these last three paragraphs is all under the assumption that the consumer is in the interior of his solution when, in fact, such a presupposition is improbable at low income.

The equation along the boundary, corresponding to Equation (C.9), is more complicated than (C.9). The solution, obtained by using Equations (C.8) and (C.3), implies that the left-hand side of (C.9) is reinterpreted as the percentage rate of change in marginal total disutility with respect to work hours [i.e., the percentage rate of change in the (negative of the) left-hand side of Equation (C.8)], while r is reinterpreted as

$$r = \frac{-f'(c)[\partial y^*(t,H)/\partial H]}{\Delta} - \frac{f''(c)}{f'(c)}\dot{c}$$

where Δ is the ratio of the marginal total disutility of work to the total disutility. With $c = y^*(t,H)$ on the boundary, this may be rewritten

$$r = f(c)\frac{[-cf'(c)/f(c)]\{H[\partial y^*(t,H)/\partial H]/y^*(t,H)\}}{H\Delta} - c\frac{f''(c)}{f'(c)}\frac{\dot{c}}{c}$$

In other words, the rate of return is reinterpreted as the probability of dying times the absolute value of the elasticity of that probability with respect to work hours divided by the elasticity of total disutility with respect to work hours (positive) *minus* the elasticity of the change in the probability of dying due to more consumption (positive or negative) times the percent rate of change in consumption. When wages are constant, as in Equation (4.7), the elasticity of the probability of dying with respect to work hours is the same as the elasticity of that probability with respect to consumption.

Appendix D

SOLUTION FOR THE GROWTH RATE OF REAL WAGES (SECTION 6.1)

First, define g_2 such that

$$g_2 \equiv \frac{\dot{Y}_2}{Y_2} - \frac{\dot{L}_2}{L_2} = b_2 + (1 - \beta_2)\left(\frac{\dot{K}_2}{K_2} - \frac{\dot{L}_2}{L_2}\right)$$

Then,

$$\frac{\dot{K}_2}{K_2} = \frac{g_2 - b_2}{1 - \beta_2} + \frac{\dot{L}_2}{L_2}$$

However, from (5.22),

$$\frac{\dot{M}_2}{M_2} = \tau + \frac{\dot{Y}_x}{Y_x} = \tau + b_x + \frac{\beta_1}{1 - \beta_1}\left(b_1 - \frac{\dot{w}_1}{w_1}\right) - \frac{L_1}{L_x}\frac{\dot{A}_1}{A_1}$$

Consequently, equating $\dot{M}_2/M_2$ with $\dot{K}_2/K_2$ and using (5.23),

$$\tau + b_x + \frac{\beta_1}{1 - \beta_1}\left(b_1 - \frac{\dot{w}_1}{w_1}\right) - \frac{L_1}{L_x}\frac{\dot{A}_1}{A_1}$$

$$= \frac{g_2 - b_2}{1 - \beta_2} + \epsilon + \frac{L_1 + L_x}{L_2}\frac{\dot{w}_1/w_1 - [b_1 - (1 - \beta_1)\epsilon]}{1 - \beta_1}$$

or

$$(1 - \beta_1)(\tau + b_x) + \beta_1\left(b_1 - \frac{\dot{w}_1}{w_1}\right) - (1 - \beta_1)\frac{L_1}{L_x}\frac{\dot{A}_1}{A_1}$$

$$= \frac{1 - \beta_1}{1 - \beta_2}(g_2 - b_2) + (1 - \beta_1)\epsilon + \frac{L_1 + L_x}{L_2}\left\{\frac{\dot{w}_1}{w_1} - [b_1 - (1 - \beta_1)\epsilon]\right\}$$

Using (5.18) and remembering that $g_2 = \dot{w}_1/w_1 - b_1 + b_x + \tau$,

$$(1 - \beta_1)(\tau + b_x) + \beta_1\left(b_1 - \frac{\dot{w}_1}{w_1}\right)$$

$$- \frac{L_1}{L_x}\left\{[1 - (1 - \beta_1)(1 - \alpha_1)]\frac{\dot{w}_1}{w_1} - [b_1 - (1 - \beta_1)\epsilon]\right\}$$

$$= \frac{1 - \beta_1}{1 - \beta_2}\left(\frac{\dot{w}_1}{w_1} - b_1 + b_x + \tau - b_2\right) + (1 - \beta_1)\epsilon$$

$$+ \frac{L_1 + L_x}{L_2}\left\{\frac{\dot{w}_1}{w_1} - [b_1 - (1 - \beta_1)\epsilon]\right\}$$

In other words,

$$(1 - \beta_1)(\tau + b_x) + \beta_1 b_1 + \frac{L_1}{L_x}[b_1 - (1 - \beta_1)\epsilon]$$

$$+ \frac{1 - \beta_1}{1 - \beta_2}(b_2 + b_1 - b_x - \tau) - (1 - \beta_1)\epsilon + \frac{L_1 + L_x}{L_2}[b_1 - (1 - \beta_1)\epsilon]$$

$$= \frac{\dot{w}_1}{w_1}\left\{\beta_1 + \frac{L_1}{L_x}[1 - (1 - \beta_1)(1 - \alpha_1)] + \frac{1 - \beta_1}{1 - \beta_2} + \frac{L_1 + L_x}{L_2}\right\}$$

or

$$\frac{\dot{w}_1}{w_1}\left\{\frac{L}{L_2}\frac{L_1}{L_x}[1 - (1 - \beta_1)(1 - \alpha_1)] + \frac{1 - \beta_1}{1 - \beta_2} - (1 - \beta_1)\right\}$$

$$= (1 - \beta_1)(\tau + b_x - b_1 - b_2) + (1 - \beta_1)(b_1 + b_2)$$

$$+ \beta_1 b_1 + \frac{L_1}{L_x}[b_1 - (1 - \beta_1)\epsilon]$$

$$+ \frac{1 - \beta_1}{1 - \beta_2}(b_2 + b_1 - b_x - \tau)\frac{L}{L_2}[b_1 - (1 - \beta_1)\epsilon] - b_1$$

Therefore, $\dot{w}_1/w_1$ becomes

$$\frac{\dot{w}_1}{w_1} = \frac{(L/L_2 + L_1/L_x)[b_1 - (1 - \beta_1)\epsilon] + [(1 - \beta_1)/(1 - \beta_2)]\beta_2(b_2/\beta_2 + b_1 - b_x - \tau)}{L/L_2 + L_1/L_x[1 - (1 - \beta_1)(1 - \alpha_1)] + [(1 - \beta_1)/(1 - \beta_2)]\beta_2}$$

Appendix E

THE PROFIT FUNCTION FOR THE THREE-FACTOR CES PRODUCTION FUNCTION (SECTION 8.3)

First, total profits π are

$$\pi = p[(\beta L)^\rho + (\alpha F)^\rho + (\gamma A)^\rho]^{1/\rho} - wL - c_f F$$

where p is the output price. Therefore, for profit maximization,

$$\frac{\partial \pi}{\partial L} = p[(\beta L)^\rho + (\alpha F)^\rho + (\gamma A)^\rho]^{1/\rho - 1}(\beta L)^{\rho - 1}\beta - w$$

$$= p\frac{y^{1-\rho}}{L^{1-\rho}}\beta^\rho - w = 0$$

and, similarly,

$$\frac{\partial \pi}{\partial F} = p\frac{y^{1-\rho}}{F^{1-\rho}}\alpha^\rho - c_f = 0$$

Therefore,

$$\frac{F^{1-\rho}}{L^{1-\rho}}\frac{\beta^\rho}{\alpha^\rho} = \frac{w}{c_f}$$

or

$$\frac{F}{L} = \left[\frac{w}{c_f}\frac{\alpha^\rho}{\beta^\rho}\right]^{1/(1-\rho)}$$

Thus, substituting back into the profit equation,

$$\pi = p\left\{(\beta L)^\rho + \left[\alpha\left(\frac{w}{f}\frac{\alpha^\rho}{\beta^\rho}\right)^{1/(1-\rho)}L\right]^\rho + (\gamma A)^\rho\right\}^{1/\rho} - wL$$

$$- c_f\left(\frac{w}{c_f}\frac{\alpha^\rho}{\beta^\rho}\right)^{1/(1-\rho)}L$$

$$= p\left\{\left[\beta^\rho + \alpha^\rho\left(\frac{w}{f}\frac{\alpha^\rho}{\beta^\rho}\right)^{\rho/(1-\rho)}\right]L^\rho + (\gamma A)^\rho\right\}^{1/\rho} - \left[w + c_f\left(\frac{w}{c_f}\frac{\alpha^\rho}{\beta^\rho}\right)^{1/(1-\rho)}\right]L$$

Now, let

$$w' = w + c_f\left(\frac{w}{c_f}\frac{\alpha^\rho}{\beta^\rho}\right)^{1/(1-\rho)}$$

$$= w\left[1 + \left(\frac{w}{c_f}\frac{\alpha}{\beta}\right)^{\sigma-1}\right]$$

and

$$\beta' = \left[\beta^\rho + \alpha^\rho\left(\frac{w}{c_f}\frac{\alpha^\rho}{\beta^\rho}\right)^{\rho/(1-\rho)}\right]^{1/\rho}$$

$$= \beta\left[1 + \left(\frac{w}{c_f}\frac{\alpha}{\beta}\right)^{\sigma-1}\right]^{\sigma/(\sigma-1)} = \beta\left(\frac{w}{w'}\right)^{\sigma/(1-\sigma)}$$

Then, we have another CES production function for which

$$\pi = p[(\beta'L)^\rho + (\gamma A)^\rho]^{1/\rho} - w'L$$

Thus,

$$\frac{\partial \pi}{\partial L} = p[(\beta'L)^\rho + (\gamma A)^\rho]^{1/\rho-1}(\beta'L)^{\rho-1}\beta' - w' = 0$$

Therefore,

$$[(\beta'L)^\rho + (\gamma A)^\rho]^{(1-\rho)/\rho}L^{\rho-1}\beta'^\rho = \frac{w'}{p}$$

or

$$\left[\beta'^\rho + \left(\frac{\gamma A}{L}\right)^\rho\right]^{(1-\rho)/\rho} = \frac{w'}{p}\beta'^{-\rho}$$

or

$$\beta'^\rho + \left(\frac{\gamma A}{L}\right)^\rho = \left(\frac{w'}{p}\beta'^{-\rho}\right)^{\rho/(1-\rho)}$$

Thus,

$$\frac{\gamma A}{L} = \left[\left(\frac{w'}{p} \beta'^{-\rho} \right)^{\rho/(1-\rho)} - \beta'^{\rho} \right]^{1/\rho}$$

Therefore,

$$\pi = p\left[\beta'^{\rho} + \left(\frac{\gamma A}{L} \right)^{\rho} \right]^{1/\rho} L - w'L$$

$$= p\left[\beta'^{\rho} + \left(\frac{w'}{p} \beta'^{-\rho} \right)^{\rho/(1-\rho)} - \beta'^{\rho} \right]^{1/\rho} L - w'L$$

$$= p\left(\frac{w'}{p} \beta'^{-\rho} \right)^{\sigma} L - w'L$$

$$= p\left[\left(\frac{w'}{p} \beta'^{-\rho} \right)^{\sigma} - \frac{w'}{p} \right] \gamma A \left[\left(\frac{w'}{p} \beta'^{-\rho} \right)^{\rho\sigma} - \beta'^{\rho} \right]^{-1/\rho}$$

$$= p\left[\left(\frac{w'}{p} \right)^{\sigma} \beta'^{-\rho\sigma} - \frac{w'}{p} \right] \gamma A \beta' \left[\left(\frac{w'}{p} \right)^{\rho\sigma} \beta'^{-\rho\sigma} - 1 \right]^{-1/\rho}$$

$$= p\frac{w'}{p} \left[\left(\frac{w'}{p} \right)^{\rho\sigma} \beta'^{-\rho\sigma} - 1 \right] \gamma A \beta' \left[\left(\frac{w'}{p} \right)^{\rho\sigma} \beta'^{-\rho\sigma} - 1 \right]^{-1/\rho}$$

$$= w'\left[\left(\frac{w'}{p} \right)^{\rho\sigma} \beta'^{-\rho\sigma} - 1 \right]^{-1/(\rho\sigma)} \gamma A \beta'$$

Therefore, maximized profits π^* are

$$\pi^* = w'\left[\left(\frac{\beta'}{w'/p} \right)^{-\rho\sigma} - 1 \right]^{-1/(\rho\sigma)} \gamma A \beta'$$

$$= w'\left[\left(\frac{\beta'}{w'/p} \right)^{1-\sigma} - 1 \right]^{1/(1-\sigma)} \gamma A \beta'$$

$$= p\left[1 - \left(\frac{w'/p}{\beta'} \right)^{1-\sigma} \right]^{1/(1-\sigma)} \gamma A \beta'^{2}$$

or, substituting for β',

$$\pi^* = p\gamma\beta^2 \left[1 - \left(\frac{w/p}{\beta} \right)^{1-\sigma} \frac{w'}{w} \right]^{1/(1-\sigma)} \left(\frac{w'}{w} \right)^{-2\sigma/(1-\sigma)} A$$

BIBLIOGRAPHY

Ahmad, Jaleel (1968). "Import Substitution and Structural Change in Indian Manufacturing Industry, 1950–1966. *"Journal of Development Studies,* 4:352–379.

Arrow, K., H. B. Chenery, B. Minhas, and R. M. Solow (1961). "Capital-labor Substitution and Economic Efficiency." *Review of Economics and Statistics,* 43:225–250.

Bardhan, Pranab K. (1970). *Economic Growth, Development, and Foreign Trade: A Study in Pure Theory.* New York, Wiley (Interscience).

Bardhan, Pranab K., and Sydney Lewis (1970). "Models of Growth with Imported Inputs." *Economica,* 37:373–385.

Barraclough, Solon L., and Arthur L. Domike (1966). "Agrarian Structure in Seven Latin American Countries." *Land Economics,* 42:391–424.

Beals, R. E., M. B. Levy, and L. N. Moses (1967). "Rationality and Migration in Ghana." *Review of Economics and Statistics,* 49:480–486.

Berry, R. Albert, and Stephen H. Hymer (1969). "A Note on the Capacity to Transform and the Welfare Costs of Foreign Trade Fluctuations." *Economic Journal,* 79:833–846.

Berry, R. Albert, and Ronald Soligo (1968). "Rural-Urban Migration, Agricultural Output, and the Supply Price of Labour in a Labour-Surplus Economy." *Oxford Economic Papers*, 20:230–249.

Böhm–Bawerk, E. von (1912). *Positiv Theorie des Kapitals*, Dritte Auflage, Buch IV, Abschnitt I. "Gegenwart und Zukunft in der Wirtschaft," pp. 426–486. (Paged references are to the English translation in (1959) *Capital and Interest*, vol. II, *Positive Theory of Capital*, book IV, section I, "Present and Future in Economic Life," pp. 257–289. South Holland, Ill., Libertanian Press.)

Bose, Sanjit, and Avinash K. Dixit (1972). *Development Planning: A Theoretical Analysis*. San Francisco, Holden-Day, forthcoming.

Box, G. E. P., and D. R. Cox (1964). "An Analysis of Transformations." *Journal of the Royal Statistical Society*, 26B:211–243.

Brainard, William C., and Richard N. Cooper (1968). "Uncertainty and Diversification in International Trade." *Food Research Institute Studies in Agricultural Economics, Trade, and Development*, 8:257–285.

Chatterji, M. K. (1962). "A Study of the Consumption Expenditure on Food in India." *Artha Vijnana*, 4:353–368.

Chennareddy, Venkareddy (1967). "Production Efficiency in South Indian Agriculture." *Journal of Farm Economics*, 49:816–820.

Cline, William R. (1970). *Economic Consequences of a Land Reform in Brazil*. Amsterdam, North-Holland.

Desai, Meghnad, and Dipak Mazumdar (1970). "A Test of the Hypothesis of Disguised Unemployment." *Economica*, 37:39–53.

Dixit, Avinash K. (1970). "Growth Patterns in a Dual Economy." *Oxford Economic Papers*, 22:229–234.

Duesenberry, James S. (1949). *Income, Saving and the Theory of Consumer Behavior*. Cambridge, Mass., Harvard University Press.

Fei, John C. H., and Gustav Ranis (1964). *Development of the Labor Surplus Economy, Theory and Policy*. Homewood, Ill., Richard D. Irwin.

Fisher, Irving (1930). *The Theory of Interest*. New York, Macmillan.

Food and Agriculture Organization of the United Nations (1967). *Agricultural Commodities—Projections for 1975 and 1985*. Rome.

Forsyth, F. G. (1960). "The Relationship between Family Size and Family Expenditure." *Journal of the Royal Statistical Society*, 123A:367–393.

Friedman, Milton (1957). *A Theory of the Consumption Function.* Princeton, N.J., Princeton University Press.

Fuchs, Victor R. (1963). "Capital-labor Substitution: A Note." *Review of Economics and Statistics,* 45:436–438.

Furtado, Celso (1970). *Economic Development of Latin America: A Survey from Colonial Times to the Cuban Revolution.* Cambridge, England, Cambridge University Press (translated by Suzette Macedo).

Giesbrecht, Martin G. (1971). "Women versus the Malthusian Trap, The Comestic Motive for Birth Control." *Journal of Political Economy,* 79:338–344.

Goreux, L. M. (1960). "Income and Food Consumption." *Monthly Bulletin of Agricultural Economics and Statistics,* 9 (October):1–13.

Greenwood, Michael J. (1969). "The Determinants of Labor Migration in Egypt." *Journal of Regional Science,* 9:283–290.

Griliches, Zvi (1967). "Production Functions in Manufacturing: Some Preliminary Results." *The Theory and Empirical Analysis of Production, Studies in Income and Wealth,* vol. 31. New York, National Bureau of Economic Research, pp. 275–322.

Hansen, Bent (1967). *Long- and Short-Term Planning in Underdeveloped Countries.* Amsterdam, North-Holland.

Harris, Donald J. (1964). "Econometric Analysis of Household Consumption in Jamaica." *Social and Economic Studies,* 13:471–487.

Hirschman, Albert O. (1958). *The Strategy of Economic Development.* New Haven, Conn., Yale University Press.

Hopper, W. David (1965). "Allocation Efficiency in a Traditional Indian Agriculture." *Journal of Farm Economics,* 47:611–624.

India, Government of, Cabinet Secretariat (1952 to present). *The National Sample Survey.* New Delhi.

India, Government of, Ministry of Food and Agriculture, Economics and Statistics Advisor (1958). *Indian Agricultural Atlas.* New Delhi.

India, Government of, Ministry of Food and Agriculture, Economics and Statistics Advisor (1958–1960). *Studies in the Economics of Farm Management.* New Delhi. Seventeen volumes covering the states of Bombay, Madras, Punjab, Uttar Pradesh, and West Bengal for the crop years of 1954–1955, 1955–1956, and 1956–1957 and also the state of Madhya Pradesh for the crop years of 1955–1956 and 1956–1957.

India, Government of, Ministry of Food and Agriculture, Economics and Statistics Advisor (1964–1968). *Studies in the Economics of Farm Management*. New Delhi. Six volumes covering the states of Andhra Pradesh and Orissa for the crop years 1957–1958, 1958–1959, and 1959–1960. A study scheduled to be undertaken for Bihar has not appeared.

Johnston, Bruce F., and John Cownie (1969). "The Seed-fertilizer Revolution and Labor Force Absorption." *American Economic Review*. 59:569–582.

Jorgenson, Dale W. (1961). "The Development of a Dual Economy. *Economic Journal*, 71:309–334.

Jorgenson, Dale W. (1967). "Surplus Agricultural Labour and the Development of a Dual Economy." *Oxford Economic Papers*, 19:288–312.

Jorgenson, Dale W., and Lawrence J. Lau (1969). "An Economic Theory of Agricultural Household Behavior." Paper presented to the Fourth Far Eastern Meeting of the Econometric Society, Tokyo, Japan, June 26–28, 1969.

Kamarck, Andrew M. (1971). *The Economics of African Development*. New York, Praeger.

Katz, Jorge M. (1969). *Production Functions, Foreign Investment and Growth: A Study Based on the Argentine Manufacturing Sector, 1946–1961*. Amsterdam, North-Holland.

Kelley, Allen C. (1969). "Demand Patterns, Demographic Change and Economic Growth." *Quarterly Journal of Economics*, 83:110–126.

Lau, Lawrence, and Pan A. Yotopoulos (1971). "A Test for Relative Efficiency and Application to Indian Agriculture." *American Economic Review*, 61:94–109.

Leibenstein, Harvey (1957). *Economic Backwardness and Economic Growth*. New York, Wiley.

Levin, Jonathan V. (1960). *The Export Economies*. Cambridge, Mass., Harvard University Press.

Lewis, W. Arthur (1954). "Economic Development with Unlimited Supplies of Labour." *The Manchester School*, 22:139–191. See also Lewis (1958). "Unlimited Labour: Further Notes." *The Manchester School*, 26:1–32.

Liviatan, Nissan (1961). "Errors in Variables and Engel Curve Analysis." *Econometrica*, 29:336–362.

MacBean, Alasdair I. (1966). *Export Instability and Economic Development*. Cambridge, Mass., Harvard University Press.

Marglin, Stephen A. (1966). "Comment," in *The Theory and Design of Economic Development* (Irma Adelman and Erik Thorbecke, eds.). Baltimore, Johns Hopkins Press.

McFadden, Daniel L. (1972). "Cost, Revenue, and Profit Functions," in *An Econometric Approach to Production Theory* (Daniel L. McFadden, ed.). Amsterdam, North-Holland, forthcoming.

Meier, Gerald M. (1970). *Leading Issues in Development Economics*, 2d ed. New York, Oxford University Press.

Nurkse, Ragnar (1953). *Problems of Capital Formation in Underdeveloped Countries*. Oxford, Oxford University Press.

Paris, Quirino (1970). "An Appraisal of 'Income' Elasticities for Total Food Consumption in Developing Countries." Technical Papers, Development Centre of the Organization for Economic Co-operation and Development. Paris.

Parks, Richard W. (1969). "Systems of Demand Equations: An Empirical Comparison of Alternative Functional Forms." *Econometrica*, 37:629–650.

Philippines, Republic of the (1964, 1968). Department of Commerce and Industry, Bureau of the Census and Statistics, *The BCS Survey of Households Bulletin*, ser. no. 14 and 22, "Family Income and Expenditures, 1961 and 1965 [respectively]." Manila.

Punjab, Goverment of, Economic and Statistical Organization (1964, 1966). *Studies in the Economics of Farm Management in the Punjab*. Chandigarh. Three volumes for the crop years 1961–1962, 1962–1963, and 1963–1964.

Rae, John (1905). *The Sociological Theory of Capital*. New York, Macmillan.

Raj, K. N. (1969). "Some Questions Concerning Growth, Transformation and Planning in the Developing Countries." *Journal of Development Planning*, No. 1. New York, United Nations, pp. 15–38.

Ramsey, James B., and Paul Zarembka (1971). "Specification Error Tests and Alternative Functional Forms of the Aggregate Production Function." *Journal of the American Statistical Association*, 66: 471–477.

Rao, C. H. Hanumantha (1971). "Uncertainty, Entrepreneurship, and Sharecropping in India." *Journal of Political Economy*, 79:578–595.

Reynolds, Lloyd G. (1969). "Economic Development with Surplus Labour: Some Complications." *Oxford Economic Papers*, 21:89–103.

Sahota, Gian S. (1968). "An Economic Analysis of Internal Migration in Brazil." *Journal of Political Economy*, 76:218–245.

Sankar, Ulaganathan (1970). "Elasticities of Substitution and Returns to Scale in Indian Manufacturing Industries." *International Economic Review*, 11:399–411.

Schlesselman, J. (1971). "Power Families: A Note on the Box and Cox Transformation." *Journal of the Royal Statistical Society*, 33: 307–311.

Schultz, T. Paul (1971). "Rural-Urban Migration in Colombia." *Review of Economics and Statistics*, 53:157–163.

Sen, Amartya K. (1966). "Peasants and Dualism With or Without Surplus Labor." *Journal of Political Economy*, 74:425–450.

Shand, R. T., ed. (1969). *Agricultural Development in Asia.* Berkeley and Los Angeles, University of California Press.

Shepard, Ronald W. (1953). *Cost and Production Functions.* Princeton, N.J., Princeton University Press.

Sinha, R. P. (1966). "An Analysis of Food Expenditure in India." *Journal of Farm Economics*, 48:113–123.

Swamy, Dalip S. (1967). "Statistical Evidence of Balanced and Unbalanced Growth." *Review of Economics and Statistics*, 49:288–303.

Todaro, Michael P. (1969). "A Model of Labor Migration and Urban Unemployment in Less Developed Countries." *American Economic Review*, 59:138–148.

Turner, H. A., and D. A. S. Jackson (1970). "On the Determination of the General Wage Level—A World Analysis; or ' *Unlimited Labour Forever.*'" *Economic Journal*, 70:827–849.

Uzawa, Hirofumi (1964). "Duality Principles in the Theory of Cost and Production." *International Economic Review*, 5:216–220.

Varma, Ravi (1959). "Income Elasticity of Demand for Food-Grains—A Regional Approach." *Artha Vijnana*, 1:271–280.

Viner, Jacob (1957). "Some Reflections on the Concept of 'Disguised Unemployment,'" in *Contribuicoes à Análise do Desenvolvimento Econômico* (Livraria Agir, ed.). Rio de Janeiro.

Wellisz, Stanislaw, with B. Munk, T. P. Mayhew, and C. Hemmer (1970). "Resource Allocation in Traditional Agriculture: A Study of Andhra Pradesh." *Journal of Political Economy*, 78:655–684.

Williamson, Jeffrey G. (1968). "Personal Savings in Developing Nations: An Intertemporal Cross-section from Asia." *Economic Record*, 44: 194–210.

Yaari, Menahem E. (1965). "Uncertain Lifetime, Life Insurance, and the Theory of the Consumer." *Review of Economic Studies*, 32:137–150.

Yoshihara, Kunio (1969). "Demand Functions: An Application to the Japanese Expenditure Pattern." *Econometrica*, 37:257–274.

Yotopoulos, Pan A., and Lawrence J. Lau (1970). "A Test for Balanced and Unbalanced Growth." *Review of Economics and Statistics*, 52: 376–384.

Zarembka, Paul (1968). "Functional Form in the Demand for Money." *Journal of the American Statistical Association*, 63:502–511.

Zarembka, Paul (1970a). "On the Empirical Relevance of the CES Production Function." *Review of Economics and Statistics*, 52: 47–53.

Zarembka, Paul (1970b). "Labor Migration and Urban Unemployment: Comment." *American Economic Review*, 60:184–186.

Zarembka, Paul (1970c). "Marketable Surplus and Growth in the Dual Economy." *Journal of Economic Theory*, 2:107–121.

Zarembka, Paul (1972). "A Long-Run Economic Growth Model for Developing Countries," in *International Economics and Development: Essays in Honor of Raul Prebisch* (Luis E. DiMarco, ed.). New York, Academic Press.

Zarembka, Paul, and Helen B. Chernicoff (1971). "Further Results on the Empirical Relevance of the CES Production Function." *Review of Economics and Statistics*, 53:106 110.

Zellner, A., J. Kmenta, and J. Drèze (1966). "Specification and Estimation of Cobb–Douglas Production Function Models." *Econometrica*, 34:784–795.

INDEX

DATE DUE

GAYLORD			PRINTED IN U.S.A.